REPRODUCING RACISM

REPRODUCING RACISM

White Space, Elite Law Schools, and Racial Inequality

Wendy Leo Moore

ROWMAN & LITTLEFIELD PUBLISHERS, INC.
Lanham • Boulder • New York • Toronto • Plymouth, UK

ROWMAN & LITTLEFIELD PUBLISHERS, INC.

Published in the United States of America
by Rowman & Littlefield Publishers, Inc.
A wholly owned subsidiary of The Rowman & Littlefield Publishing Group, Inc.
4501 Forbes Boulevard, Suite 200, Lanham, Maryland 20706
www.rowmanlittlefield.com

Estover Road
Plymouth PL6 7PY
United Kingdom

British Library Cataloguing in Publication Information Available

Library of Congress Cataloging-in-Publication Data

Moore, Wendy Leo, 1971–
  Reproducing racism : white space, elite law schools, and racial inequality / Wendy Leo
Moore.
     p. cm.
  Includes bibliographical references.
  ISBN-13: 978-0-7425-6005-5 (cloth : alk. paper)
  ISBN-10: 0-7425-6005-8 (cloth : alk. paper)
  ISBN-13: 978-0-7425-6006-2 (pbk. : alk. paper)
  ISBN-10: 0-7425-6006-6 (pbk. : alk. paper)
  1. Law—Study and teaching—Social aspects—United States. 2. Law schools—Social
aspects—United States. 3. African American law students—United States. 4. Racism—
United States. I. Title.
  KF272.M66 2008
  340.071'173—dc22   2007027302

Printed in the United States of America

⊗™ The paper used in this publication meets the minimum requirements of American
National Standard for Information Sciences—Permanence of Paper for Printed Library
Materials, ANSI/NISO Z39.48-1992.

In loving memory of Dr. Robert B. Bailey III

and

To Nikki and Malcolm

May you never be too tired to fight

Contents

Foreword

IN THE SUMMER OF 1787, fifty-five men met in Philadelphia to craft a U.S. Constitution, a constitution that would become world famous and the legal understructure for what has been called the first democratic country. These founders were all white and of European origin. The constitutional convention was conspicuously "white space," to accent a concept central to this savvy analysis by social scientist and lawyer Wendy Moore. In the assertively white space of Philadelphia, the important understructure for the new country's legal and political system was built under the articulated fiction that it was representative, just, and democratic. Yet, some 40 percent of the delegates were or had been slaveowners, and many others had profited from the dominant slavery-centered economy as merchants, lawyers, and bankers. The wealthy slaveholder George Washington, presiding as chair over this constitution-making, and his colleagues created a nation where only self-defined "whites" were rights-guaranteed "citizens." In the U.S. Constitution's much-quoted preamble, these founders accented "We the People," but for them only whites were "people."

From the beginning, the fictionally representative and democratic U.S. political and legal system has been grounded in the quicksand of a Constitution, and subsequent long constitutional tradition, that have never come to terms with the society's antidemocratic and enduring reality of racial oppression. This oppression was the foundation of the new nation created by European entrepreneurs and colonists in the seventeenth and eighteenth centuries. For more than two and a half centuries these invading colonists and their descendants killed off Native Americans and enslaved African

Americans. This savage era was followed, in turn, by many long decades of extensive reservation and Jim Crow segregation. Such extreme racial oppression lasted for about the first three and a half centuries of this country's existence. Only for the past four decades (since 1969) has the United States even been a theoretically "free" country. Over the entire course of U.S. history, whites as a group have been unjustly enriched by an economic, political, and legal system of their own crafting, one chronically nonmeritocratic in operation and routinely favoring white interests. Today, as earlier, African Americans and other Americans of color are racialized "others" and are not fully included in "We the People."

For most of our history, slavery and the Jim Crow apartheid were enshrined in law and constantly reinforced by the highest courts and legislative bodies. Until the 1950s, very few state or federal government officials (all being white at the time) in areas of the country with large black populations showed interest in extending the principle of equality in access to, or of treatment in, the legal or political system to African Americans. Until the late twentieth century, African Americans and other Americans of color had virtually no role (apart from a brief Reconstruction era) in making significant state and federal laws.

The fabled U.S. legal and political system was originally constructed, and for the most part is still being made or remade, by white legal and political officials. For example, only 110 justices have ever served on the U.S. Supreme Court, arguably the world's most powerful legal institution. Some 98 percent of these justices have been white. No African American served on the highest court until 1967, and only two have ever served. No other Americans of color have served on the Court. For decades, most justices have been drawn from the country's important law schools, indeed often from elite law schools such as those researched in this pioneering book. (Indeed, *all* nine current Supreme Court justices are from historically white, elite law schools, including five from Harvard and two from Yale.) Below the Supreme Court, the upper echelons of the legal system include relatively few Americans of color. Recent studies have shown that black Americans make up less than 2 percent of important legal officials, including state attorneys general, district attorneys, leading civil and criminal lawyers, and the judges in major state and federal courts. For the most part, the high court's white elite, together with their white brethren in state and federal governments, have shaped and controlled the major changes in the U.S. legal and political system since the founding era.

In this well-researched book, Moore provides substantial empirical evidence on how law schools, especially elite schools, play a key role in society as they groom and indoctrinate this country's future important lawyers, who often later gain powerful positions in the legislative, judicial, and corporate spheres. Given the significance of elite law schools in creating societal leaders, their everyday racialized norms, spaces, performances, and practices are particularly important to study empirically.

Those in authority in elite and other law schools spend much time and effort in helping perpetuate a white-normed legal system that is imposed on all Americans, a great many of whom have never had significant input into fashioning that system. Historically and in the present, indeed, our law schools have been particularly important in officially legitimizing and rationalizing patterns of U.S. racial oppression. Not surprisingly, thus, mainstream analysts inside or outside academia have seldom critically examined the important racialized features of the U.S. legal system and its law schools. While law professors and students often engage in intense discussions and debates of particular laws and legal proposals as they relate to racial and ethnic conflicts, few there, especially among whites, perform deep critical examinations of their own problematic law school contexts or the larger racialized societal contexts within which they are situated.

In this book, Professor Moore helps to remedy this serious neglect with substantial interview and ethnographic data on two elite law schools. In a perceptive and documented analysis, Moore draws on the critical race theory tradition of legal scholars, but adds to these ideas and data from a much older tradition of critical racial analysis in the social sciences. Moore backs up her conceptually honed analysis with much new data drawn from the lives and experiences of numerous law students and faculty within these white-controlled legal institutions.

Moore's data show well that these elite law schools are white spaces, in terms of a majority of their occupants' characteristics, their normative structures, their power hierarchy, and their racial pathologies. Law schools are racialized spaces where whites rarely think about that racialization. One dramatic dimension of this white-normed space is documented in Moore's observations about portraits of important legal figures in the atrium, halls, and classrooms at Midstate Law School. Not one lawyer of color was represented among these portraits at this major law school, although some artwork on the walls did show people of color engaged in various civil rights movements. The implicit message of this whitewashed space was that whites were the legal and political insiders, while, if present at all, Americans of color were outsiders trying to get treated fairly by the legal or political system. At the Presidential School of Law, Moore did find one wall that had a racially diverse set of photographs of recent alumni, but in the rest of the law school the portraits were similar to those at Midstate—again, virtually all white men in legal regalia. The only exception was a portrait of Supreme Court justice Thurgood Marshall, also the only portrait at either law school of a lawyer of color.

Moore demonstrates other substantial aspects of the white-normed space of these elite law schools. The Asian American, Latino, Native American, and African American students that she interviewed describe an array of interactions with and commentaries from white students and faculty, including classroom discussions, that confidently exhibit what I have elsewhere described and conceptualized as the "white racial frame" of society. This law school space is problematic because most whites there think unreflectively from within this old racial frame. Central to the persistence of racial oppression in the United States has been the development of this white racial frame—an organized set of racialized ideas, images, emotions, and inclinations, which are closely connected to recurring discrimination and constitutive of still-racist institutions.[1] Today, as in the past, this white racial frame includes much negative material concerning Americans of color, as well as assertively positive views of whites and white-controlled institutions. The North American version of this white frame originated to rationalize slavery in the seventeenth century, also the same period during which the legal system was becoming more developed. This racial frame has long rationalized and buttressed slavery, legal segregation, and contemporary racism.

The reality of white university students and other whites operating from the white racial frame, and commenting and otherwise discriminating in blatantly and subtly racist ways, is unsurprising in light of much recent social science research indicating that many white minds are filled with such framing. For example, in recent research, Leslie Houts Picca and I had 626 white college students at more than two dozen colleges and universities across the country keep journals of racial events that they observed, for a month or two on average. In relatively brief journals, these students reported nearly seven thousand events of a clearly racist nature. Much of the reported racist activity was in backstage social settings with white relatives or friends, and white college students were often central to the racist performances. Such data reveal that many educated whites still aggressively think and act out the old white racial frame, behavior that often slips out of the backstage into multiracial frontstage settings such as the halls and classrooms of the law schools described in this book.

White students are not the only problem for students of color in these law schools. Often in classroom discussions, as Moore documents thoroughly, well-educated law professors also operate out of this white racial frame as they analyze U.S. laws and the larger society. They clearly have great difficulty in moving outside that frame, even briefly, to adopt a more probing and critical antiracism perspective, such as that which is common among Americans of color. Such a strong, white interpretive frame captures territory in the mind and makes it difficult to think about that captured territory in terms other than those of the accepted frame.

Signs of this can be seen in attempts by some law faculty members to rationalize what is morally indefensible (now *and* in that era), such as the holding of African Americans as enslaved servants and laborers by whites, including the slaveholding founders George Washington and Thomas Jefferson. Other classroom examples include making arguments and using language about U.S. political leaders reasonably "compromising" over issues of slavery or legal segregation in particular historical eras. These leaders were, of course, white, and their "compromising" is considered from within a white racial frame, not from the point of view of the centrally effected African Americans, whose view sought elimination of racial oppression. Yet other examples in Moore's data are of white faculty members making sarcastic jokes about African Americans or their communities in connection with law cases involving slavery, Jim Crow, or civil rights movements and laws. Among other things, such faculty commentaries indicate a minimization of the racial oppression that is still systemic in U.S. society.

Many white faculty seem unable to look at society from a deeper systemic racism perspective like that developed from life experience by many students and faculty of color. Moore cites the example of legal analysts like Stanford Law School's Richard Sander. Sander has argued that it does not serve African American students well to admit them to elite law schools where they make lower grades, and then later have trouble in the job market. He suggests encouraging them to go to lower-tier law schools where they can make better grades and move on to secure jobs. Sander accents conventional measures of performance into and out of law schools, yet ignores the systemic racism of the law schools and surrounding society. Like most white analysts in education, he looks at these issues from within a white racial frame and cannot see the world from the point of view of African American students, who know from experience that historically white law schools and the legal employment system are often discriminatory in their treatment of black students and other students of color. Analysts like Sander, as Moore suggests, seem very concerned that African Americans only have limited capital to spend with whites, so they must be careful not to alienate whites. Such analysts typically do not study or question the many racist practices that operate inside law schools and employing firms that channel, restrict, or eliminate law students or lawyers of color. Moore also notes that analysts like Sander, relying on conventional white-created measures of "merit," pay no attention to the high intelligence and advanced skills that it takes for African American students and other students of color to navigate through, and often succeed in, highly racist settings.

One cannot evaluate the success or failure of white law students and students of color with white-created measures that ignore the reality of the white-space oppression faced by them.

Moore also wryly suggests that white analysts who accent "merit" as a standard for educational performance need to consider the nonmerit-related privileges that all whites have inherited from their ancestors. A reflective academic analysis of white and black students should thus single out *white students* as the nonmeritorious group because their socially protected white privilege has given them many unearned and unjust advantages not connected to their individual merits. Thus, white college students and law students should be those with the social *stigma* of having had many unfair advantages and unjust admissions, promotions, and placements in educational settings, *not* the students of color.

Moore's analysis makes evident the conclusion that white students and students of color live in different worlds, even within the same law school walls. One further demonstration of this is seen in the data on the effect of quotidian racism and in the related racism-countering tactics used by the students of color. Students of color must regularly endure the great pain of racist events at the law schools, and thus are often very uncomfortable in these white-normed spaces. Moore's data reveal that students of color must do much emotional work, individually and collectively, just to survive these settings. Students of color must daily decide whether and how to reject the white racial framing of everyday events. They may disengage in various ways from the law school experience, or they may choose to fight daily against the racism of their law school space. In either case, great emotional labor is required. In addition, recurring encounters with blatant or subtle racist attacks are often handled by describing these events to other students of color within informal or formal support groups, which can provide emotional support and advice on countering strategies. Indeed, students of color must often participate in such extra group activities just to make it—time-consuming efforts not required of white students. Many succeed, not only because they are talented students, but also because they create critical social support networks where they can be somewhat protected. These racism-countering efforts are rarely recognized by those who run law schools or those who hire their graduates.

Irony is written on most pages of this book, for those running U.S. law schools regularly assert or repeat, much like elementary school children everywhere, that U.S. society is truly one of "liberty and justice for all." Historically, this liberty-and-justice framing of U.S. society grew up alongside the white racial frame. This liberty-and-justice frame accents certain values that most Americans, including most whites, hold in their minds, at least at a rhetorical level. Yet most whites violate these liberty-and-justice values in numerous ways in their everyday racist thinking, commentaries, perform-ances, and practices. These whites live lives that often are at great odds with what they claim to believe about liberty, fairness, and justice, mainly because the more important framing of society is the old white racial framing. As a result, the U.S. legal system and its constituent parts, including law schools, are structured so that there is mainly racial equality in the public rhetoric, and not in many areas of everyday practice. Indeed, white law school faculty and law schools often hold themselves up as a major source of reason and ob-jective analysis, yet most remain uncritical in their acceptance of a legal sys-tem that has created and maintained a large-scale system of racial oppression for centuries. (Thus, I have yet to see a sustained analysis by a contemporary white law professor arguing that a U.S. Constitution made by slaveholders and their minions should be replaced by one made by representatives of all Americans—that is, a democratically made constitution.)

Great irony can also be seen in the reality that it is the African American law students and other law students of color whose communities have carried the deepest currents of commitment to liberty and justice for all for centuries. For much of this country's long history, white Americans collectively have not been the main carriers of the robust ideals of freedom and justice, especially since 1800. Actually, African Americans have played a more consistent and on-going role as the primary carriers of the ideals of freedom and justice. Perhaps the first great manifesto for full human equality in the history of the United States was the 1829 *Appeal to the Coloured Citizens of the World* by the black abolitionist David Walker. In his *Appeal*, Walker quotes the words "All men are created equal" from the Declaration of Independence and then adds this com-ment for white readers: "I ask you candidly, was your suffering under Great Britain one hundredth part as cruel and tyrannical as you have rendered ours under you?" After the Civil War, black Americans pressed hard to secure greater freedom and equality, and in the early 1900s there were yet more new movements for civil rights. Whites resisted hard. During the 1950s and 1960s the country again witnessed a reinvigorated movement for freedom and equality for African Americans. Many in that movement, like Dr. Martin Luther King, Jr., regularly noted that the major problem was getting whites to understand the real meaning of the black struggle for liberty and justice in U.S. society. Whites again resisted. Important changes resulted in the direction of greater freedom and justice, but much was left undone. Today, most whites still remain opposed to the aggressive eradication of all forms of racial dis-crimination and to the large-scale racial integration of society.

The only way out of the racial pathology so well described here by Wendy Moore is for all Americans who really care about "liberty and justice for all" to band together to rebuild this society on a more democratic foundation than that provided by the existing U.S. Constitution and the legal system grounded in it. One key step is to reframe the dominant understanding of this society's racial contours away from the white racial frame to the liberty-and-justice frame that, at some level, most Americans seem to accept. Reframing away from this traditional white racial frame will certainly require great effort, yet we must aggressively seek such a reframing in order to get people to focus authentically on articulating, living, and implementing the human values of justice, inclusiveness, and equality so long a part of the rhetoric of U.S. legal institutions.

Joe R. Feagin
Texas A & M University

Note

1. Joe R. Feagin, *Systemic Racism: A Theory of Oppression* (New York: Routledge, 2006).

Introduction

Georgetown "Dixie"

O N MARCH 31, 2003, the evening before the Supreme Court was to hear two cases concerning the affirmative action policies of the University of Michigan,[1] the Women of Color Consortium at Georgetown University Law Center hosted a debate on affirmative action. The participants in this debate included the Rev. Jesse Jackson and Pulitzer Prize-winning columnist Clarence Page in support of affirmative action and Roger Clegg from the Center for Equal Opportunity in opposition to affirmative action. As the debate progressed, the arguments became more vehement on both sides, and the responses from the audience made it clear that its members were largely in support of affirmative action. At some point, Clarence Page and Roger Clegg went head to head in debate, and as Mr. Page was discussing the relevance of the history of racism in the United States to the affirmative action debate, a cell phone went off toward the back of the room. I turned to look at the location of the noise, and I saw that the white man with the phone was standing very near the door, so I assumed he would quickly leave the room. He did not leave, however, and as the cell phone continued to sound, it became clear that the song playing from the phone was "Dixie," a song tied to the institution of slavery both in its origin as a song originally written in a mocking black dialect and in its popular recognition as a theme song of the Confederacy during the Civil War.

On the eve of a Supreme Court hearing concerning affirmative action, at an elite law school located in Washington, D.C., the political center of the nation, a white man played "Dixie" on his cell phone as an African American scholar delineated the historical consequences of racism in this country. The irony of the moment was punctuated by the fact Roger Clegg and the other opponents of affirmative action policies were arguing that blatant racism was a thing of the past and that the law in post–civil rights America need only guarantee equal access. As "Dixie" echoed in the hall over the voice of Clarence Page (who responded by joking, "Ah, one of my favorite songs"), the assertion that blatant racism had passed into history was vividly challenged. But there was another challenge in the moment, one that was perhaps covert, if not subtle. The playing of "Dixie" signified a time in America's brutally racist history when an African American man would never have been *permitted* to speak about policies to end racism in an elite law school. The white man with the phone invoked historical white racism to silence Clarence Page, and in doing so, he implicitly challenged his right to be heard in the space of the law school. This more covert message, whether it was intended or not, suggested something deeper and more foundational than an expression of white racist sentiment. It signaled the presumptive whiteness of this elite institutional space, the boundaries of which are explicitly challenged by a call for affirmative efforts to increase the presence of students of color in historically white universities and law schools.

It is not insignificant that this example of racism took place within an elite U.S. law school. Law schools are more than educational institutions or institutions of professional socialization; they are fundamentally connected to the political system and the political economy of race. Elite law schools represent a gateway to positions of power in the American political system. And the power of lawyers in the American political landscape cannot be overemphasized. As Mark Miller has pointed out, the profession of law has "colonized the political domain" in this country (1995, 3). In fact, lawyers have long dominated the sphere of politics in the United States. Beyond the obvious presence in the judiciary, since 1850 between one-half to two-thirds of all state governors have been lawyers, and since 1855 almost every U.S. congressional committee and subcommittee has had at least one, often more than one, lawyer on its staff. Today, lawyers represent the most dominant profession in Congress, as well as in state legislatures. Furthermore, by 1980 there were more than twelve thousand "lawyer-lobbyists" working to represent the interests of big business before Congress, federal courts, and regulatory agencies (Miller 1995). Since the early 1900s, law schools have served as gate-keeping institutions, functioning as the primary socializing mechanism for people who wish to enter this powerful profession. The impact of racism within these institutions is thus potentially very far-reaching.

The connection between law schools as elite institutions and the broader social and political realms of power in American society makes these institutions important sites for examining race and racism. But the connection between law schools and the law reveals an even more essential reason for critically examining the racial dynamics of power in law schools. Law is an extremely powerful profession; it is also deeply racialized. Throughout U.S. history, the law has operated as a central political institution in the construction and maintenance of the racial state. Race, racism, and the American legal system grew up together. The law has historically been used as a tool of the state to construct and enforce a white citizenry (and government), to justify the theft and exploitation of land and human bodies for white economic gain, to define the boundaries of the racial categories used to convey unearned privilege to whites and the forced subjugation of people of color, and to prevent interracial alliances between those legally defined as racially distinct.[2] Law schools, as institutions of professional socialization, were constructed to teach but simultaneously to rationalize and justify the legal structure. As such, they are fundamentally connected to the racial legal structure.

The intersecting relationship between racism, the law, and law schools is perhaps the most central impetus for the development of the field of critical race theory. Coming out of a legal academy that law scholars of color found both epistemologically skewed and personally hostile, critical race theory developed as a method of critically analyzing sociolegal constructions of race and racial oppression.[3] Many critical race scholars have explicitly discussed their experiences in law schools and connected their legal scholarship to their alienation from legal pedagogy and the law school community. For example, describing her experience in law school, legal scholar Patricia Williams says,

> My abiding recollection of being a student at Harvard Law School is the sense of being invisible. I spent three years wandering in a murk of unreality. I observed large, mostly male bodies assert themselves against one another like football players caught in the gauzy mist of intellectual slow motion. I stood my ground amid them, watching them deflect me, unconsciously, politely, as if I were a pillar in a crowded corridor. Law school was for me like being on another planet, full of alienated creatures with whom I could make little connection. The school created a dense atmosphere that muted my voice to inaudibility. All I could do to communicate my existence was to posit carefully worded messages into hermetically sealed, vacuum-packed blue books, place them on the waves of that foreign sea, and pray they would be plucked up by some curious seeker and understood. (1987, 55)

A central aspect of the alienation experienced by Professor Williams and other law students of color was a curriculum that presented law as a neutral and impartial body of unproblematic, legitimate authority, a presentation that is sharply contradicted by the entire legal history of the United States.[4]

A new framework of legal analysis developed from within the legal academy, at least partially as a result of the experiences of people of color that echo the experience of Professor Williams. With this in mind, perhaps there is no irony in the racist invocation of the theme song of the slave South, used to drown out the words of a black Pulitzer Prize-winning journalist speaking about racial equity. Viewed in the context of a deeply racialized institution, this explicit example of racial antagonism becomes less out of place. While this form of racism is less prevalent in the post–civil rights era than during earlier moments in U.S. history, the foundation that supports such racist expression remains in place. Although elite law schools, which were formerly restricted to only white people, have opened their doors to students of color, the white frame that organizes these institutions remains intact. Certainly, the white student who played "Dixie" at Georgetown Law expressed a racialized idea or emotion, but the ideological expression has its power in the deeper structures and practices that maintain and reproduce elite law schools as white spaces.

Scholars like the ones who participated in the creation and proliferation of critical race theory had access to legal education in elite law schools, but within these schools, their experience was quite different from that of white men and women. This fact belies the assertion made by opponents of affirmative action that the "playing field is level" as a result of civil rights laws that erased legally sanctioned racial inequality. If the space of the law school "field" represented the dense atmosphere that muted Patricia Williams's voice in law school such that her experience was substantively different from that of the white men and women who went to law school with her, what meaning can be given to abstract, individualistic terms like "equal access"?

While critical race theorists have written a significant amount on race and racism in legal education, very few scholars have engaged in any form of systematic empirical analysis of race in elite law schools. Given the relationship between race and the law, as well as the fact that law schools, especially the most elite American law schools, provide access to important and powerful positions in politics and business, such an analysis is extremely important. More than that, however, understanding the racial structure and culture of law schools provides insight into the institutional reproduction of racism in the post–civil rights era. Thus, in this book I attempt to transcend the boundaries of the rhetoric, like that employed in affirmative action debates, that confines analyses of race in institutions like law schools to racial comparisons of outcomes, such as grades and exam-passage rates. Drawing from two years of ethnographic research at two elite American law schools, which I call Presidential University School of Law and Midstate Law School, I examine the racialized *process* of legal education. An ethnographic methodology was particularly well suited to this task as it allowed me to examine the deep racial structures, racialized everyday practices, and racial ideologies and discursive frames that work in combination to organize these elite law schools as *white institutional spaces.*

The contemporary racial disparities in law student populations, which were the subject of the Georgetown Law debate, provide one surface indicator of white space, and this disparity often becomes the main focus when discussions about "diversity" or "affirmative action" arise. But racial disparities are connected to much deeper racial structures and practices. For this reason, I selected two schools with distinct racial demographics, Presidential having one of the highest percentages of students of color among elite law schools and Midstate having among the lowest.[5] At both schools, I found that deep normative structures and institutional practices contribute to the racial organization of the law schools. Extending the work of critical race theorists to examine the very institution from which this body of knowledge developed, I interrogated the mechanisms that function to reproduce white institutional space, even as the populations of these institutions become more diverse. My hope is that this more nuanced understanding of race in elite institutions like law schools will challenge contemporary social discourses about race and racism, which are generally limited by a failure to account adequately for the structural depth and permanence of racism in American society.

Acknowledgments

This book would not have been possible without the assistance of the many people who supported me throughout the research and writing process. I sincerely thank the law students and law faculty who took the time to talk with me—particularly those law students of color who became invested in this study and spent many hours talking to me and helping to facilitate my research in so many ways. And to the several law faculty, who I will not mention by name for the sake of anonymity, who believed in me and this research so much that they helped me to gain access to the law schools, thank you so much. I must also note that this project would not have been possible without the intellectual foundation provided by the many scholars of color who, despite personal and professional risks, developed and continue to insist upon a framework of critical race theory in socio-legal studies. I thank you for your insights and your courage. I would also like to thank the Law School Admission Counsel for trusting me with financial support without which this research would never have been possible. And, of course, the institutional support I have received from the Sociology Department at

Texas A&M University has been incredible. I feel incredibly lucky to have been able to work on this book within the context of such an unconditionally supportive department.

In addition to the institutional support I received on this project, there are many individuals who have supported me professionally. I must give thanks to Jennifer Pierce, Rose Brewer, Douglas Hartmann, and Roderick Ferguson for their mentoring, support, and constructive criticism throughout the research and writing process (not to mention the personal support that they gave as I negotiated the world of graduate education). I would also like to thank the students of my Fall 2006 Critical Race Theory class who challenged me at least as much as I challenged them and gave me the final push I needed to complete this book. In addition, I appreciate the thoughtful comments of the Race and Ethnicity Workshop group at Texas A&M University. To the many people who read (many) drafts of my work, including Zulema Valdez, Sara Gatson, Joseph Jewell, Eduardo Bonilla-Silva, Jackie Jebens, Ryan Jebens, Ruth Thompson Miller, Glenn Bracey, Jennifer Mueller, Lorena Murga, Rosalind Cho, David McIntosh, Oliver Kim, TiShaunda Jamison, and Sara Bolden, thank you so much for your insights. And most notably, I feel very privileged to have had the exceptional mentoring and support of Joe Feagin; you are truly an inspirational mentor, friend, and human being.

And to my family-friends, I have asked far too much of you, far too many times, but you have been there and without you I would not be here. Thanks to my mom Kathleen Leo, and my stepdad, Subir Chatterjee for always challenging me, forcing me to continually develop better and stronger arguments. Heidi Barajas, Juan and Arien Telles, and the rest of the family, you have never failed to make me feel loved and supported when I needed you. The greatest lawyers I know, Oliver Kim, Jennifer Nimmons Herman, and Eric Chen, without you how could I ever have finished law school??!! To my babies, Nikki and Malcolm, you are my life. I hope you will forgive me all the evenings and weekends I worked and know that you are the reason I do what I do. Also to all those who taught me those things I never could have learned in any school, especially my brother Kemet Imhotep, and my heart Choyce D. Young, you are the reason I am who I am. And of course, I am blessed to have three of the most beautiful, supportive, intelligent women as my sisters and friends: Joyce Bell, Tiffany Davis, and Lisette Haro; I hope that you know you are truly amazing. I love you, and I will never be able to thank you enough for being there when I needed you.

Finally, in my intellectual journey I lost three people who developed and guarded my heart. To my godfather, Dr. Robert B. Bailey III, my great-gran, Rosa Beatrice Bailey, and my grandpa, Ray Graham, your spirits are within me and my work. I hope I will make you all proud.

Notes

1. *Gratz v. Bollinger*, 539 U.S. 244 (2003), *Grutter v. Bollinger*, 539 U.S. 982 (2003).

2. For a review of the legal and political construction of race and white racial supremacy, see, for example, Derrick Bell, *Race, Racism and American Law*, 4th ed. (New
York: Aspen Press, 2000), and Joe Feagin, *Racist America: Roots, Current Realities and
Future Reparations* (New York: Routledge, 2000). For a discussion of the intersection
of the law and the white citizenry, as well as the construction of racial-group bound-
aries, ⸱ Adrienne D. Davis, "Identity Notes Part One: Playing in the Light," *American
Univer⸱   ⸱w Review* 45 (1996): 695–720; Ian Haney Lopez, *White by Law: The Legal
Constr⸱   f Race* (New York: New York University Press, 1996); Ariela Gross, "Lit-
igating   ess: Trials of Racial Determination in the Nineteenth-Century South,"
Yale Li⸱   al 108 (1998): 109; and Matthew Frye Jacobson, *Whiteness of a Differ-
ent Co⸱   pean Immigrants and the Alchemy of Race* (Cambridge, MA: Harvard
Univer⸱   , 1998).

3. C⸱   ⸱e theory was formed out of a movement by legal scholars of color
who fo⸱   ailure of legal educators to interrogate the connection between race,
racism,   aw, combined with the presentation of legal education as a neutral
and obj⸱   eavor, extremely problematic. See Kimberle William Crenshaw, "Forward: T⸱   Race-Conscious Pedagogy in Legal Education," *National Black Law
Journal⸱   1–14. See also Charles R. Lawrence III, "The Word and the River:
Pedagog⸱   arship as Struggle," in *Critical Race Theory: The Key Writings That
Formed⸱   ent*, ed. Kimberle Crenshaw, Neil Gotanda, Gary Peller, and Kendall
Thomas⸱   k: The New York Press, 1995): 235–256. For a more complete
overviev⸱   mings of, and developments in, critical race theory, see Kimberle
Crensha⸱   nda, Gary Peller, and Kendall Thomas, eds., *Critical Race Theory:
The Key⸱   hat Formed the Movement* (New York: The New Press, 1995);
Richard⸱   *itical Race Theory: The Cutting Edge* (Philadelphia: Temple Uni-
versity P⸱   Richard Delgado, *Critical Race Theory: An Introduction* (New
York: Ne⸱   iversity Press, 2001); Adrien Katherine Wing, ed., *Critical Race
Feminisn⸱   : New York University Press, 1997); Francisco Valdes, Jerome Mc-
Cristal Ci⸱   ⸱ela P. Harris, eds., *Crossroads, Directions, and a New Critical Race
Theory* (⸱   Temple University Press, 2002).

4. Kim⸱   ⸱aw has called this "perspectivelessness," or the notion that the
law and l⸱   ⸱ion contain no particular perspective but are, rather, representative of a ⸱   ⸱sal perspective. She suggests that there is an assumption of perspectivelessness in legal academia that perpetuates both a white normative perspective and
ignores the relevance of the long history of racism in the law. See Kimberle William
Crenshaw, "Forward: Toward a Race-Conscious Pedagogy in Legal Education," *National Black Law Journal* 1 (1994): 1–14. See also Charles R. Lawrence III, "The Word
and the River: Pedagogy as Scholarship as Struggle," in *Critical Race Theory: The Key
Writings That Formed the Movement*, ed. Kimberle Crenshaw, Neil Gotanda, Gary
Peller, and Kendall Thomas (New York: The New York Press, 1995): 235–256.

5. I discuss my methodology in depth in the appendix.

1

White Space

IN APRIL 2002, the Black Law Students Association (BLSA) at Harvard Law School organized a class walkout and silent protest in response to several racist incidents that occurred in the winter and spring of 2002. The first incident occurred when a white law student used the law school website to outline the facts of a property case involving racially restrictive covenants and used the term "nigs" to refer to African Americans. In response, the BLSA publicly registered its disgust and demanded that the administration take some action. After this public outcry, another white male student sent an anonymous e-mail (though he was later identified) to a first-year black woman law student that said, among other things,

> We at the Harvard Law School [are] a free, private community, where any member wishing to use the word "nigger" in any form should not be prevented from doing so. . . . I have actually begun using the "nigger" word more often than before the incident. . . . If you, as a race, want to prove that you do not deserve to be called by that word, work hard and you will be recognized.[1]

That e-mail message was then reproduced on fliers, which also contained anti-Semitic comments, and widely distributed to the law school community (those responsible for the reproduction and dissemination of these fliers were never discovered). In reaction to these events, a Harvard Law professor proposed holding a mock trial in his class, with the white student who sent the e-mail as the defendant and the professor himself serving as the white student's defense counsel.

Separately, but during this same period, another Harvard Law professor told his first-year torts class that "the blacks" (as well as Marxists and feminists) had contributed nothing to tort law theory.[2] When black students complained to the administration about his comment and said that they were uncomfortable with him teaching the class, the professor publicly asserted that his opinions concerning tort law theory were an expression of academic freedom. He said, "Imagine what would happen in the classroom if everyone has to walk on eggshells. Scholars have to be prepared and motivated to think about subjects without limitation, especially in teaching people to be lawyers, since virtually everything in the legal realm is open to debate."[3]

Although these are particularly explicit examples of racial hostility at Harvard Law, these incidents, as well as the response of the administration to the incidents, provide a situational lens through which to interrogate racialized institutional norms in the law school. White students and faculty in the law school are, according to their own analysis, asserting a *right* to publicly express antiblack racism in the space of the law school. African American students, on the other hand, suggest a competing interest, their interest in attaining a legal education free from dehumanizing stereotypes and insults. The competing interests of white students and faculty who wish to express their racial hostility and the interests of students of color to be free from such hostility are clearly not equally situated for several reasons. First, when white students use the racial epithet "nigger," they are tacitly drawing upon a legacy of white racial oppression, exclusion, and violence. The white student who sent the e-mail understood this connection in as much as he suggested that if African Americans "as a race" want to prove that they "do not deserve" to be called by the racial epithet, they should "work harder" and then white people will "recognize" them. In framing his use of racist speech in this manner, he simultaneously relies upon the history of white racism attached to the epithet he uses, while shifting the blame for that racism away from himself (and whites generally) and onto African Americans. Similarly, when a professor suggests that "the blacks" have contributed nothing to an entire body of legal theory, then responds to criticism of this racist assertion by suggesting that "everything in the legal realm is open to debate," his assertion is necessarily connected to the history of racial exclusion in the law and an unspoken norm of white superiority in legal scholarship (which is, of course, connected to this exclusion). This assumption in place, he is able to assert that he would be forced to "walk on eggshells" if he could not openly express his racially stereotypical perspective.

Not only do the constructions of the interest of whites to openly express their racism in the law school draw power from their tacit reliance upon the long history of racial oppression and exclusion to which they are connected, but they also rely upon both legal and institutional support. The white student suggests that he has a right, which invokes a legally constructed entitlement, to use the racial epithet "nigger." Furthermore, this right to racist speech was validated as an entitlement respected in the law school when a faculty member offered to publicly defend the student as part of a classroom exercise. Through this action, he confirmed both the right of whites to assert racist speech and the institutional norm of support for that right. Furthermore, when another professor asserts that his racist comments about legal scholarship are an aspect of his academic freedom, he is relying upon a particular speech right in the context of teaching, a central institutional norm in the realm of education. The underlying history of racist oppression, combined with an institutional norm that protects the right to invoke epithets that signify that history, leaves African American students in an unequal position from which to assert their interest (not recognized as a right) in pursuing a legal education free from racial hostility.

After these incidents of racism occurred at Harvard, BLSA members and other students who supported their position met with members of the law school administration. They presented a concrete list of demands for action, which included sanctioning the white students who publicly expressed their racism, preventing the two professors implicated in the incidents from teaching first-year classes, and developing a law school policy against racial harassment. The reaction of administrators again constrained the discussion of these events and BLSA's demands within the boundaries of the institutional norm of protecting free speech. Dean Todd Rakoff said to reporters, "I would say that it is clear that we have got a problem or set of problems to address. Some of these are substantive problems—what are the limits of community on one side and free speech on the other?"[4] The phrase "limits of community" is instructive in that it tacitly signifies a racial norm with regard to the "community" of the law school. The construction of racist speech as a right of white people generally, and a right of white students and faculty in the law school in particular, sets up a particular frame within which to constrain dialogue about whose interests are definitive in the construction of the Harvard Law community. Certainly all forms of speech are not, and never were, protected under the law or in private institutions. By way of example, if a law student publicly threatened to shoot and kill the faculty and deans of the law school, it is extremely unlikely that there would be such public attempts to defend his right to speak in this manner. Yet, despite their connection to horrible, not to mention state-sanctioned, racial terrorism and violence, racist epithets are not viewed as threatening speech in this "community," or at least not by these white students, the faculty, and the administration. Black students, as well as other students of color who participated in the protests, certainly view the speech as both potentially threatening and harmful to their attempt to gain a legal education. But the institutional logic that shapes the boundaries of the discussion is ultimately based upon a white normative frame that gets used to define both "the limits of community" and "free speech."

While racism and racist discourse is usually subtler in the post–civil rights era, even traditional Jim Crow racism, such as open use of racist epithets and explicit stereotypes, gets afforded protection in the space of the law school. Offering any protection for this egregious form of racism sends a clear message that contestation of subtler forms of racism will be fruitless. This message was further conveyed when the administration responded to the demands of BLSA with hesitation and disingenuous surprise. In response to the BLSA request for a policy against racial harassment, the dean of faculty, Robert Clark, said, "That's a major undertaking" and suggested that while the administration would "consider" such a policy, it would not happen quickly.[5] Furthermore, both Dean Clark and Dean Rakoff publicly stated that although they "care about" the perspectives of students, they would not allow students to dictate who would teach first-year classes.[6] Thus, BLSA's request to prevent the two faculty members who were involved in the incidents from teaching these classes was denied. And finally, while the administration said that they would "consider" how best to sanction the white students who were involved, because the use of racial epithets and stereotypes was presumptively framed as a right of free speech, the possible approaches for sanctions were limited by the institutional norm in support of this right. As a result, practically speaking, the school failed to support the interest of African American law students to receive a legal education free from racism (and, quite obviously, there exists no historically or legally supported right to be free from racism in education for students of color).

In declining to institutionally enforce a right of students of color to be free from racism in the space (or "community") of the law school, the administration effectively minimized the relevance of racism. They did this both tacitly, by constructing the issue as one centering on protected speech rights, and explicitly, by reacting with surprise to the anger of African American students. After meeting with BLSA, Dean Clark said publically that he was surprised by the reaction of black students to the incidents. He said, "By themselves [the individual incidents] weren't all that catastrophic." So, he concluded, "There must be some sense that there's a more general racist feeling around."[7] The question of whether these individual incidents were "catastrophic" was clearly up for debate, as the organized protest of students of color illustrated. More importantly, the surprise registered by Dean Clark concerning the reaction of students of color to the incidents was unconvincing given the broader historical context of racism and racial protest at Harvard Law. In fact, throughout the 1980s and 1990s, students of color at Harvard Law organized numerous protests in various forms to problematize the lack of racial diversity in the curriculum and among students and faculty. Robert Clark was dean of faculty in 1990, for example, when prominent critical race scholar Derrick Bell, who was the first tenured African American faculty member at Harvard Law, went on an unpaid leave from his position to protest the failure of the law school to hire an African American woman. Professor Bell remained on unpaid leave for two years, and during that time, students continually lead silent protests to support his actions (see also Bell 1996). Professor Bell eventually lost his position at the law school because the school did not move to meet his demands, and after his two-year leave, he was fired. Dean Clark, however, had previously registered his lack of support for these forms of racial resistance at Harvard. In 1987, when Professor Bell had held a silent protest in his office as a result of the denial of tenure to two professors who were proponents of critical legal studies, then professor Robert Clark dismissed the relevance of Professor Bell's efforts, publicly stating, "This is a university, not a lunch counter in the Deep South."[8]

Situated within the context of this institutional history, the minimization of racism seems to be part of a broader white framing of the issues that excuse racism, whether expressed subtly or explicitly, and decenter the perspectives of students and faculty of color with regard to race and community within the law school. And while Harvard Law School may be the most prominent, it is not unique among elite law schools with regard to racial criticism. In 1990, students at over forty law schools across the country boycotted their classes in order to protest the dismal record of hiring faculty of color in elite law schools.[9] Since that time, the racial demographics of faculty, as well as students, at elite law schools have changed little.[10] And Robert Clark's suggestion that Harvard Law is "not a lunch counter in the Deep South" is powerful, if not in the way he originally intended. Elite law schools are the political institutions in which people are trained to become lawyers, lawyers who will gain access to powerful positions in government and business as a result of their affiliation with these prominent schools. Racism and racially exclusive practices in elite law schools have far more politically significant consequences than racism in public accommodations like restaurants.

In this chapter, I situate law schools within the broader political economy of race in the United States. I suggest that these schools are uniquely located to reproduce notions of legal authority and sociolegal racial ideologies. Despite this fact, and despite continual recognition from professional organizations like the American Bar Association (ABA) that racial equity in the profession of law should be a central concern for the legal profession,[11] very little empirical research has been conducted to examine the racial dynamics of elite law schools. More importantly, even the research that has been conducted on legal education, which has tended to focus on class and gender, has not adequately considered the interaction between structural attributes of elite law schools, everyday cultural and institutional practices, and dominant ideologies and discourses in the schools. In order to create a framework that adequately accounts for all of these dimensions of the law school space, I extend the work of race-critical scholars, developing an integrated conception of *white institutional space*. I suggest that this conception of white space provides an analytical tool with which to interrogate the intersecting mechanisms that contribute to the reproduction of white privilege and power within elite institutional spaces like law schools.

The Political Relevance of Law Schools

The United States developed as a nation characterized by systemic racism in all its major economic, political, and social institutions.[12] As Joe Feagin has aptly described it, "Race relations—or more accurately, racist relations—are not *in*, but rather *of* this society" (2000, 17; emphasis added). The construction of race and racist hierarchy was used as a political tool by white elites to justify the exploitation of human beings and land, while simultaneously asserting the rhetorical principles of freedom, democracy, and equality under the law. Upon this nation's inception, and throughout its racially violent history, the protection of the economic interests of white elites has been a central, guiding principle in the social contract that organizes the state.[13] Cheryl Harris (1993) suggests that the economic interests of whites were so fundamental to the development of this country's legal structure that whiteness took on the legal characteristics of property. Initially, she suggests, this was based upon legal and political theories concerning who had the right to own property (whites), who did not (American Indians), and who became the object of property (African Americans). As time went on, however, whiteness came to be treated as a property interest in itself. Harris says,

> The law's construction of whiteness defined and affirmed critical aspects of identity (who is white); of privilege (what benefits accrue to that status); and, of property (what legal entitlements arise from that status). Whiteness at various times signifies and is deployed as identity, status, and property, sometimes singularly, sometimes in tandem. (1993, 1725)

Racial pseudoscience, in the form of studies designed to biologize race and simultaneously provide scientific support for racial hierarchy, became an important mechanism for constructing and justifying systemic racism (Harding 1993, Gould 1996). But, as Harris's analysis suggests, the most powerful political tool employed for the construction of white racial supremacy was the U.S. legal system.

Beginning with the construction of a constitution that recognized and politically protected racialized slavery, white supremacy was deeply embedded in the U.S. legal structure. One of the first acts of Congress in the newly developed state was the statutory construction of the 1790 Immigration and Naturalization Act, which restricted citizenship to "free white persons." This restriction posed a problem for U.S. courts of naturalization because the term "white person" was far from unambiguous. Through legal cases involving individuals who sought to become U.S. citizens, the law codified the boundaries of whiteness. This occurred largely through a process of judicial decision making about who was not white (and therefore could not naturalize) so that the boundaries of whiteness got constructed through negation, by legally identifying those who were not entitled to the privileges of whiteness (Lopez 1996; see also Jacobson 1998). Thus, the law played a central role in actually establishing racial boundaries—that is, who was designated a member of what race—and racial boundary construction was deeply connected to the institution of slavery and the notion of Manifest Destiny, the ideology that advocated the geographical spread of white power across the country (Takaki 1993, Lopez 1996).

The legal construction of racial group boundaries as a mechanism for parceling out economic and political rights (or the denial of such "rights") was not the only way in which the law influenced the construction of race. As Ian Haney Lopez (1996) points out, the racialized legal structure had an impact on actual phenotypical characteristics in a very real sense. Explicitly racialized immigration and naturalization laws remained in effect in this country from its inception until the mid-1950s, restricting who could come into and remain in the United States, thereby manipulating the demographics of persons with particular phenotypical characteristics present in the country (see Lopez 1996, Allen 1997, Jacobson 1998, Glenn 2002). This limited the range of possibilities with regard to normal human procreation, thus manipulating the phenotypical landscape that allegedly signified racial group boundaries. Furthermore, until the early 1960s, many states enacted and enforced antimiscegenation laws, again using the authority of the state to prevent unions between people that would likely have made the boundaries of "whiteness" or "blackness" even more of a physiological blur than they already were.[14] Race and the law were fundamentally interconnected, and sociolegal constructions of race were at all moments connected to the preservation of white economic and political power.

Not only did the law concretely impact the physiological markers of race and define the economic and political interests that corresponded to race, but it also served, and continues to serve, as a mechanism of hegemonic ideology with regard to white privilege and power.[15] Eduardo Bonilla-Silva notes that racial ideology and racialized social structures are always interconnected and suggests that once a society becomes racially structured, "there develops a racial ideology. . . . This ideology is not simply a 'superstructural' phenomenon (a mere reflection of the racialized system), but becomes the organizational map that guides the actions of racial actors in society. It becomes as real as the relations it organizes" (1997, 470).[16] But, as Kimberle Crenshaw (1988) has pointed out, the law represents an ideological framework that, in itself, structures society. In other words, while the language and analysis of the law is fundamentally discursive and expressive of ideology, it simultaneously carries the force of the state to shape the racial structure. The law is an organizational map that coercively guides the actions of racial actors by, for example, legally proscribing whom one can and cannot marry or legally protecting the right of white people to publicly express racial hostility. The law is both ideological, in its discursive frame, and proscriptive so that it draws upon the power of the state to influence the citizenry, both through actual physical coercion and as the hegemonic moral voice of state authority (see also Mills 1997).

Toward the end of the nineteenth century, law schools began to develop as an institutional power with regard to the profession of law (see Seligman 1978 and Stevens 1983). The traditional model of lawyer apprenticeship was gradually being replaced by a regular course of study in institutions of higher education. The most influential push in the movement to require attendance in law schools as a prerequisite for entering the profession of law came from elite legal institutions, most notably, Harvard Law School. Christopher Columbus Langdell, dean of Harvard Law from 1875 to 1895, is widely recognized as the founder of the model of legal education that predominates today. Under his model, the course of study in law school was extended from eighteen months to three years, and a standardized curriculum was established. This new curriculum focused on the analysis of judicial case law in order to facilitate the internalization of the doctrinal logic used in the judicial process—or, as it is commonly stated, to learn to "think like a lawyer" (Seligman 1978, Granfield 1986, 1992, Schleef 1992, Brooks 2006). This method, termed the "case method," was combined with a style of teaching whereby professors challenged students to tease out the information in cases through rapid and forceful question and response, the Socratic method. Developed at Harvard, this combination of the case-method curriculum and the Socratic method of instruction soon became the model of legal education followed by law schools throughout the country and continues to the present.[17] So, at the very foundation of the law school curricular model, there rested an assumption that law students must internalize the logic, hence the ideological frame, of the law.

The interaction present in legal education between the power of the law as an ideological frame and the power of education in the reproduction of ideology should not be minimized. Education, as a social institution, is widely recognized as a source of ideological reproduction and social control.[18] Pierre Bourdieu (1990) has gone so far as to suggest that through tacit ideological reproduction, education becomes a form of symbolic violence (see also Bourdieu and Passeron 1990). Symbolic violence, according to Bourdieu, is perpetrated by "every power which manages to impose meanings and to impose them as legitimate by concealing power relations which are the basis of its force" (1990, 4). Education, in all its forms, gets presented as neutral, yet it imposes meanings and symbols that are associated with dominant culture, thus reproducing an ideological frame that rationalizes and reproduces structures of inequality.[19] This, according to Bourdieu, typifies symbolic violence. And as Crenshaw (1994) has pointed out, one of the central problems with race and legal education is the implicit assertion of "perspectivelessness" in the teaching of a fundamentally racialized body of law, precisely the kind of symbolic violence to which Bourdieu alludes.

The law, as an institution, functions in the same way. A seemingly (and often asserted) neutral method for organizing economic, political, and social interactions, the law actually serves to protect the economic interests of the ruling class—elite white men. The realm of legal education, then, contains the interacting power of two social institutions, law and education, both of which operate to reproduce structures, as well as hegemonic ideologies that support those structures. Yet, within legal education there remains an insistent claim that the teaching of law is a neutral, objective, and impartial endeavor. As Duncan Kennedy asserts, "Law school teaching makes the choice of hierarchy and domination, which is implicit in the adoption of the rules of property, contract, and tort, look as though it flows from legal reasoning rather than from politics and economics" (1983, 21).

So, the very institution that trains the people who will be most influential in creating and interpreting the legal structures that organize U.S. society socializes them not to problematize the connection between law and domination. Given the central importance of the law with regard to race and racial hierarchy in the United States, this fact powerfully implicates law schools in the reproduction of racial inequality. Furthermore, the reproductive power of law schools is exacerbated by the fact that the law has been the central institution through which people of color have attempted to challenge racial oppression by appealing to legally protected civil rights. This raises the question that Audre Lorde (1984) identified and that spurred the development of critical

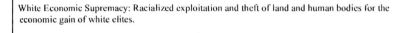

White Economic Supremacy: Racialized exploitation and theft of land and human bodies for the economic gain of white elites.

Legal Structure: Creates and supports political system for the proliferation of white economic supremacy, and aides in the construction of political and social racial domination. Simultaneously justifies, normalizes, and enforces the racial oppression of the state.

Law Schools: Rationalize and normalize the legal structure; socialize those who will have the most control over the legal structure to uncritically internalize the ideological frames of the law.

Figure 1.1.   The Political Location of Law Schools

legal studies: can the master's house be dismantled with the master's tools? Although its discussion is beyond the scope of this book, this question speaks to the important political location of law schools. Figure 1.1 illustrates how law schools became embedded within the social structure of racial domination.

Situated as such, law schools become an important institutional site for empirical investigation with regard to race and reproduction. Yet, surprisingly little research examining the racial dynamics of law schools and legal education has been conducted. The bulk of the studies either focus on the relevance of "diversity" in legal education (see, for example Allen and Solorzano 2001, Dowd 2003, and Buckner 2004), or on gender or class in the law schools. However, these studies do provide insight into the power dynamics of these schools.

Thinking Like a Lawyer:
The Social Transmission of Knowledge and Power

In the famous book *One L* (1977), Scott Turow writes of his own experience as a first-year law student at Harvard Law School. Turow suggests that not only did law school demand that he change the way he thought about law and social issues but that this process of learning to think in a new way occurred within an extreme hierarchy of the powerful professor and the (relatively) powerless student. In his description, the process is at times painful and is ultimately life altering. At one point, Turow describes an uncomfortable exchange between one of his classmates, "Mooney," and Professor Perini, their contracts professor, in order to illustrate the power dynamics in the classroom. On this day, the student came to class unprepared, and Professor Perini randomly called on him (picking his name off a seating chart).

> "I'm sorry, sir," Mooney said. "I'm not prepared." Perini froze over the seating chart, stock-still, one elbow hooked in the air as he held his pencil. His jaw rotated once or twice before he spoke. "You mean you didn't think we'd get that far," he said. He was looking up at Mooney with horrible hatred in his face and his voice was icy with contempt. . . . I'd heard this had happened once several years before and that Perini had stood over the student and made him read the case right there, answering questions line by line as he went through it, a torture of exposure which had lasted nearly forty minutes. (Turow 1977, 129)

Describing many experiences like these, Turow explains how the process of legal education took place in a context within which public humiliation became a mechanism for enforcing law school socialization. In the above example, the humiliation came as a result of being unprepared for class, but at other times it came as a result of failing to properly internalize the interpretations of the law expected by professors. In law school, as Turow notes, the hierarchy of power is inherent in the version of the Socratic method employed to teach law. Professors fire hard-hitting questions, often calling on students randomly, then draw upon tactics ranging from open hostility to mild sarcasm in an effort to compel students to both carefully read and internalize case law.

Law professor Paul Wangerin (1986) has suggested that the process of socialization involved in learning to think like a lawyer is so totalizing that he likens it to the story in the movie *Invasion of the Body Snatchers*. Wangerin analogizes a fictional tale of law school in which law students are lulled to sleep during their three years in law school, and in their third year, they are secretly placed in a basement room. At that time, giant pods stored in the secret basement room open, and out come new people in the exact likeness of the students who have disappeared. While these new people look exactly like the students they have replaced, their ideological perspectives and cognitive styles have been forever transformed. The story, though meant to invoke humor, reveals a socialization process so intense that the students are completely, irreversibly changed.

Stories like the ones told by Turow and Wangerin represent many of the narratives of law students and law professors, and they provide us with a particularly personal and emotive perspective on the power of law school socialization. Political scientist Mark Miller has said, "Learning to think like a lawyer is analogous to giving birth to a new person with a new personality, or at least it feels as painful as childbirth for most law students" (1995, 21). These narratives are supplemented by empirical research on law school education that suggest this view of the process of socialization involved in learning to think like a lawyer is widespread (Erlanger and Klegon 1978; Granfield 1986, 1992; Schleef 2001). More importantly, this research indicates that while the process of teaching students to think like lawyers is generally presented as a neutral, impartial endeavor, the law school space is clearly marked by class, gender, and racial hierarchies. Again, Bourdieu's conception of symbolic violence is useful, and in the context of law schools, the symbolic violence of imposing meaning while concealing power relations (the power relations embedded in the law) occurs in a particularly coercive manner.

The titles of two major books coming out of empirical investigations of the power dynamics in law schools are revealing of the class and gender hierarchies in law schools. Robert Granfield's *Making Elite Lawyers: Visions of Law at Harvard and Beyond* (1992) and Lani Guinier, Michelle Fine, and Jane Balin's *Becoming Gentlemen: Women, Law School, and Institutional Change* (1997) both suggest that legal education is a process of conversion for those who are not elite white men. Granfield's research at Harvard suggests that elite law schools are classed institutions and that the process of law school socialization assumes a standpoint of elite class status. Students from working-class backgrounds must learn to "fake" the dominant cultural representations of elitism to be successful in law school, and this creates an identity crisis for many students from such backgrounds seeking out the law as a mechanism for social change, only to find that they themselves are changed (Granfield 1986, 1991 and Granfield and Koenig 1992). Similarly Guinier, Fine, and Balin's examination of gender in elite law schools suggests that law school education is normed toward the learning and problem-solving styles of men. According to these authors, the dominant teaching approach in law schools, which involves frequently adversarial and sometimes hostile questioning of students by professors, tends to be reflective of more masculine learning styles and often becomes problematic for women. They further suggest that the emphasis on objective and neutral styles of argumentation is more challenging for women, who are generally socialized to problem solve in a more contextualized manner.

Of course, if learning to think like a lawyer involves learning to think and act like a man, some women will make the choice to do just that in law school, just as some working-class students attempt to take on elite culture. Yet, while working-class students who find themselves in elite law schools can buy into the ideologies and reap the economic and cultural rewards of elite legal education (albeit with an emotional cost), the situation for women in law school is qualitatively different. Even women who choose to accept the dominant ideologies of law schools cannot become gentlemen. The consequences of this are made clear by the research of several legal scholars who find that even women who strive to think and act like men may be the victim of sexual bias and harassment in law school. For example, Joan Krauskopf (1994) conducted survey research at nine Ohio law schools and found that 69 percent of female students in Ohio law schools reported sexual harassment in the form of improper comments. In addition, Taunya Lovell Banks (1986, 1990) found in her research, collected over three years from eighteen different law schools, that sexually offensive comments in the classroom were a common occurrence and that some professors even referred to women as "bitches" in class (1986, 144). Thus, even women who say they enjoy the masculine pedagogical approach in law school education still sometimes find themselves facing these forms of gender bias in their education—even learning to think and act like a man cannot prevent women from being treated as inferior to men.[20]

Where Is Race?

Race, like gender, is qualitatively different from class in that most of the time individuals cannot (even if they want to) fake their race.[21] And the research of Guinier, Fine, and Balin (1997) contains powerful anecdotal evidence suggesting that race is a central component of how students experience law school. For example, one Latina woman law student who was interviewed said, "I think that there is a lot of discrediting on the side of the white students. . . . I get the sense that, perhaps, people won't listen to me as much as if I was a white person saying it. I think when they listen to me, they say, 'of course she is going to say that because she is speaking for her own self-interest'"(51). And in another interview with two African American women law students, one of the students said, "I think that still most people do not understand that African Americans are still struggling or why they are struggling. To me, it's incredible because it's like blindness, and I listen to some of the comments in class, and I realize that I am coming from an entirely different world in that perspective than most people" (51). And finally, according to Guinier, Fine, and Balin, a Latino male law student reported that "the press for objectivity in his three years of law school [had] forced him to remove his mind from his Latino body" (1997, 53). These comments suggest that race and racial dynamics of power impact the law school experience in both overt and subtle ways. Yet, while scholars who have examined gender and class acknowledge the relevance of race, with notable exceptions, none has attempted to examine the dynamics of race in law schools systematically.

Two notable studies of legal education have included an empirically based examination of race in law schools, one exploring the intersecting identities of race, class, and gender (as well as several other aspects of social identity) in the law school and the other examining how class participation varies by race as well as gender. Carrie Yang Costello (2001) conducted ethnographic research at Boalt Hall School of Law (the law school at the University of California, Berkeley). Costello suggests that students of color (as well as women and people from "less privileged backgrounds") experience an identity dissonance because their own identities and experiences do not fit well with the appropriate "professional identities" expected in the law school. Costello acknowledges that the expected "professional identity" is connected to white, elite, male identity but frames her analysis from a social-psychological perspective, suggesting that the source of the problem for students of color stems from identity dissonance as opposed to the structural relations of power in the law school and society. As a result of this framework, she makes two major mistakes in her analysis of race and racism in the law school. First, Costello reduces race to merely an aspect of identity, then equates it to other aspects of identity, including gender and class, but also includes political ideological standpoint and what she terms "empathic orientations" (2001, 178). In her attempt to analyze many different aspects of identity with regard to success in law school, she fails to take note of the structural aspects of race and the ways in which these structural dynamics differentiate racial identity from other aspects of identity. Conflating gender identity and race identity, for example, is problematic because gender and race hierarchies operate differently in society.[22] But equating racial identity with political perspectives or orientations illustrates a complete disregard for the social-structural aspects of race, the relative permanence of racial group membership in U.S. society, and the centrality of racism in society and in the law.

Costello's reduction of race to the level of identity is related to the second major flaw in her analysis. Just as she reduces race to merely an aspect of identity, she reduces the notion of racism to the level of the individual. As she discusses the possibility of racial discrimination or systemic racism in law schools, she equates racism with intentional acts on the part of bad actors. She suggests that she is examining "institutional discrimination," then tacitly defines institutional racism as "overt bigotry" or "a conspiracy to discriminate." Then, having set up a straw man—individual overt bigots or groups of individuals engaged in conspiracy—she easily knocks it down, suggesting that she did not find evidence to support either of these as an explanation for the problems of students of color at Boalt Hall. A more structural definition of race and racism would have been far less easy to dismiss, given her findings suggesting that students of color often felt out of place in the law school and as though they were losing both their identities and touch with the communities they lived in before coming to law school. These problems in Costello's analysis of race at Boalt Hall leave serious gaps in our understanding of the racial dynamics of that elite law school.

Another empirical study that explicitly looked at the racial dynamics of law schools involved an examination of the levels of student participation in class discussions. This research, conducted by Elizabeth Mertz, Wamucii Njogu, and Susan Gooding (1998), compared participation in contracts classes in different law school settings, at law schools of different ranks (not just elite law schools) in classes taught by professors with differing races and genders, with student demographics in the classes, and in classes in which the professors utilized varying teaching styles. Having videotaped the classes, they were able to analyze variations in participation in these settings by both race and gender. These scholars found that students of color tended to participate less in class than white students but also that the amount and substance of class participation was influenced by the race of the person teaching the class (students of color tended to participate and volunteer more in classes taught by faculty of color). However, because this research only examined class participation, it reveals little about *why* students of color participate less frequently in classes. Nor does it attempt to examine other aspects of the racial structure or culture of legal education that might interact with, and help to explain, the lack of class participation.

The major shortcoming of these studies represents a shortcoming of much of the research evaluating the power dynamics in law schools; there is a failure both to contextualize race within the broader social-structural aspects of law schools and legal education and, correspondingly, to situate law schools within the broader social and political context in which they operate. No study of race in law schools has captured the totality of the racialized structures within them, nor within the law. Neither do they capture the everyday racialized practices and normative discourses that function to reproduce and justify these structures. In fact, none of the literature on legal education attempts to critically analyze the most deeply embedded and authoritative voice in the law school: the law. Given the central role of the law in the construction and maintenance of relations of power, and especially relations of power based upon race, as well as the hegemonic power of the law which is, if anything, more controlling in law school education than in society at large, this is a major shortcoming of this entire body of literature (see also Sarat and Felstiner 1989, and Kennedy 1983).

In Guinier, Fine, and Balin's analysis of gender in law schools, they say, "There is something about the law school *environment* that has a negative academic impact on female law students" (1997, 9; emphasis added). Invoking the word "environment" suggests that there is something about the space of the law school that is negative for women law students, yet while these authors do a good job of capturing the gendered process of learning and thinking dominant in the law school, their structural analysis stops there. In Costello's research at Boalt Hall, one African American woman law student (whom she also describes as having "lower-middle-class origins") said in her interview, "At first I used to feel weird walking around the halls, like I didn't belong. I couldn't really believe I was here" (2001, 40). This comment, while it does indicate a feeling of dissonance with regard to upward mobility as Costello suggests, also suggests an emotive reaction to nonbelonging in the physical space of the law school. Much of the work of scholars that examines law schools and legal education contains these types of cues, pointing to something totalizing about the law school space that is operating upon different students differently.

To extend this literature and construct a framework with which to understand the racial dynamics of elite law schools, attention must be paid to these totalizing invocations of space. Feagin suggests that "white racism today remains normal and is deeply imbedded in all historically white institutions. Every such institution is mostly whitewashed in its important norms, rules, and arrangements" (2006, 190). In order to understand *how* elite law schools are whitewashed, I suggest the need for an analytical framework that captures the broad range of mechanisms—structural, cultural, ideological, and discursive—that converge to reproduce whiteness in elite American institutions like law schools—a theoretical framework of white space.

White Space: A Framework

The notion of racialized space is not new to the social science literature, but it has generally been theorized with respect to geographical areas, specifically racially marked residential segregation (Massey 1993, Jargowsky 1997, powell 1999). As a result of racialized government housing and lending policies, racist practices in the real estate industry, and private discrimination in white communities, the United States has become one of the most race-segregated countries in the world (Massey and Denton 1993). Racially segregated neighborhoods have functioned to spatially isolate black (and increasingly Latino) communities from the wealth and resources that have accumulated in white communities as a result of racial exploitation and oppression. Speaking about the implications of residential segregation for democracy in the United States, Iris Young has noted, "Residential segregation enacts or enlarges many material privileges of economic opportunity, quality of life, power to influence actions and events, and convenience. At the same time it obscures the fact of such privileges from many of their beneficiaries" (2000, 196). Racialized spatial segregation becomes a mechanism for the reproduction of racial inequality without regard to the intent of racial actors in different communities. In fact, as Young notes, the material and ideological privileges that whites receive as a result of racial segregation get rendered invisible because they require no individual racial animus (see also Frankenberg 1993). As a result, spatial segregation functions as a central element of institutional racism.

As the case of residential segregation illustrates, the concept of institutional racism is essential to a complete understanding of the reproduction of racism in U.S. society. The concept of institutional racism captures how racist relations can be reproduced without individuals' intentional racist acts, because racism is deeply entrenched within our institutions (see Knowles and Prewitt 1969, Blauner 1972, Carmichael and Hamilton 1977, and Wellman 1993). Louis Knowles and Kenneth Prewitt note, "Institutions are fairly stable social arrangements and practices through which collective actions are taken" (1969, 5). As I have discussed above, law and education are key social institutions through which social reproduction takes place. And because these institutions are fundamentally racialized, they function to reproduce racist social relations and ideologies that support these relations as institutions (as opposed to as individuals, or even collections of individuals). Stokely Carmichael and Charles Hamilton provide a clear articulation of the connection between institutions and actors in the U.S. racist order:

> Institutional racism relies on the active and pervasive operation of antiblack attitudes and practices. A sense of superior group position prevails: whites are "better" than blacks; therefore blacks should be subordinate to whites. This is a racist attitude and it permeates the society, on both the individual and institutional level, covertly and overtly. "Respectable" individuals can absolve themselves from individual blame: *they* would never plant a bomb in a church. . . . But they continue to support political officials and institutions that would and do perpetuate institutionally racist policies. Thus *acts* of overt, individual racism may not typify the society, but institutional racism does. (1967, 5, emphasis added)

This conception of institutional racism reveals a connection between racist ideology and racialized practices at both the level of individuals and institutions, resulting in the reproduction of racist social structure.

As the research on residential segregation illustrates, racialized space is one mechanism of institutional racism through which white power and privilege are reproduced in often tacit and relatively invisible ways.[23] Several scholars have extended the notion of race and space beyond the context of geographical neighborhoods. Amanda Lewis (2003) has discussed the racialization of space in grammar school settings, noting that racial segregation in education has lead to white and nonwhite educational spaces. In characterizing schools as a white or nonwhite space, however, Lewis seems to rely solely upon the racial demographics of the schools. Yet, in her analysis she finds that even in schools that are demographically nonwhite spaces, tacit white norms remain embedded in the school institution as a result of broader institutionalized racism in education. Feagin, Hernan Vera, and Nikitah Imani (1997) discuss the spatial dynamics of historically white colleges and universities with more of a focus toward identifying the institutional characteristics that result in racialized space in these institutions. They point out that many institutional norms, policies, and procedures make these institutions normatively white spaces, including the history of the institutions, the racialized practices and policies of administrators, and the dominant white culture and discourse that often employ racism to signify students of color as outsiders in these spaces. But no one has yet gone so far as to delineate the many interacting mechanisms by which white institutional space is constructed and reproduced. I suggest that a model of white space will provide a more comprehensive and useful tool for interrogating the "whitewashing" of powerful social institutions and, thus, shed light on the tacit reproduction of white power and privilege that occurs within these institutions.

Joan Acker (1990) has discussed the processes by which organizational institutions become gendered. This process, according to Acker, is explained through an analysis of the ways that "advantage and disadvantage, exploitation and control, action and emotion, meaning and identity are patterned through and in terms of a distinction between male and female, masculine and feminine" (1990, 146). Extending this analysis to the context of race, a theoretical model of white space should explicate how advantage and disadvantage, exploitation and control, action and emotion, and meaning and identity get patterned in terms of a distinction between whiteness and nonwhiteness. The concept of "nonwhiteness" fails to capture the very different histories and experiences of nonwhite racial groups; for example, the racialized history and experience of African Americans is quite different from that of Asian Americans. However, while the experience of race and racism by different groups of people of color in the United States has been quite distinct, they all share a denial (albeit in different ways and to different extents) of access to the privileges that correspond to white racial identity. Thus, turning the gaze upon whiteness (which contains an implicit concept of nonwhiteness) as the source of oppressive racial control provides a good starting point for examining the etiology of white institutional space.[24]

Acker's conceptualization of gendered organizational institutions captures the notion of institutional power, who has it, and who does not within the institution. But her discussion about action, emotion, meaning, and identity also captures the ways in which tacit gendered norms are embedded in allegedly neutral practices and policies within these spaces. Her theoretical framing draws attention to the interactions, of which I have already spoken, between institutional structures, everyday practices and policies, and dominant ideologies and discourses that construct the normative understanding of the space and the unequal power relations within the space. However, as Feagin, Vera and Imani (1997) have discussed, attention must also be paid to the historical racial exclusion that accompanied the development and organization of institutional settings like educational institutions. It is this historical exclusion that provided the context for the uncontested construction of white institutional space that is the foundation for contemporary white institutional norms and policies that reproduce white privilege and power within these spaces. Taking into account the foundational history of racist exclusion that characterized elite law schools, like most other powerful social institutions in the United States, I suggest the following model of the formation of white institutional space (see figure 1.2).

The white institutional space of elite law schools has as its foundation a history and legacy of white racist exclusion of people of color. Not only did this result in the white accumulation of economic and political power reaped from these institutions, but it also permitted an exclusively white construction of the norms, values, and ideological frameworks that organize these institutions. This resulted in the development of a white frame that organizes the logic of these institutions. Feagin defines a white frame as "an organized set of racialized ideas, emotions, and inclinations, as well as recurring or habitual discriminatory actions, that are consciously or unconsciously expressed in,

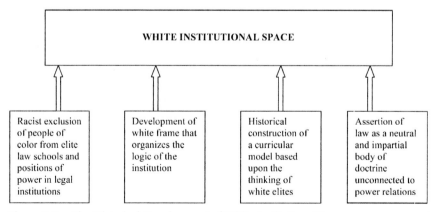

Figure 1.2. The Historical Development of White Institutional Space

and constitutive of, the routine operation and racist institutions of U.S. society" (2006, 23). A history of racist exclusion meant that this frame was generally formed without *any* input from racially excluded groups.[25] Yet, because most people in these institutions, as well as most social scientists who study institutions, fail to make the connection between historical racist exclusion and contemporary institutional norms, much of the white frame remains tacit, thereby reifying whiteness within the space without need for intentional action to do so.

In chapter 2, I discuss the history of legal education, revealing the tacit norms upon which legal education has been based, and I connect this history to contemporary law school structures. The history of elite law schools and other elite U.S. institutions organized white institutional space and provided the foundational support for the reproduction of white privilege and power in these institutions—but this history alone is not enough to reproduce white space. Set in motion by the history of exclusion but remaining relevant today, racially disparate demographics of a space become a relevant (though neither necessary nor sufficient) aspect of white institutional space. Just as the racial makeup of segregated neighborhoods signifies racial space, so, too, in institutions like elite law schools, the vast underrepresentation of people of color becomes a signifier. But to truly capture the relevance of racial demographics, just as Acker suggests with regard to gender demographics, one must assess how race marks positions of institutional power.

Looking to the administration, faculty, and staff in elite law schools, one can see that white people are consistently (and extremely) overrepresented in positions of institutional power. Thus, the demographics of law students of color, while relevant to the institutional space, is less significant in terms of institutional structure than the racial demographics of power holders in these schools. In the two elite law schools at which I conducted my research, the vast majority of people of color working in the schools were concentrated in low-level administrative posts, untenured instructor positions, or staff positions. Furthermore, as a cursory analysis of the websites of all of the top-tier law schools in the United States reveal, these demographics of power hold true in all elite law schools.[26]

Other relevant racial signifiers of power mark the racialized structure of institutional spaces, and in educational settings these are considered what Eric Margolis (2001) has identified as the hidden curriculum (see also Apple and Kegan 1982 and Apple 1986, 1990). For example, elite law schools typically have portraits of important legal actors lining the halls and classrooms within the space of the law school, and nearly all of these are portraits of white men. At one of my research sites, the law school added a great deal of art to the hallway walls while I was conducting my research, and much of this art depicted scenes of the civil rights movement. Notably, in these scenes all of the legal actors, the lawyers and judges, were white men, whereas the people represented as protestors, carrying signs and sitting in courtroom balconies, were African American. Given the fact that this law school, like many, contained a huge portrait of a white man in every large law school classroom, this artwork sent a tacit (and perhaps unintended) message that legal authority is properly in the hands of white people. People of color can participate as outsiders to the system, as protestors and observers, but not as legal actors.

As I have already mentioned, the most deeply embedded white normative structure in law schools is the law itself. The legal cases that make up the thousands of pages of reading law students do each semester of their three-year law school experience represent the most prominent voice in legal education. Yet, none of the studies examining legal education, whether in terms of race, class, or gender, has situated this voice within its analysis, revealing that this, too, is part of the hidden curriculum in legal education. Case law is presented to students as the voice of authority, as though handed down by God. In chapter 3, I interrogate the discursive framing of the law historically and today, noting that our legal frame was constructed with the same racially exclusionary practices that provided the institutional white frame for legal education. In doing so, I reveal the explicitly racist frame that characterized U.S. law and legal reasoning for the vast majority of U.S. history. This analysis sheds sharp light upon the hypocrisy of the dominant ideology and discourse in the law and in the law schools.

The legal system in the United States has historically been, and remains today, a structural support for white privilege and power. The post–civil rights legal frame, which is based upon an abstract liberalism that confines racial analysis to the level of the individual completely disconnected from the racial social structure, has stalled the progressive legal reforms that may have dismantled white supremacy. This impacts elite law schools in two major ways. First, post–civil rights law provides structural and ideological support for the reproduction of institutional racism throughout society. In this sense, the post–civil rights legal reasoning that supports white racial group interests influences all institutions in the United States. But, with regard to law schools in particular, the force of these laws is heightened because the law also serves as the main source of authority in the legal curriculum. As such, it carries both the authority of an educational knowledge source, as well as the legal and political force of the state. Thus, the law represents one of the deepest racialized normative structures functioning to enforce and reproduce white institutional space.

The deep structural features of white space embedded in law schools serve as the tacit shelter of support for the microlevel, everyday racialized interactions and discourses within the schools.[27] Eduardo Bonilla-Silva (2001, 2003) suggests that in the post–civil rights United States, whites have developed certain "story lines" or "frames" to create an ideology that supports a racialized structure based upon white privilege and power. One of the most powerful frames of color-blind racism is abstract liberalism, or the notion that equality means treating all individuals the same without regard to social structure or history. Abstract liberalism, which is the basis for contemporary legal reasoning in the law, organizes the dominant ideology and discursive frame at both Presidential and Midstate. Many students, for example, expressed sentiments similar to that of Ken, a white male law student, when he said, "I don't know, I guess, when it comes to the Constitution anyway, um [long pause], a lot of things have become more, more black and white. You know, there's a clear line. . . . I think admissions to the university should be race blind." His comments reveal a sentiment that views race issues as "black and white" (no pun intended) with regard to the law, meaning that college admissions and interpretations of the Constitution should not consider the racist history of the law (in particular the Constitution) or the contemporary racial social structure.

But the color-blind racism that characterized the dominant discourse in the schools was sharply contrasted by the normatively white (and sometimes explicitly racist) cultural and institutional practices in the law school space. White students, for example, had an expectation that law school social events would be held in white venues (for example, white bars) in white areas of the cities in which Presidential and Midstate were located. To examine the contradictions between the color-blind ideologies and discourses and the racialized culture and institutional practices in the law schools, I draw upon observations of classes, public spaces, and social events, as well as interviews with students, faculty, and staff. In chapter 4, I delineate the normative white perspectives and practices that make up the *practice* of color-blind racism.

Another central element of color-blind racism in elite law schools is the minimization of racism, illustrated by the administrative reaction to the racist incidents at Harvard discussed in the opening of this chapter. One of the major mechanisms utilized to minimize racism is the reconstruction, by white people in the law school, of the experiences of students of color. When administrators and faculty at Harvard discussed the racist incidents that took place there, they rejected the perspectives of students of color and reframed the race issues by stating that they were not "catastrophic" and by binding them within the discursive frame of speech rights in a manner that denied the relevance of racism to the law school community. As Margaret Andersen (2003) has noted, a major failing of the newly expanding social science literature on "whiteness" is the failure to connect explications of white privilege and power to the lived experiences of people of color. In chapter 5, I center the voices of students of color, disrupting the dominant white frame, to present the racialized picture of these law schools from the vantage point of the law students of color who must continually negotiate these white institutional spaces. The experiences of students of color reveal that this negotiation represents a major component of their legal education. In order to affirm their own human dignity, students of color must contend with, and resist, white space and the dominant white frame in elite law schools.

In chapter 6, I continue to center the voices of students of color, specifically examining the process of resistance these students engage in when contesting the boundaries of white institutional space. Law students of color (and often law faculty of color as well) expend a great deal of time and energy resisting the white frame that tends to dehumanize them in the space of these elite law schools. Coping with everyday racism in the law school frequently produces frustration, anger, or sadness, but the institutional logic of the law school does not recognize expressions of these emotions as legitimate. Students are thus forced to manage their emotions in order to avoid further marginalization. Moreover, students of color are forced to become student-educators as they attempt to bring the histories and experiences of people of color into their legal education. This demands that students of color perform invisible and emotional labor that their white counterparts are not required to perform. Both in the law school and in the profession of law, this labor is expected of law students of color, yet it goes unrecognized and unrewarded in the structure of legal education and the law profession.

Within the white institutional space of elite law schools, students of color find their very presence continually questioned, as Clarence Page's presence was questioned at the affirmative action debate at Georgetown (see the introduction). Although what happened to Mr. Page was an example of blatant racism, the white space of elite law schools is generally established in a more insidious manner through the interaction between deeply racialized organizational structures, everyday racialized practices, and justifying color-blind racist discourses. Law schools socialize individuals into the profession of law through the lens of a white frame. This white frame normalizes white racial superiority in the law school, in the law, and in society at large. And while students of color are constantly forced to negotiate and contest this white frame and the white space of the law schools, rarely do these struggles become a relevant component in discourses like the affirmative action debate. In the conclusion of this book, I connect the impact of white institutional space to race-related policy discussions like the affirmative action debate, as well as to race scholarship more broadly. By conceptually delineating the etiology of white institutional space in elite law schools, I am able to reveal the rhetorical boundaries of the white frame as it shapes the broader political discourse of race and racism.

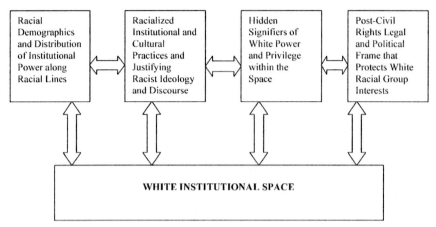

Figure 1.3.   The Reproduction of White Institutional Space

Historical racial exclusion provided context for the development of complete white institutional space. Having formed a white space through racially exclusive means, the other mechanisms of white space operate to reproduce the racial dynamics of the law school space without the need for enforced racial exclusion or open racial animus. Thus, in figure 1.3 I provide a contemporary model of white space and the mechanisms by which it is reproduced.

It is important to recognize, as the arrows on the diagram illustrate, that the mechanisms of white institutional space operate recursively and in conjunction with each other to enforce and reproduce the racial structure and culture. Because these mechanisms intersect with one another, they often overlap, and each mechanism is supported by and supports the other mechanisms. Although there may be varying degrees of each of these mechanisms with regard to distinct institutional spaces, in the following chapters I explicate how all of these mechanisms operate at Presidential University School of Law and Midstate Law School. My goal is to use these two cases to illustrate the processes that reproduce white institutional space. And, of course, the logical place to begin this project is with the history of law schools and legal education and its connection to the contemporary racial structure of the schools.

Notes

1. This e-mail was not reprinted in full in any news account of the incident, but these particular quotations from the e-mail were reported in the *Harvard Law Record* (the law school's newspaper), the *Harvard Crimson* (the main Harvard University

newspaper), and the *New York Times.* See "Administration Responds to BLSA Demands as Students Stage Protest," *Harvard Law Record,* April 18, 2002; "Law Students, Faculty Protest Racial Incidents," *Harvard Crimson,* April 16, 2002; "Comments Concerning Race Divide Harvard Law School," *New York Times,* April 20, 2002.

2. Tort law is the body of law that concerns civil liability for injury (physical and nonphysical injury), as differentiated from criminal law, which concerns criminal liability. This incident was reported in several news articles, including "Administration Responds to BLSA Demands as Students Stage Protest," *Harvard Law Record,* April 18, 2002; "Law Students, Faculty Protest Racial Incidents," *Harvard Crimson,* April 16, 2002; "Comments Concerning Race Divide Harvard Law School," *New York Times,* April 20, 2002.

3. *"New York Times'* Comments Concerning Race Divide Harvard Law School," April 20, 2002.

4. Quoted in "Administration Responds to BLSA Demands as Students Stage Protest," *Harvard Law Record,* April 18, 2002.

5. Quoted in "Administration Responds to BLSA Demands as Students Stage Protest," *Harvard Law Record,* April 18, 2002.

6. The students of color who were actually enrolled in the class of the professor who suggested that African Americans had not contributed to tort theory were provided the option of not attending class. The administration offered to tape the classes and allow students who did not feel comfortable attending to watch the class on video. While many faculty and administration expressed that they found this remedy reasonable, forcing the students of color to be segregated from the class, instead of taking action against the faculty member, was reminiscent of the days of separate but equal, when states that did not provide segregated black law schools or professional schools were forced to admit black students to white schools and responded by segregating them within the space of the law school. See *McLaurin v. Oaklahoma State Regents,* 339 U.S. 637 (1950), in which McLaurin was made to sit in a special roped off seat, eat at a segregated space in the cafeteria, and sit in a segregated desk in the library.

7. Quoted in "Administration Responds to BLSA Demands as Students Stage Protest," *Harvard Law Record,* April 18, 2002.

8. As quoted in "Old Rights Campaigner Leads a Harvard Battle," *New York Times,* May 21, 1990.

9. "Law Schools Boycotted Over Lack of Minority Teachers," *New York Times,* April 6, 1990.

10. The statistics for student body and faculty at all U.S. law schools can be found on the Law School Admission Counsel's website (www.lsac.org) or on the American Bar Association website (www.abanet.org).

11. See the ABA website (www.abanet.org) for information about the statements of commitment to racial diversity and the reports on race in the profession that have been sanctioned by this professional organization.

12. A vast literature discusses the centrality of racism in the U.S. nation-state, historically and today. But see, in particular, Oliver Cox, *Caste, Class, and Race* (New York: Modern Reader Paperbacks, 1948); Stokely Charmichael (Kwame Ture) and Charles V. Hamilton, *Black Power: The Politics of Liberation in America* (New York: Random

House, 1967); Michael Omi and Howard Winant, *Racial Formation in the United States from the 1960s to the 1990s,* 2nd ed. (New York: Routledge, 1994); Joe R. Feagin and Hernan Vera, *White Racism: The Basics* (New York: Routledge, 1995); Eduardo Bonilla-Silva, "Rethinking Racism: Toward a Structural Interpretation," *American Sociological Review* 62 (1997): 465–80; Charles Mills, *The Racial Contract* (Ithaca, NY: Cornell University Press, 1997); Derrick Bell, *Race, Racism and American Law,* 4th ed. (New York: Aspen Press, 2000); Joe R. Feagin, *Racist America: Roots, Current Realities and Future Reparations* (New York: Routledge, 2000); Joe R. Feagin, *Systemic Racism* (New York: Routledge, 2006).

13. See Charles Mills, *The Racial Contract* (Ithaca, NY: Cornell University Press, 1997). Mills discusses the way in which white racist interests have fundamentally influenced modern Western conceptions of government and the political and moral justifications for the formation of the nation-state.

14. The law also operated to protect the right of white men to have sexual access to black women's bodies, without risking a loosening of the boundaries of the racialized institution of slavery. Laws such as "the one-drop rule," which legally defined the boundaries of "blackness" according to the notion that any trace of African ancestry made one legally "black," were tied to the systematic rape of black women by white men. See, for example, Derrick Bell, *Race, Racism and American Law,* 4th ed. (New York: Aspen Press, 2000); A. Leon Higginbotham Jr. and Barbara Kopytoff, "Racial Purity and Interracial Sex in the Law of Colonial and Antebellum Virginia," *Georgetown Law Journal* 77 (1967): 1989.

15. Alexis De Tocqueville makes a similar point when he notes that "the language of the law . . . gradually penetrates . . . into the bosom of society . . . so that at last the whole people contract the habits and tastes of the judicial magistrate" (Alexis De Tocqueville, *Democracy in America,* ed. Bowen (1876), 358. See also Austin Sarat and William L. F. Felstiner, "Lawyers and Legal Consciousness: Law Talk in the Divorce Lawyer's Office," *Yale Law Review* 98 (1989): 1663.

16. He explores the dominant racial ideology of the post–civil rights era in more detail in Eduardo Bonilla-Silva, *Racism without Racists: Color-Blind Racism and the Persistence of Racial Inequality in the United States* (Lanham, MD: Rowman & Littlefield, 2003); Eduardo Bonilla-Silva, *White Supremacy and Racism in the Post–Civil Rights Era* (Boulder, CO: Lynne Rienner, 2001).

17. This is not to suggest that there has been no change in the way in which the case method and the Socratic method are presented or utilized in legal teaching today or that there are no differences in how they are employed in different law school institutions. But, variations aside, these methods are widely recognized as the foundational aspects of the legal curriculum. Robert Stevens has gone so far as to suggest that these methods became so powerfully entrenched, and the race to model all legal education after the practices in elite law schools like Harvard so intense, there is actually very little substantive variation in the process of legal education among all the law schools in the United States. Robert Stevens, *Law School: Legal Education in America from the 1850s to the 1980s* (Chapel Hill: University of North Carolina Press, 1983).

18. See, for example, Emile Durkheim, *Education and Sociology* (Glencoe, IL: The Free Press, 1956 [1922]); Michael Apple, *Ideology and Curriculum,* 2nd ed. (New York:

Routledge, 1990); Michael Apple, *Cultural and Economic Reproduction in Education* (London: Routledge and Kegan Paul, 1982). Note, however, that whereas Durkheim views the socializing effects of education as a function, and moreover as a positive function, of education, Michael Apple, as well as other scholars who have researched what scholars call the "hidden curriculum," suggests that ideological reproduction in education serves to reproduce structures of power and inequality. For a good discussion of the hidden curriculum, see Eric Margolis, ed., *The Hidden Curriculum in Higher Education* (New York: Routledge, 2001).

19. Michel Foucault offers a similar analysis of the relationship between power, violence, and knowledge; he says, "[W]e should abandon a whole tradition that allows us to imagine that knowledge can exist only where the power relations are suspended and that knowledge can develop only outside its injunctions, its demands and its interests . . . power and knowledge directly imply one another. . . . [T]here is no power relation without the correlative constitution of a field of knowledge, nor any knowledge that does not presuppose and constitute at the same time power relations." Michel Foucault, *Discipline and Punish: The Birth of the Prison*, trans. Alan Sheridan (New York: Vintage Books, 1977), 27.

20. There has been a great deal more research on gender than on class in legal education. Other studies that have examined gender in law schools include, see for example, Taunya Lovell Banks, 1986. "Gender Bias in the Classroom." *Journal of Legal Education* 38: 137–46; Taunya Lovell Banks. 1990. "Gender Bias in the Classroom." *Southern Illinois Law Journal* 14: 527–39. Joan M. Krauskopf. 1994. "Touching the Elephant: Perceptions of Gender Issues in Nine Law Schools." *Journal of Legal Education* 44: 311–40; and Debra Schleef. 2001. "Thinking like a Lawyer: Gender Differences in the Production of Professional Knowledge." *Gender Issues* 19(2): 69–86.

21. This is not, of course, always the case, as the history of white supremacy in the United States has led to the phenomenon of "passing." African Americans and other people of color with light skin and other Anglo features have attempted to represent themselves as white in order to reap the material privileges of whiteness that accompany white supremacy. See, for example, Ian Haney Lopez, "The Social Construction of Race: Some Observations on Illusion, Fabrication, and Choice," *Harvard Civil Rights–Civil Liberties Law Review* 29 (1994): 1–62. However, "passing" is something that only those with Anglo physical features can accomplish; it is also most often a degrading and painful experience. See Cheryl Harris, "Whiteness as Property," *Harvard Law Review* 106 (1993): 1709–89.

22. One example of this is that women are not underrepresented in law schools; in fact, the gender demographics at most elite law schools mirror gender demographics in society at large. But, as the research indicates, sexism continues to be a problem in law schools. The situation for students of color is more complex. Students of color are severely underrepresented at all elite law schools.

23. Whiteness becomes tacit and invisible because it operates through institutions and cultural representations that become normative and are, thus, rarely explicitly examined. These cultural norms, however, are in fact racialized, and they enforce white privilege and white cultural signifiers as if they were race-neutral societal norms. See Ruth Frankenberg, *White Women, Race Matters: The Social Construction of Whiteness*

(Minneapolis: University of Minnesota Press, 1993); David R. Roediger, *Colored White: Transcending the Racial Past* (Berkeley: University of California Press, 2002); David R. Roediger, *Black on White: Black Writers on What It Means to Be White* (New York: Schocken Books, 1998); David R. Roediger, *Towards the Abolition of Whiteness* (London: Verso, 1994); David R. Roediger, *The Wages of Whiteness: Race and the Making of the American Working Class* (London: Verso, 1991).

24. Note that this should only be a starting point that lends itself to an interrogation of whiteness and white domination, but a full understanding of the racial dynamics of white institutional space must also contain a nuanced analysis of how whiteness imposes its exploitative gaze upon different racial groups differently (see Athena D. Mutua, "Shifting Bottoms and Rotating Centers: Reflections on LatCrit III and the Black/White Paradigm," *University of Miami Law Review* 53 [1999]: 1177–1217). In my analysis of race in two elite law schools, I am attentive to these differences.

25. Derrick Bell provides a good analysis of the consequences of racial exclusion to the formation of political and legal frames in his fictional critical analysis of the Constitutional Convention in his book *And We Are Not Saved: The Elusive Quest for Racial Justice* (New York: Basic Books, 1987).

26. The race statistics with regard to faculty and administration can be located on the Law School Admission Council's website (www.lsac.org). Individual law school websites confirm the pattern, in particular with regard to faculty, that is, the comparison of race statistics between tenured and tenure-track faculty and nontenure-track instructors or clinical staff.

27. As Michael Omi and Howard Winant suggest, race takes place on the macrolevel, signifying structural racial inequality, and the microlevel of everyday interaction. We notice race, we notice the race of individuals we come into contact with, and we draw upon "commonsense" understandings of what it means to be a particular "race" (*Racial Formation in the United States from the 1960s to the 1990s*, 2nd ed. [New York: Routledge, 1994], 59). Through structural inequalities, and the racial meanings we draw upon to account for these inequalities, race becomes "real" in the lived experiences of individuals. And, as Eduardo Bonilla-Silva points out, microlevel processes of everyday interaction and ideological beliefs about race are connected to and tend to reproduce the macrostructural organization of race ("Rethinking Racism: Toward a Structural Interpretation," *American Sociological Review* 62 [1997]: 465–80).

2

The Imperious Law School

The Deep Structure of White Institutional Space

W HEN YOU WALK THROUGH the front doors of Midstate Law School (like many elite law schools), you are met with a larger-than-life portrait of a white man; he is a former vice president and a graduate of Midstate Law. As you move further into the school, you will see more portraits of white men, the legacy of alumni who have become powerful attorneys, judges, law professors, and politicians. At Presidential University School of Law, several hallways are lined with black-and-white prints of historical white men in white wigs, engaged in various aspects of the practice of law. At both schools, you will find large, richly detailed portraits in elaborate frames in nearly every classroom you enter. These portraits reveal an immense pride in the history of these elite institutions. At the same time, the walls of the schools reveal that this history was racially exclusive. They are an immediate visual signifier that one has entered a historically white space.

The legacy of racial exclusion, revealed by the portraits on the walls of elite law schools, are not the only indicator that these elite law schools are white institutional spaces. Certainly, in terms of racial demographics, the vast majority of the students and professors (and even staff) you encounter as you walk through the halls will be white. But to truly understand the pervasiveness of white space, one must look deeper. The racially exclusive history of these schools and the profession of law comprise the context within which the American legal framework was formed. The buildings in which students learn to become lawyers are racially marked, but so are the legal frames within which students will be taught to construct legal arguments. The elite white men whose portraits line the walls are the very people who constructed this law, as well as the pedagogy utilized to reproduce their legal frames in the minds of budding lawyers. The history of law and law school education provides a racialized foundation and a frame that permeates legal education. History provides an unspoken *precedent* for the racialized practices and discourses that dominate the contemporary law school experience.

In *Whitewashing Race: The Myth of a Color-Blind Society* (2003), Michael Brown et al. challenge scholars who suggest that the U.S. government and law must adhere to a principle of color blindness. As their title suggests, they challenge the assertion that color blindness is a desirable principle, noting that those who assert this principle ignore the relevance of structural racial inequality and documented present-day discrimination, which results in the perpetuation of white privilege. The term "whitewashing" suggests an all-encompassing process, one that taints everything it touches. Yet, the authors do little to develop the term. In delineating the meaning of the term "white space," the concept of "whitewashing" is potentially useful.[1]

The white institutional space of elite law schools is all encompassing, as if it has been whitewashed. The process of whitewashing began with the construction of elite law schools as explicitly and exclusively white institutions. Embedded within these "white-only" institutions was a pedagogical framework that asked students to internalize the logic of a deeply racist legal structure. U.S. law created, reproduced, and maintained whiteness as a marker of power and privilege, making law a most powerful tool in the construction of the racial state. I discuss this legal frame explicitly in the following chapter. Relevant here is the fact that the dominant method of legal education, which was based upon the reading of case law, required students of law to internalize an epistemological frame, a way of knowing or, as law schools describe it, of "thinking." As law schools became the gateway into the profession of law, teaching students to think like lawyers simultaneously became the stated goal of law schools. And thinking like a lawyer meant learning to think and reason like the exclusively elite white male judges who produced the openly white racist law that organized U.S. society. But this process was made even more insidious by the presentation of law and legal principles as neutral, impartial, and objective (Crenshaw 1994, Williams 1991). While contemporary elite law schools have seen changes in racial demographics, as well as some changes in curriculum, racial minorities remain severely underrepresented, and the deep normative structures of the curriculum remain deeply embedded in a white frame. The remnants of the racially exclusive history remain visible on the walls of elite law schools, but a deeper analysis of the institutional organization of elite law schools reveals the totality of white institutional space.

The History of Legal Education:
Constructing the Foundation for White Space

Because of *stare decisis,* you hear the voices of the past. . . . When we decide a difficult case [in the Supreme Court], our only resource is the capital of trust from the public. . . . We replenish the trust by adhering to our history.

—A white man and sitting Supreme Court justice,
speaking at a forum at the Presidential School of Law

It falls to each of us to make sure that the lessons of history are learned—
if for no other reason than our own protection.

—A black woman and current congresswoman,
also speaking at a forum at the Presidential School of Law

In the late 1800s, there was marked debate within the American Bar Association (ABA) concerning the structure of legal education. The main issue of the time was whether there should exist a bifurcated bar—in other words, whether there should be a working-class bar, with corresponding law schools, and an elite bar, with members from elite law schools. During this period (first in the 1860s), there developed a notable number of part-time law schools, proprietary schools that taught a more "pragmatic" law (local rules of law rather than legal jurisprudence, or theories of law and legal principles) and often catered to European immigrants (Stevens 1983, 74–84).[2] As a result, for a brief period, law schools became accessible to all white males, even recent immigrants who often faced discrimination upon arrival to the United States (Allen 1997, Jacobson 1998). Yet, this did not imply equality even for white males in the profession of law. Obviously, the very idea of a bifurcated bar indicated a desire among some in the profession to create exclusivity in law schools and the legal profession (Seligman 1978). But the bifurcated bar was never fully realized; instead, the push for exclusivity became a defining characteristic of the legal profession. Members of the bar who desired elitism in the form of higher educational standards and selectivity in admissions fundamentally influenced the development of law schools.

The historical moment during which these debates concerning the nature of legal education took place corresponded with other educational transformations in the United States. There was a general movement in higher education toward a more scientific study of the social world at the end of the nineteenth century. Departments of political science and sociology, constructed with the intent of bringing the scientific method to the study of social life, cropped up in universities across the country in the late 1800s and early 1900s. In addition, the profession of medicine instituted a regularized program of study within institutions of higher education—and the field of medicine was particularly well suited to a scientific model. It was within this social context that Harvard Law School dean Christopher Columbus Langdell instituted a three-year regularized legal curriculum at Harvard (Seligman 1978, Stevens 1983).

Dean Langdell was heavily influenced by the transformations in education toward a more scientific method (Seligman 1978). He believed that the analysis of appellate-level case law would establish a disciplined manner of thinking—thinking like a lawyer—which would be the basis for a scientific study of law. Rather than read statutory law to understand what the law *was* in a particular jurisdiction, he suggested that reading cases written by sitting judges would reveal the correct *process* by which law was interpreted and constructed. He also conducted his classes not by lecturing, the method dominant at that historical moment, but by utilizing the Socratic teaching method. In other words, he posed questions to his students so that they could tease out the reasoning of the cases on their own, rather than simply lecturing to explain the logic of the case law. This, he argued, would enable students to understand the logical methods being applied by the judges who wrote the cases they read and to develop ways of thinking that mirrored those of the great judges of the time.

Developing the minds of law students so that they would learn to think like lawyers was essential for the profession of law, according to Dean Langdell and those who supported his methods, and required the "best" students and the "best" minds because the legal principles they would need to learn were based upon the thinking of the best legal minds: appellate judges. Qualifications required for admittance to law school increased, and a simultaneously increasing demand led to greater selectivity (Stevens 1983).[3] Soon, other law schools followed suit, and the ABA (as well as the Association of American Law Schools, an organization founded in 1900) eventually came to sanction this three-year model of legal education (though not, I must add, without debate), and the case method, combined with the Socratic method of question and response in the classroom, became the dominant model for legal education (Stevens 1983). The Langdellian model became, and remains today, *the* model for law school education. Elitism in law schools and the profession also won out, and eventually the part-time schools disappeared.

The study of law was limited to those with the "best minds" because it was said that these students could best internalize the case-method model of instruction. Professor Langdell's colleague, James Barr Ames, who became dean at Harvard when Langdell left the post, defended the case method, noting that it was designed to inculcate students with a new method of thinking—one modeled upon that of "the greatest judges the English Common Law System has produced" (Stevens 1983, 59). Implicit in this reasoning was the fact that the greatest judges that the English common law system had produced at that historical moment were exclusively propertied white men. Furthermore, white superiority was so entrenched within the legal system that the Supreme Court, the highest of appellate courts, took judicial notice in the 1896 *Plessy v. Ferguson* case of the fact that white people had a privileged status to which African Americans were not legally entitled.[4] Thus, the "scientific method" of legal education was tacitly based upon the idea that epistemological constructions of legal principles should be based upon a white frame that privileged whiteness and oppressed nonwhites. The fact that these cases were viewed and presented as "objective" and "neutral" establishments of legal principles, thereby likening legal education to science, perpetuated and reproduced as natural the assumptions and perspectives of this white frame.[5]

The racialized ideological biases in the legal curriculum fit with contemporary definitions of the "best minds" because the students in law schools like Harvard were almost exclusively elite white men. As the part-time law school passed into history and tuition rates increased throughout the 1900s, law school became less of a possibility for working-class white men. For African American men, there were some opportunities for legal education in black law schools, but explicit legal segregation before the late 1950s kept African American men from having access to white law schools and to the bar. The facilities and opportunities available at white law schools were not available at black law schools in the first half of the 1900s. Furthermore, though Howard Law School, a historically black law school, produced exceptional and renown lawyers, including National Association for the Advancement of Colored People lawyers Charles Houston and Thurgood Marshall, who later became the first African American Supreme Court justice, it was not regarded as an elite law school in the white legal power structure (and in fact, it is still ranked as a third-tier law school today).[6]

White women outnumbered African American men in the bar in 1900, though they faced similar prejudice and exclusion. In 1896, a white woman, Myra Bradwell, brought suit in the federal courts to be admitted to the Illinois Bar. In an infamous Supreme Court holding, Justice Joseph Bradley wrote in his opinion that

> the natural and proper timidity and delicacy which belongs to the female sex evidently unfits it for many of the occupations of civil life. . . . The paramount destiny and mission of women are to fulfill the noble and benign offices of wife and mother. This is the law of the creator. And the rules of civil society must be adapted to the general contribution of things and cannot be based on exceptional cases. (Quoted in Stevens 1983, 82)

The comments of Justice Bradley were heavily racialized in the sense that African American women were never granted the privilege of having their femininity constructed as "timid" or "delicate" as white women did (see, for example hooks 1987, 1992; Collins 2001). However, it goes without saying that Justice Bradley would not have viewed African American women as fit for the occupations of civil life; thus, the intersecting oppressions of race and gender completely excluded African American women from law schools and the bar.

The law school as an institution developed within a society that was deeply and openly racist (not to mention sexist) (see Feagin 2000, 2006). The explicit racism of the time, along with the elitism that flourished in the profession of law, facilitated the development of law schools that were entirely and explicitly whitewashed institutions. They were designed to admit those individuals who shared the demographic and ideological characteristics of the elite white male bench. Thus, the portraits of historical legal figures that line the walls of these elite institutions today, while they represent to some a proud history of academic integrity and professional success, signify to others this explicitly racist past. This history represents the foundation upon which modern law schools have been built. It provides the underlying support for the contemporary structure of white institutional space.

Contemporary Law School Structure:
White Space at Midstate and Presidential

The very concept of "structure" often invokes images of physical spaces (especially for those who are not sociologists). Yet, generally the physical spaces of institutions are not the subject of sociological analysis. Carrie Yang Costello (2001) suggests that in an educational context like law schools, ignoring the physical structure of the space is a mistake because the physical surroundings represent an important aspect of the learning that takes place within the space. It is, she suggests, part of the hidden curriculum (see also Margolis 2001):

> [I]t is important to note . . . that while everyone is constantly subject to the socializing influence of their surroundings, most people are typically unaware of being so influenced. . . . It is this fact that makes the influence of schools' built environment a paradigmatic example of how certain curricula remain hidden, even though they are in plain sight. Of course, physical settings do not function as socializing agents *sua sponte*; they are things. The people who design, ornament, and maintain them are the true sources of socializing messages, and the settings are merely the means by which these messages are propagated. (Costello 2001, 44–45)

As I have already noted, the message conveyed by those responsible for designing and maintaining the law schools in which I conducted my research was heavily racialized. The physical structure of both schools, like the physical structure at Boalt Hall where Costello (2001) conducted her research, revealed a message of elitism and grandeur. And elitism and grandeur are closely associated with whiteness. As I mention above, the walls of the school are lined with pictures—some photographs, some expensive portraits—exhibited in ornate frames. The most important people in the history of the schools and the legacy of the legal profession are white men; the implicit message here is that the history of the law school and the legal profession is of extreme importance irrespective of its racist boundaries.

If you attend Midstate Law School, you will see painted portraits, beginning with the life-size portrait of a former vice president at the entrance, as you walk to your classes and into your classrooms. The entrance, the atrium where students socialize and work, the library, and each of the large classrooms contain portraits and photographs of historic legal figures. There are no portraits of people of color in the halls or in the classrooms. And the photographs that line the walls of the library reveal a history of exclusion: as you walk from the entrance around the outside walls of the library, you see the photographs of graduating classes with the year posted under them. In the early photographs, there is rarely a person of color. After the 1960s, you see a smattering of faces of people of color, but all of the images are overwhelmingly white. There is not one portrait of a person of color in Midstate Law School. The summer before I began my research there, Midstate added artwork to the walls in the hallways of the main classroom building. Many of the pictures were of abstract art, but there were three pictures in which African Americans were portrayed in various civil rights activities, for example sitting in a courtroom or marching with a sign that said "Equal justice for all." When juxtaposed with the large number of pictures and portraits depicting legal professionals who were white men, these pictures suggested another role for African Americans—battling through grassroots activities, like marching, for civil rights. Another unstated message was that white men are lawyers, politicians, and judges—the civic elite. African Americans are outsiders, battling to be recognized by a white legal system.

If you attend Presidential School of Law, you will see more images of people of color in the pictures on the walls. One of the first things I saw when I arrived at the law school was a wall of photographs of graduates from the last two decades who have become prominent figures in society and the legal profession. This wall revealed a different picture than the walls of the library at Midstate. The faces of Presidential's recent past were presented as much more racially diverse than at Midstate. Within the last twenty years, a number of

Presidential's alumni of color have become very prominent lawyers. However, when you attend your classes, you will see that in the rest of the law school, the portraits look very similar to those at Midstate. Nearly all of them are of white men in prominent legal roles, and there are many more ornate portraits at Presidential than at Midstate, suggestive of an even more elite history. Several hallways in the older buildings of the school are also lined with black-and-white sketches of British barristers, as I mentioned in the opening of this chapter. The vast number of portraits of white men reveals a long history of racial exclusion that overshadows the more recent racial diversity. Moreover, during the course of my research, I entered a classroom at Presidential one morning and saw on the wall a portrait of Supreme Court Justice Thurgood Marshall, the first African American Supreme Court justice. This was the only *portrait* at either law school of a lawyer of color. After I left that class, following a section of students into their next class, I was exasperated to find that the walls of that classroom were lined with no fewer than six portraits of white men. And each of these portraits was significantly larger than the portrait of Justice Marshall. Though I am certain this was no intentional slight against Justice Marshall or African Americans in the legal profession, the visual message, though tacit, was powerful; the white men of history are the most important figures in the profession and in this space.

The visual messages of racialized elitism sent by the physical structure of these law schools were juxtaposed with another visual indicator of racialized space: the racial disparities that exist in the population of people in this space, as well as in the positions they hold. When I began my research in the spring of 2002 at Midstate Law School, Midstate had a minority population of approximately 16 percent. This is among the lowest at top-twenty law schools; only one school had a lower percentage. African Americans made up only 2.5 percent of the student body (Asian Americans were the largest minority group at 10 percent). Two years before I began my research at Midstate, the first-year class—or "1L" class in law school parlance—enrolled only one African American student. Thus, though statistically the student body remained at between 2 and 3 percent African American (of an entering class of approximately two hundred fifty), the percentage of African Americans fluctuated from year to year such that some classes were even less racially diverse than the statistical norm. The same pattern held true for American Indian and Latino students.[7] And among the faculty, the statistics for that year stated that 11 percent of the faculty were minorities. However, the year that I began my research, there were only two tenured faculty members of color, an African American man and an Asian American man. And in the middle of my research, the tenured African American man left Midstate. Two African American junior faculty members were on the tenure track, a man and a woman, but the other faculty members of color were clinical faculty who worked on contract and were not on tenure tracks. While contract professors do have a great deal of contact with students, their contracts do not give them the same protections offered by tenure, and they have respectively less power among, and less input into, the law school faculty and curriculum than do tenure-track faculty. The vast majority of visible staff members at Midstate were also white, as were the vast majority of administrators. In the middle of my research, Dean Edwards, a white man, was replaced by a man of color, so Midstate became one of the few law schools with a dean of color. But the majority of the faculty and administration in roles that came with decision-making power in law schools were white (and male).

Presidential, a private law school, had a total "minority" student population of approximately 30 percent, a high percentage relative to other top law schools. The percentage of African American students at Presidential, 7.5 percent, is not the highest among the elite law schools, but interestingly, Presidential also has a rather high percentage of Latino students, 7.9 percent, as well as Asian American students, 13.7 percent. Although their American Indian student population is very small (less than 1 percent), they have a significant number of each of the other ABA-measured racial minority groups, which provides a range of racial diversity in the student body. In addition to the racial diversity of Presidential, the law school is structurally distinct from most elite law schools in that it has an office of minority affairs with a director position. In a conversation with Dean Hill, the dean of Presidential (who is a white man), I learned that this position was constructed when the law school received grant money targeted for racial diversity purposes. According to Dean Hill, the administration was planning to utilize the money to create some form of minority-targeted scholarship, but students requested that the money be spent on setting up a permanent position and office of minority affairs. The position was titled "Director of Minority Affairs," and when I conducted my research at Presidential, Chandra Banerjee, a South Asian woman, held this position.[8]

Despite the racial diversity among the student body and the structural addition of a director of minority affairs position, minority faculty at Presidential were vastly underrepresented. In 2003 (when I began my research), only 3 percent of Presidential faculty members were racial minorities. There were two tenured women of color and no men of color. The numbers of faculty of color and women were, surprisingly, even lower than the numbers at Midstate and contrasted with the student body strikingly. And as at Midstate, there was a higher concentration of white women, and men and women of color, in clinical faculty positions as opposed to tenure-track positions at Presidential. Presidential had also lost a tenured African American man to another law school the year before I conducted my research. Unlike at Midstate, the staff at Presidential was largely made up of people of color. In the student affairs office, the office with which students had the most contact, the entire staff, with the exception of one white man, comprised people of color. The dean of students was also a woman of color, though none of the other deans were, and the year after I conducted my research at Presidential, she left and was replaced by a white man. During my research at Presidential, a number of students of color and several white students commented to me that the largely all-white faculty, contrasted by the staff made up disproportionately of people of color, sent a message to the students in the law school about the racial dynamics of power.

When I arrived at Presidential, having just completed my research at Midstate, I was initially struck by the amount of racial diversity among the students. At Midstate, I generally saw one or two people of color in a room, perhaps four or five at a large social event at the law school. By contrast, when I entered the atrium at Presidential, many students of color were working and socializing. Initially, I believed that this would mean that there were significant differences in the racial practices and discourses at Presidential. However, as I sat and looked around the atrium for several hours that first day, I began to notice that although there were many students of color, they were not interacting with white students. In fact, I came to see that despite the first appearance of racial diversity, there was a great deal of segregation within social spaces and even in classes in which students were allowed to select their own seating.[9] This sometimes occurred by group—in other words, as I watched the spaces, I would see separate groups of African American students, Asian American students, Latino students, and white students—but in some cases, the split was dichotomous, with white students seated apart from students of color. In fact, many of the students of color at Presidential worked with several different student-of-color organizations (which I discuss in more detail in chapter 5). For example, a Latina woman who was the president of the Latino Law Students Association was also very involved in the Black Law Students Association. Yet, no white students were formally involved with any of the student-of-color organizations.

The racial segregation at Presidential was emphasized for me during my last visit to the law school when I met with several students of color in the atrium. During the course of the conversation, people joined and left our group—many students came who had wanted to talk with me but had not had time for an interview; others wanted to talk with me again to tell me about things that had happened or that they had remembered after our interview. I sat in the atrium that day with students for over five hours, and students came and went throughout the day so that the group composition was

continually changing. Yet, over the entire period, no white students ever
joined the group. Several times a white student would stop to talk to one of
the people in the group about a class or a project but did not join the conversation. And near the end of the day, Tyson, an African American third-
year, or "3L," man, was telling me a story about an experience he had had at
a law firm after his first year of law school (the story is discussed in detail in
chapter 5). Everyone in the group was amazed by the racism he had faced at
the law firm, and we were all reacting so that the conversation became loud,
and there was a lot of laughter. While Tyson was talking, a white man whom
Tyson clearly knew walked past, and as he did, he turned to Tyson and mo-
tioned with his hand imitating a puppet talking, then rolled his eyes sarcastically. The student made it clear that he felt Tyson was talking about something unimportant and that he perceived him as complaining unreasonably.
He also made it clear that he felt empowered enough to mock Tyson in front
of an entire group of people (there were approximately ten people in the cir-
cle at that time) who clearly agreed with what Tyson was saying. This act
punctuated the racial segregation in the law school; it was spatial segregation,
but it was deeper than that.

The extremely low level of racial diversity at Midstate meant that the people one interacted with in the school were extremely disproportionately
white. At Presidential, the picture was more complex. There were people of
color in the school, but among administrators, staff, and faculty, people of
color tended to be those with less prestigious positions or less power in the
school. Among students there was more racial diversity than at Midstate, but
there was also racial segregation within the school. The one portrait of Justice Marshall, which was significantly smaller than other portraits of white
men, was metaphorically symbolic in representing what one African American student called "diversity as window dressing." Presidential sent out a
message of commitment to racial diversity and even changed the structure
of the institution by adding the director of minority affairs position. Yet the
racial dynamics within the school writ large were not significantly different
at Presidential than at Midstate. The reaction of the white man to Tyson's
conversation with our group illustrated the implicit power that white students have within white institutional spaces; he felt no pressure to take care
in his interpretation of the relevance of Tyson's experience, even when he
was in the minority (racially, as well as politically, in the sense that we were
all in clear agreement with Tyson's expression of anger at the racism he experienced). Students of color consistently bumped up against a tacit white
frame, as well as explicit racism, and this often led them to find social spaces
that were racially exclusive (see Tatum 1997). The consequence was that, despite the differences in the racial demographics of the two law schools, both

Midstate and Presidential were white institutional spaces characterized by a deeply entrenched white frame.

The visual messages at the law schools, the messages sent by the physical structure as well as the racial demography of the people in the space and the positions they held, revealed tacit assumptions about whiteness, privilege, and power. However, the comparison of the demographically distinct Midstate with Presidential revealed underlying tacit norms that also quietly reinforce and reproduce white privilege even as racial demographics change. The portraits and pictures that reveal the legacy of elite law schools signify, intentionally or not, a particularized historical memory. The portraits tell a story: history is important and relevant, and the exclusionary and violent racism that marks history is less important to us in this space than is the image of professional success, power, and elitism that we seek to portray. In this sense, white historical memory, as Joe Feagin (2006) has noted, is selective such that it privileges the successes of whites without accountability for the violent oppression that facilitated this success. The contemporary racial dynamics in the law school echo the racist past. White power and privilege permeate the space, but the dominant collective narrative dismisses the relevance of white racism in the law and in the law schools. This is revealed most clearly in everyday discourse in the law school (which I take up in chapter 4). But this discursive white frame has its foundation in the deep normative structures that organize the way the law is taught in law schools, in other words, in the process of learning to think like a lawyer.

Thinking Like a Lawyer—Thinking White

The research provides a clear indication of exactly what it means to think like a lawyer. Howard Erlanger and Douglas Klegon, who conducted a survey questionnaire of law students entering a state law school, then another in the students' second year of instruction, say that learning to think like a lawyer means forming the ability "to distinguish a legal from nonlegal issue, to see the various sides of a problem, to reason formally and logically, and to express themselves clearly, concisely, and unemotionally" (1978, 30). Robert Granfield similarly notes, on the basis of ethnographic research, followed by in-depth interviews and a survey at Harvard Law School (called Ivy Law School in this article), that thinking like a lawyer is a "rationalistic style . . . generally considered imperative by faculty and students alike for developing the characteristics associated with the legal profession's ethos which include objectivity, emotional neutrality, and impartiality" (1986, 516). But in the context of the racialized power dynamics of the law schools, as well as society more broadly, the discursive and analytical frame of "thinking like a lawyer" tacitly functions to justify and reproduce white power and privilege.

The process of learning to think like a lawyer occurs within a very clear power hierarchy in law schools. Professors have the power, and the relatively less powerful students must respond to the will of the professor. The Socratic method, as it is used in modern law schools, often becomes adversarial and even hostile, and the professors (because they presumably know the answers to their own questions) maintain the power in this adversarial exchange. Some professors call on students randomly, "putting them on the spot," with questions regarding the material they should have read. This often takes place from the moment class begins, so the professor may begin class by asking a student to "state the case," in other words, to describe the facts, legal issues, and court holdings in the cases they have read. Even when professors make an attempt not to be hostile in their classrooms, the law school experience is tinged with the potential power dynamic in which a student may get "slammed" by a professor, which means that they have been publicly called out through humor or hostility as not understanding the material.

As scholars suggest, the law is presented in law schools as though it were a set of objective, impartial, logically reasoned principles. This imposes a deep contradiction within the process of thinking like a lawyer. A fundamental aspect of the process is accepting as neutral principles that function to justify and reproduce white racist social structures. And this assertion of neutrality is made, usually tacitly, in a context in which the power dynamic functions to discourage challenges to hegemonic understandings of the law, particularly when presented by law professors. As Michel Foucault (1977) suggests, power relations are always implicated in the construction of knowledge, and the assertion of legal objectivity in law schools represents a form of discipline, imposed upon law students, from which lawyers are trained to disregard the reproduction of power hierarchies implicit in their learning of the law. Thus, a fundamental aspect of thinking like a lawyer is the implicit internalization of a white racial frame.

The Ethics of Thinking Like a Lawyer

Lawrence Kreiger argues that "thinking 'like a lawyer' is fundamentally negative; it is critical, pessimistic, and depersonalizing" (2002, 117). This is true, according to Kreiger, because the essence of legal argumentation is adversarial, and all perspectives are considered equally defensible if one can make a legal argument that follows the logic of legal doctrine (the principles set forth in case law), regardless of the ethical or moral implications of the argument.

In fact, bringing up ethical or moral considerations is frowned upon in law school classes. Professor Bisby instructed his students as such in his jurisprudence class. He told them, "If you look at any controversial case, there are likely to be principles on either side. The sophisticated lawyer . . . in most cases [doesn't] really think there's a right answer." If there is no moral or ethical "right answer" in the law, as Professor Bisby suggests, then moral or ethical arguments are not good *legal arguments*. In addition to being removed from ethical or moral considerations, legal analysis takes place by decontextualizing the legal principle from the larger social context (Epstein 1999, Kreiger 2002). In practice, of course, this is not always true. Law students (and professors) frequently bring up issues of ethics and discuss the moral underpinnings of legal outcomes by connecting them with broader social-structural issues. However, ethical and moral concerns are not respected as "legal" arguments, and they are easily dismissed with arguments that focus solely upon the principles set forth in case law, as Professor Bisby's comments make clear. Given that U.S. law has been largely constructed by white men and that for the vast majority of history, it was explicitly constructed to legally enforce and protect white privilege and power, the relative irrelevance of the ethical, moral, and social-structural consequences of legal arguments can create a troublesome racial consequence as students are learning to think like lawyers.

For example, in one of the constitutional law classes that I observed, Professor Davante asked students to read the case of *Prigg v. Pennsylvania*.[10] In this case, Edward Prigg and Nathan Bemis "captured" Margaret Morgan, an African American woman (and her children), whom they asserted were their slaves. According to the record of the facts of this case, Morgan's parents had "informally" been set free by Bemis's father. When Bemis inherited the property of his father, he went to Pennsylvania to forcibly take Morgan and her children to reenslave them. Under an 1826 Pennsylvania statute, "self-help" was not permitted in the return of "fugitive slaves." As a result, Prigg was arrested by Pennsylvania authorities and convicted of unlawfully forcibly taking Morgan and her children. To contextualize the classroom discussion that I observed, I present an edited excerpt of the holding in this case, written by Supreme Court Justice Joseph Story:

> [The clause of the Constitution invoked by this case comes from the second section of the fourth article, which reads:] "No person held to service or labor in one state, under the laws thereof, escaping into another, shall in consequence of any law or regulation therein, be discharged from such service or labor; but shall be delivered up, on claim of the party to whom such service or labor may be due." . . . Historically, it is well known, that the object of this clause was to secure to the citizens of the slave-holding states the complete right and title of ownership in their slaves, as property, in every state in the Union into which they might

escape from the state where they were held in servitude. The full recognition of this right and title was indispensable to the security of this species of property in the slave-holding states. . . . If the Constitution had not contained this clause, every nonslave-holding state in the Union would have been at liberty to declare free all runaway slaves coming within its limits, and to have given them entire immunity and protection against the claims of their masters; a course that would have created the most bitter animosities and engendered perpetual strife between the different states.

The Supreme Court then ruled that Prigg had the constitutional right to take action to forcibly capture Morgan and her children and that the Pennsylvania law prohibiting this was unconstitutional and void.

The Prigg case not only presents a legal framework that values the preservation of the union between states over the human rights of African Americans, but it also uses horribly dehumanizing language to preserve the rights of "masters" to protect their "property rights" in human beings, which the court refers to as a "species of property." Such principles and language evoke painful emotions and ethical crises for many who read the case today, yet this fact was not relevant in the classroom discussion about *Prigg*.

At the beginning of the class, Professor Davante set up the discussion of *Prigg* as follows:

Article IV Section II was the fugitive slave law . . . [S]laves who escape from their masters have to be handed back. . . . [Y]ou should know that at the time that the framers were drafting the Constitution, there was more of a belief that slavery was on a path to gradual extinction than there was in the mid-1800s when [this case was] decided. There were many indicators that the framers had a problem with slavery. George Washington made a point of freeing his slaves after he and his wife were dead—in doing that he made a point that slavery was problematic. . . . In 1870 Congress faced a major controversy; what to do with new states. The compromise was that for every one free state, they would admit one slave state. The Missouri Compromise said that slavery would be allowed to spread into western territories only below a certain line. . . . In the 1840s, something happened to upset the balance. In 1845 America fought the Mexican-American war, and Mexico annexed Texas, California, Arizona, and New Mexico, and this raised a question about whether slavery was going to spread into these areas. . . . All of this sets the background for [the *Prigg* case].

Professor Davante then called on a white woman, Julie, and asked, "Can you set forth the case of *Prigg*?" The ensuing conversation went as such:

JULIE: "The case involved a Pennsylvania law which said that you couldn't have self-help with regard to fugitive slaves; you have to get a court order to get a slave back. . . . The issue was about the constitutionality of the law."

PROFESSOR DAVANTE: "Right. Why is it a constitutional question?"

JULIE: "I think it violates the right of the slave owner or . . . is it a property issue?"

PROFESSOR DAVANTE: "Well, I think it relates to the fugitive slave clause. Let me just clarify what Justice Story says about that clause. He says that the clause imposes a duty to slave states to return slaves to where they've escaped from. So with that duty, there must implicitly be a duty for Congress to act to legislate about this. Congress passes the Fugitive Slave Act, and in doing so, Congress is acting under the necessary and proper clause. It is a means to a constitutional end; the fugitive slave clause must allow Congress to act. Let me ask you, are you persuaded so far by Justice Story's constitutional analysis?"

JULIE: "Not really." [Then hesitantly,] "I guess I'm just so biased by the fact that I think its such a bad decision. It's hard to separate emotion and logic."

PROFESSOR DAVANTE: "Right, right. Well, Justice Story's argument is a plausible argument, but it's not necessarily the only way. Story is using a broad understanding of the commerce clause. . . . Story says that the Constitution gives an exclusive power to Congress to act [on the issue of fugitive slaves], and so this means states cannot act; therefore the Pennsylvania statute is unconstitutional."

JULIE: "It seems like the state should be able to act to fill in the gaps."

PROFESSOR DAVANTE: "What is the state interest of Pennsylvania?"

JULIE: "Well, protection of its citizens."

PROFESSOR DAVANTE: "Yeah, in particular protection of its African American citizens, so people from Maryland can't just come across and claim that an African American citizen is a slave. Even beyond that, they want to protect the public peace and safety regarding the laws. Now Justice Story is saying these interests don't matter because it's an area of exclusive federal power. . . . One interesting thing to note about this is that Justice Story was from Massachusetts and was an opponent of slavery—so why this decision? One possible answer was that he was freeing Northern states from having to act on this issue. The federal government in 1842 was very dependent on state enforcement personnel. He was trying to relieve this burden."

I must note that this particular classroom discussion of *Prigg* was one of the most historically contextualized discussions that took place in all of the classes I observed. Professor Davante at least made the attempt to discuss the issue of slavery as a relevant historical issue, something most other professors avoided altogether. That said, his entire analysis of the *Prigg* case and the historical context in which it was decided was situated within an unidentified white racist frame. Professor Davante began the class by lecturing, explaining the political compromises concerning the enslavement of human beings in newly forming states. He notes that the framers of the Constitution did not believe that slavery would be an issue for Congress by the mid-1800s because they thought slavery was gradually ending. Then he offered as evidence the fact that George Washington and his wife freed their slaves when they died. This apologetic analysis of the protections of slavery contained within the Constitution rings hollow when the statement is reframed: Washington freed his slaves *only* after he and his wife had died. The Washingtons lived their entire lives served by enslaved African American people, including Martha Washington's half-black sister, the product of her father's rape of a woman he enslaved (see Feagin 2006). Furthermore, congressional protection of the institution of slavery can only be viewed as a "compromise" within a white frame. White people compromised with other white people about the violent dehumanization of African Americans, who were not viewed as human enough even to participate in the discussion (see Bell 1987).

Situated within a white racist frame, this class discussion also makes clear which facts and issues are relevant to the *legal* discussion and which are not. Professor Davante asked Julie, "Why is it a constitutional question?" She responded, uncertainly, that she thought it had to do with the rights of slave owners, or "property rights." He then clarified that it was a constitutional issue because of the fugitive slave clause written into the Constitution (the legal principle on which the case analysis was based). He focused the discussion on Justice Story's argument that the clause gave Congress the exclusive right to act on the issue of "fugitive" slaves. Then he asked Julie whether she was convinced by this legal argument. She initially said that she was not but then quickly dismissed her opinion by noting that she was biased because she did not like the decision and had emotional reaction to the ethical problems with the arguments and the outcome. He responded by saying "right" (confirming, perhaps, that she was biased by her emotions) and then refocused the discussion on the issue of whether Justice Story's argument that Congress should have "exclusive" power in the area of fugitive slaves was the only plausible legal argument. Her empathic response to an ethically questionable decision that protected the institution of slavery was diminished through the redirection of the discussion to "constitutional principles." She followed the redirection, coming up with an alternative argument that did not invoke emotional or ethical considerations: couldn't the states act to fill in the gaps concerning the return of "fugitive slaves" by acting where Congress had not acted; might not this make Pennsylvania's law constitutional. Professor Davante helped her to make this argument, the *legal* argument, by offering her the question, "What is the state's interest?" The state's interest is explicitly recognized in the Constitution and principles of federalism; thus it is a good basis for making the legal argument. She offered "protection of its citizens," and he elaborated on this argument, confirming that she was at that point thinking about the issue the way he wanted her to think about it.

Professor Davante avoided any discussion of the moral ramifications of constructing a group of human beings into a form of (or "species of") property. Instead, he presented the legal issues as balancing the interests of "slave states" and "free states," the rights of Congress and states' rights. His perspective illustrates selective historical memory. Despite the fact that this was a class about constitutional law, there was no discussion of whether the document itself may be tainted because of the protections of slavery it contained. Furthermore, though he made the suggestion that the state of Pennsylvania had an interest in protecting its black citizens, he failed even to consider the implications of power, white supremacy, and "compromise" for African Americans. The perspective he presented contains an implicit bias for the interests of white men in the formation of a government to protect their interests, certainly not the interests of African Americans. The white frame used by white elite men to construct the document that organized the state as a slave state at the founding of our nation became the very frame that limited the boundaries of the legal discussion. Most troublesome about the discussion, however, is that this bias is so deeply embedded in the legal framework that Professor Davante's focus on "legal" arguments appeared to the students to be a neutral and objective reading of the law (Williams 1991, Crenshaw 1994, Bell 1987, Lawrences 1995).[11]

On the surface, the refusal to consider the ethical or moral implications of laws and legal decisions or the rejection of the appropriateness of emotional responses to racial violence may appear to be "neutral" or "objective." One line of argument suggests that these issues are social or "policy" issues that should be left to legislatures, not to judges who are interpreting legislation (see, for example, Brooks 2002). In fact, this argument is problematic given the number of lawyers in state and federal legislatures (Miller 1995).[12] Beyond that, relegating moral and ethical concerns to the area of "policy" and subordinating social or policy concerns in legal argumentation functions to block critical analyses of power and privilege in the implementation of the law. This serves power because it silently bolsters the status quo. Structural racial inequality in society and in the law is reified through the passive acceptance of the legal principles that produced and continue to maintain white power and privilege. *Thinking like a lawyer requires a manner of thinking that acquiesces to a white normative framework and simultaneously facilitates the invisibility of whiteness by precluding forms of argumentation that seek to identify the power and privilege that mark it.*

A key aspect of the supposed neutrality and objectivity in this discussion is the rejection of emotional response to racial oppression, in this case the reenslavement of a woman and her children. Julie explicitly stated that she was swayed by her emotional reaction to this case and that this prevented her from conducting a good legal analysis. The notion that a good legal analysis excludes emotion is rooted in the legal education of the late 1800s that led Harvard Deans Langdell and James Barr Ames to attempt to construct a study of law using a scientific framework. Scientific study, according to the argument, must be based upon reason and rationality, not emotion (see also Weber 1925). Emotion must be excluded because it prevents the very neutrality and impartiality that lead to objectivity, and objectivity is the key to reason and rationality. This argument rests on the assumption that human beings are capable of emotionless objectivity, a tenuous argument at best. As physical scientist Stephan Jay Gould has noted,

> Impartiality (even if desirable) is unattainable by human beings with inevitable backgrounds, needs, beliefs, and desires. It is dangerous for a scholar even to imagine that he might attain complete neutrality, for then one stops being vigilant about personal preferences and their influences—and then one truly falls victim to the dictates of prejudice. Objectivity must be operationally defined as fair treatment of data, not absence of preference. Moreover, one needs to understand and acknowledge inevitable preferences in order to know their influence—so that fair treatment of data and arguments can be attained. (1996, 36)

Gould refers to the "preferences" of individuals, not specifically emotions but the idea that human beings can, or should, block normal human emotions in the name of rational argumentation, which raises important questions about power, hierarchy, and oppression. Despite this fact, in elite law schools there is an open disdain for emotion in legal argumentation, and the rejection of emotion is taught as a component of thinking like a lawyer. Yet, on closer examination, all expression of emotion is not rejected in legal argumentation, only a particular type of emotion: those that tend to accompany the rejection of power hierarchies, like racial hierarchy.

Reason and Rationality versus Emotion and Empathy

Based upon her research examining professional socialization at Boalt School of Law, Costello (2005) concludes that the Socratic method, as it functions in contemporary law schools, teaches students to internalize the power associated with the professional status they are attempting to achieve, as well as to reject emotion for, or empathy with, disempowered members of society. She notes that oftentimes this takes place through the use of a particularly callous form of humor:

> The humor employed by the professors at Boalt Hall played generally on the
> theme of power. Professors made light of their power over students, and of the
> power students would hold over others as lawyers and as members of the ruling
> class. . . . The message professors seemed to send was for students to grow a cal-
> lus over their bleeding hearts and learn not to take things so seriously. (Costello
> 2006, 92)

Like Costello, I found that at Midstate and Presidential, sarcasm and sarcastic
humor characterized the vast majority of classes I observed. Sarcasm became
a tool for reinforcing divisions of power between professors and students and
between the elite and the nonelite, as well as a way to block empathic responses to inequality and oppression. But something subtler also came out of
the use of sarcasm as a teaching tool: a simultaneous engagement in emotion
and rejection of empathic connections with those experiencing oppression
that lead to interesting contradictions with regard to issues of reason versus
emotion in legal argumentation.

The use of sarcasm in law school classes is tied to power because, as I have
discussed above, the setup of law school classes and the adversarial use of the
Socratic method create an atmosphere of competition, as well as a hierarchy
of power between professors and students. In my observations, sarcastic jokes
sometimes took the form of emphasizing to law students their entrance into
the ruling class, as Costello suggests. For example, Professor Stanford's criminal law course discussed the reach of criminal liability. She asked the class,
"You're a businessman, and you know that people are doing prostitution in
your doorway. You know about it, but you don't stop it. Are you liable?" When
no one responded, she continued, "This happens. Hotels think its part of their
business to provide this service to clients—prostitutes." Then, in a sarcastic
tone, she added, "You all don't know about this now, but wait 'til you become
partners in firms." The class erupted in laughter.

At other times, sarcastic humor was utilized more directly to emphasize
the power hierarchy within the classroom. For example, in Professor Riley's
contracts class, a student struggled to answer a question the professor had
asked, and Professor Riley interrupted the student, saying sarcastically, "I'm
glad I'm not in your study group." Similarly, in Professor Whitfield's contracts class, a student suggested that the court should have considered issues
of fairness in making its decision. Professor Whitfield said disdainfully, "Did
you learn that in kindergarten?" In these cases, the jokes were made at the
expense of the student, by the professor, in a mocking tone. Although professors often said that they did not intend to mock students, situated within
the power structure of the law school, jokes like these were necessarily
mocking. They functioned (sometimes completely intentionally) as a sanc-

tioning mechanism in an atmosphere of competition. But many students and faculty, when I asked them about this form of sarcasm, minimized it as irrelevant. As one white male student said, students who were uncomfortable with jokes such as these should "just get over it." As a result, this form of sarcastic humor and the inherent legitimating of power inequality became a tacit component of the process of learning to think like a lawyer.

Sarcasm reinforces both the dynamics of power within the classes and the law school, as well as subtly justifying the power that students will one day have as members of an elite class of law professionals. More than that, sarcastic humor allows professors to minimize the relevance of inequality and oppressive uses of power. The mocking of students that goes on in the classroom, which is generally juxtaposed with hard-hitting questioning through the Socratic method, sets up a dynamic in which those with power, the professors, are free to assert that power, occasionally abusively, against those with less power, the students. And within the structure of the legal system more broadly, this power dynamic is justified when students are repeatedly told that they can expect judges to question them with similar vigor and sarcasm when they become lawyers. Teaching students to get used to oppressive expressions of power, or, as Costello says, to "grow a callous over their bleeding hearts," simultaneously teaches them to disconnect emotionally from the social consequences of structural inequality and oppression. Nowhere was this more clear than in classroom discussions that were explicitly about race.

In classroom discussions where race came up explicitly, sarcastic humor was used, though it was not directed at individuals in the class. Instead, sarcastic humor about race was used to diminish the horrors of racism. For example, in his constitutional law course, Professor Roth discussed a 1964 civil rights case in which the issue was whether Congress had the right, under the Constitution, to prevent a local restaurant in Birmingham, Alabama, from excluding African Americans.[13] One issue in the case was whether discrimination on the part of a local-level restaurant might impede interstate travel. In order to assert that this discrimination did impede travel, Professor Roth asked the class sarcastically, "If I'm a black engineer, do I want to move my family to Alabama when they're feeding their police dogs little black kids?" By sarcastically joking about the violent abuses of African Americans by police officers during the civil rights era, Professor Roth turned a horrific image of a black child being eaten by a vicious dog into a moment of comedic wit. The sarcasm minimized the emotional horror of the violence committed against African Americans, who were, in fact, attacked by police dogs at that historical moment (see Branch 1988). Without intention, Professor Roth effectively provided people with a way to avoid an empathic response to the experiences of the violence faced by African Americans as a result of white racism.

This minimization of racism fits with the selective historical memory that characterizes the white institutional space of the law school; racism is not of central importance, so we should take it less seriously. But in the case of race and racial oppression, dangerous consequences go along with not taking racism seriously. First, sarcasm allows people to discuss racial violence without having to connect emotionally or empathically to the pain of it, an essential step in the process of creating a racial "other" that can be justifiably oppressed. Feagin notes,

> Thinking and practicing racism requires a breakdown in empathy across the color line. Racism is about the destruction of natural human empathy; it means a lack of recognition of the humanity of the racialized other. Identification across the color line is hard for most whites to make. It involves understandings and emotions. (2000, 254)

Though subtler than explicitly racist jokes, the effect of sarcastic humor is to diminish the real pain and suffering that occur as a result of the violent oppression of African Americans (see also Feagin 2006, Houts and Feagin 2007). In addition to numbing people to the pain of racism, this type of racist humor also has a disproportionate emotional effect upon people of color. Just as the jokes directed at individuals ("I'm glad I'm not in your study group") are more emotionally provocative for them than for others in the class, the mocking of an image of police dogs eating little black children will have a more personal impact on those who are intimately connected to black children. It is not as easy to block an empathic response when the image invokes a picture of violence, an image with historical reality, enacted upon a child that you know and love. In this instance, it is more likely that African American students will be personally emotionally affected by Professor Roth's comments than the white students in his class.[14] If they are, they will have the extra challenge of either having to suppress an emotional reaction or of being labeled as emotional, a sin against the constraints of legal argumentation (see Hochschild 2003; I return to this issue in more depth in chapter 6).

Sarcasm and humor become teaching tools in law school classes, one consequence of which is the reduction of empathy and emotional response. This corresponds to a broader disdain for emotion and for ethical and moral concerns, which are often connected to emotion. The notion that rational legal arguments exclude emotion or empathy feeds into the normalization of white power and privilege by facilitating the ability to analyze violence, racism, and oppression without normal human empathy. It also camouflages a lie that perpetuates the invisibility of power and privilege. The reality is that emotions are a central component of legal analysis and argumentation. Sarcastic humor is, in fact, a manifestation of emotion: perhaps amusement, disgust, or denial. Law professors and lawyers utilize various forms of emotional expression frequently in order to make their arguments more compelling. Sometimes those emotions are explicit, as in the emotional reaction of disdain illustrated by Professor Whitfield when he asked his student, "Did you learn that in kindergarten?" More often, it is merely the normalized, unquestioned, definition of emotion as dichotomous to rationality that perpetuates a hegemonic construction of emotion that privileges those with power.

Anger, sadness, and even confusion get constructed as emotional states, but calm and reasonableness do not. In fact, emotion is a much more complex human feature than this simple dichotomization would imply (Hochschild 2003, Bellah et al. 1985). A state of calm is as much an emotional state as a state of anger, but connecting calm with reason and rationality and anger with emotion in an institutional setting in which emotion is disparaged results in a deep structural protection for power and the reproduction of the status quo. It is much easier to be calm and collected about oppression when you are not the one being oppressed. Privileging calm and reason in legal argumentation serves those in positions of power, or as one African American male student said, "Patience is a privilege of those with power." Yet patient, calm, *reasonable* arguments are privileged in legal argumentation. The use of sarcastic humor, combined with a dichotomous definition of rationality versus emotion and the rejection of emotional or empathic responses to inequality, sends a tacit, never-articulated message to law students. Not only will those in power oppress those without access to power, but if those without access to power respond with open anger or sorrow, they can be dismissed as irrational, thereby reinforcing the notion that those in power are deserving of that status.

The use of sarcastic humor in law school classrooms, in conjunction with the other racialized dynamics of the schools, reproduces and entrenches white institutional space. On the one hand, sarcastic humor functions as a mechanism to stifle emotional, or sometimes even calm and rational, but also morally guided, legal arguments. This puts a major hurdle in front of those who would attempt to legally challenge white privilege and power in a way that suggests a major break from laws that have merely reproduced white supremacy. On the other hand, sarcasm provides students with a means to create distance from pain and suffering. It diminishes the capacity for empathy, thereby allowing those with privilege and power to enjoy their supremacy without guilt. Furthermore, examination of the use of sarcastic humor reveals a glaring contradiction in the dichotomy between reason and rationality and emotion and empathy. The dripping tones of sarcastic wit that dominate so many law school classrooms belie the stated sin of emotion in legal argumentation. And this reveals the true, but unstated, sin, which is not about emotion

per se but the discouragement of progressive arguments based upon an expressed opposition to racial (or class or gender) inequality.

Conclusion

Midstate Law School and Presidential School of Law are whitewashed spaces.
As institutional spaces descended from explicitly racist institutions, they retain the remnants of the historical legacy of racial exclusion. The physical
structures of the buildings that make up these schools reveal the connections
between elitism and whiteness, and they present a selective memory in which
the racism that defined their histories gets minimized or ignored. The continuing racial disparities among students and faculty, particularly in positions of
power, in these law schools represent one illustration of the embeddedness of
structural racial inequality in these institutions. But, more insidiously, the
deep normative structures that organize the teaching method dominant in
legal education are tinged with biases and assumptions that reproduce a white
racist frame while purporting to be impartial and objective.

In another constitutional law class that I observed, the professor discussed
racial segregation in education, and his interaction with the students in his
class provided a most illustrative synthesis of the white frame embedded
within the deep normative structures of legal education.[15] Professor Turner
utilized sarcasm and humor to assert his own power in the classroom, as well
as to decontextualize the discussion from social-structural realities and to
minimize the relevance of racism.

> PROFESSOR TURNER: "What's wrong with separate but equal? . . . [I]f my recollec-
> tion [from last class] is right, some of you said there's something wrong if equal
> is not equal, but suppose it was [equal]? . . . What's wrong with separate but
> equal, and I don't think I called on you, Ms. Newby."
>
> NEWBY: "Are you asking me?"
>
> PROFESSOR TURNER (with sarcasm): "Yes, unless you're only posing as Ms. Newby."
>
> NEWBY: "Um . . . it's inherently unequal."
>
> PROFESSOR TURNER: "But suppose we make it completely equal?" [Then, gestur-
> ing with his arms and with a tone of mocking,] "Everything is all equal—black
> is beautiful, Asian is beautiful, the [segregated] schools [are] exactly the same in
> all material respects. Exactly the same."
>
> NEWBY: "I guess I just don't know. . . . I don't know, why . . . why separate them
> if no one is inferior?"

PROFESSOR TURNER: "But assuming that we can assure that no one feels inferior, are you still against it?"

NEWBY: "Yeah."

PROFESSOR TURNER: "Why?"

NEWBY: "Because if we're gonna ensure that everybody has an equal chance . . . you're telling me all this, but, like, why? Why separate them?"

PROFESSOR TURNER: "Because we're the state, and I'm the professor, so in this class, I'm the state."

By decontextualizing the "constitutional" issue from the realities of social structure, Professor Turner was able to ask Newby to make an argument that racial segregation could be justified if "no one felt inferior." She was unable to respond in any way but to ask, why? Why separate people if none are superior or inferior? It makes no sense by virtue of the fact that there is no social reality within which to mark it. However, when a white male student in the class attempted to make an argument that racial segregation was inherently unequal, as Newby's confusion had implied, Professor Turner responded with anger.[16] The student, Mr. Smith, said, "There are some things that are intangibles in education. Interaction with other races makes them more socially and educationally advanced." Professor Turner responded forcefully, but this time he switched from a tone of sarcastic humor to a tone of disgust. He said, with condescension, "Do you really believe that? And do you believe that it ought to be constitutional law? Because the next question is going to be, why aren't you out picketing?"[17] Smith retreated and said, quietly, "I don't know if it should be part of constitutional law."

During this discussion about racial segregation in education, Professor Turner utilized sarcasm both to assert his own power and to force the students to engage in an argument that was completely decontextualized from social reality. There has never been a historical moment in which racial grouping or segregation was separate from racial hierarchy or privilege and inferiority (see, for example, Takaki 1993, Gould 1996, Feagin 2000). In setting up the question as he did, he minimized the relevance of race and racism, and when a student attempted to reassert the relevance of race, he responded by exerting even more power. He suggested that if the student really believed that interracial interaction was an educational benefit, he should be "out picketing," not in law school. This reaction by Professor Turner shut off the discussion. Mr. Smith retreated, suggesting that maybe his point of view should not be a matter for constitutional law, and no other student attempted to assert the relevance of racism after this.

Any moral or ethical discussion about inequality that may have come up in this discussion about racial segregation in education was stifled by Professor

Turner's hypothetical reality in which racial inferiority did not exist. His setup
of the discussion removed any potential for a discussion about the ethics of a
constitutional law that allows the level of racial segregation and inequality in
education that we maintain in the United States (Orfield and Eaton 1996). By
decontextualizing the discussion, exerting his power to decide the boundaries
of the discussion, and using sarcastic humor to minimize racism and mock
students who attempted to discuss it, he ensured that the discussion remained
rooted in a white frame, a frame that allowed no space for critical evaluation
of the law or interrogation of white racial privilege and power. But there is
something else in Professor Turner's question to Newby about the relevance
of the fact that "no one feels inferior." Implicit in his question is a vision of an
individual who does not feel inferior and whose feelings are more relevant
than the structural dynamics of racial inequality. This form of abstract individualism is a deeply entrenched discursive frame in law schools. It is made
more powerful by virtue of the fact that an individualist frame is supported
by modern legal authority. Yet an analysis of U.S. legal history reveals that, abstract individualistic legal analyses of race-related issues are a post–civil rights
construction. Thus before discussing the ways that abstract individualism and
color-blind ideologies dominate the law school discourse, it is important to
contextualize this discourse within the legal history of race and individualism.
In chapter 3, I present a critical examination of the historical treatment of race
in the *law*, the most deeply embedded normative structure in law schools.

Notes

1. I would like to thank Joe Feagin for suggesting that I develop this concept.

2. Here I refer to immigrants, as opposed to white Anglo-Saxon Protestants, who at
this historical moment were reaping the highest rewards of whiteness. See Matthew
Frye Jacobson, *Whiteness of a Different Color: European Immigrants and the Alchemy of
Race* (Cambridge, MA: Harvard University Press, 1998).

3. Note that the process of increased selectivity occurred at elite law schools like
Harvard early on as these schools gained a reputation early in the 1900s, and, thus,
there was competition for acceptance. However, most law schools had space for more
students and far less competition for admittance at the beginning of the 1900s. However, in the mid 1900s, the demand to get into law school increased; thus, most ABA-
certified law schools had more students applying than they were able to accept. This
made law school more competitive, and schools again became more selective. See
Robert Stevens, *Law School: Legal Education in America from the 1850s to the 1980s*
(Chapel Hill: University of North Carolina Press, 1983); J. Seligman, *The High Citadel:
The Influence of Harvard Law School* (Boston: Houghton Mifflin Co., 1978).

4. When I say that the Court took judicial notice, I am suggesting that the Court
recognized white superiority as a *fact* that served as a basis for the logic of the Court's

decision in *Plessy*. The issue in the case was whether the racial segregation of railroad cars was permissible under the Fourteenth Amendment of the Constitution. The Court said, among other things, "If he be a white man, and assigned to a colored coach, he may have his action for damages against the company for being deprived of his so-called 'property.' Upon the other hand, if he be a colored man, and be so assigned, he has been deprived of no property, since he is not lawfully entitled to the reputation of being a white man" (*Plessy v. Ferguson*, 163 U.S. 537 [1896]). I discuss race, the law, and the racial state in greater detail in chapter 3.

5. This is not to suggest that science is "objective" or "neutral," but the rhetoric of science and the scientific method is one of objectivity—and an absence of subjectivity. For critiques of science as an objective and neutral field, especially with regard to race and gender, see Stephen Jay Gould, *The Mismeasure of Man, Revised and Expanded* (New York: W. W. Norton & Company, 1996); Sandra Harding, *Whose Science? Whose Knowledge? Thinking from Women's Lives* (Ithaca, NY: Cornell University Press, 1991); Sandra Harding, *The Racial Economy of Science: Toward a Democratic Future* (Bloomington: Indiana University Press, 1993). Note, however, that sociologist Max Weber insisted that the law must be constructed and interpreted in a completely value-free manner, using inductive logical methods that preclude the inclusion of individual subjectivity. As I discuss further below, Gould (1996) has suggested that it is not humanly possible to separate one's knowledge and knowledge construction from one's own subjective state. I agree with Gould in this assessment and submit further that no scientific or social-scientific evidence has ever been offered to suggest that this might be possible; yet, we have substantial evidence indicating that an individual's subjective state will impact the internalization and interpretation of data and/or new knowledge (again, see Gould and Harding).

6. See *U.S. News and World Report*, law school rankings, http://grad-schools.usnews .rankingsandreviews.com/usnews/edu/grad/rankings/law/brief/lawrank_brief.php.

7. The ABA statistics report the percentage of "Hispanic" students and separate "Mexican" students, but do not use the term "Latino." However, at both law schools where I conducted research, individuals generally used the terms "Latino" or "Latin" to describe themselves, and the student organization at both was called the Latino Law Students Association. Because it is a term of self-expression among people of Latin American descent, I use the term "Latino" here rather than "Hispanic" (which is a census-created term), but I recognize that "Latino" and "Hispanic" are often used interchangeably.

8. I must note that this position became a source of severe contention in the law school. White students were vocally upset by the addition of the position, and the woman who held the position prior to Ms. Banerjee left, at least in part, because of constant verbal challenges and attacks to her position. During my research, I witnessed both explicit and subtler challenges to Ms. Banerjee and to the position. The year after I left, Ms. Banerjee, along with others in the office of student affairs, were considering changing the position's title from "director of minority affairs" to "director of diversity," largely to appease the animosity of white students.

9. Professors sometimes assign seating alphabetically so that they can make up seating charts to better learn the names of students.

10. *Prigg v. Pennsylvania,* 41 U.S. (16 Pet.) 536 (1842).

11. The frame of Professor Davante's analysis of the *Prigg* case, in particular his failure to explicitly discuss the moral and ethical issues associated with white supremacy, illustrated the manner in which the vast majority of professors I observed analyzed case law in the classroom. For an example of a similar frame of legal reasoning applied to this very case, see James Boyd White, "Lecture: Constructing a Constitution: 'Original Intention' in the Slave Cases," *Maryland Law Review* 47 (1987): 239.

12. Some might argue that this fact presents a problem for the justification of the case method as the primary basis for legal education. If, in fact, many lawyers become legislators, as opposed to trial lawyers or judges, then perhaps statutory construction would be a better source of instruction than case analysis. Indeed, others have made the argument that the focus on the case method ignores the empirical fact that only a minority of lawyers become trial lawyers or judges, so the reliance on the case method in law school education is actually good training for only a minority of future lawyers. See Lani Guinier, Michelle Fine, and Jane Balin, *Becoming Gentlemen: Women, Law School, and Institutional Change* (Boston: Beacon Press, 1997); Duncan Kennedy, *Legal Education and the Reproduction of Hierarchy: A Polemic against the System* (Cambridge, MA: AFAR Press, 1983).

13. *Katzenbach v. McClung* (1964) 379 U.S. 294.

14. This is especially true because white people in American society learn, as part of learning the racial social structure, not to empathize with African Americans with regard to racism. This is a fundamental aspect of the reproduction of white racism. For more discussion, see Joe R. Feagin, *Racist America: Roots, Current Realities and Future Reparations* (New York: Routledge, 2000); Joe R. Feagin, *Systemic Racism* (New York: Routledge, 2006).

15. As I mentioned, sarcasm and sarcastic humor was characteristic of nearly all of the law school classes I observed. It was not unique to constitutional law classes. However, because constitutional law classes represent one of the few classes in which issues of race and racial inequality come up explicitly, I draw upon examples from these classes disproportionately.

16. I should also note that the argument this student was attempting to make was, in fact, what the Supreme Court held in *Brown v. Board of Education,* 347 U.S. 483 (1954). Thus, the student was actually making an argument based upon legal precedent, just not an argument the professor seemed to want him to make.

17. Professor Turner was probably referring to the fact that schools in the United States today are as racially segregated as they were at the time of the *Brown* decision, more in some areas. See Gary Orfield and Susan Eaton, *Dismantling Desegregation: The Quiet Reversal of Brown v. Board of Education* (New York: The New Press, 1996). However, why this matter should be excluded from a constitutional discussion is unclear. Perhaps if he had explicitly brought up continuing racial segregation in schools, they could have discussed the relevance of this structural reality to constitutional law. As it was, he relegated that matter to "the streets," where he suggested Mr. Smith should be picketing.

3

Selective Legal Memory and the Discourse of Abstract Individualism

"THE UNITED STATES OF AMERICA is unique among the nations of the world in that it is not built on group or cultural rights but rather on individual rights," wrote Jonathan, a white male law student, in Presidential's school newspaper. Later in his article, which he entitled, "Group 'Rights' and Unearned Guilt," he proclaimed, "I do not accept unearned guilt. I have *no responsibility* for the suffering that was caused by slavery (or to the person who is stopped by the police for 'driving while black') . . . [R]ights and responsibilities are attributes of *individuals*, not groups" (italics in the original). This comment illustrates a discourse dominant at both Midstate and Presidential that confines discussions about race and racial inequality within a frame of abstract individualism, or the notion that equality means treating each individual the same under the law without regard to social-structural or historical conditions. The tenets of abstract individualism represent an ideology that has long been central to American cultural identity (see Bellah et al. 1985). For example, social theorist James Coleman asserts that "modern Western law . . . is based on the conception of purposive individuals with rights and interests, who are responsible for their actions" (1986, 1302).[1] Yet, the notion that the U.S. legal system is based upon the concept of identifiable individuals with individual rights is a gross mischaracterization of American legal history. Racial group–based interests have, from this country's inception, been a central organizing principle of the U.S. nation-state. More specifically, U.S. law has historically operated, and continues to operate today, to protect the economic, political, and social-psychological interests of whites.

Abstract individualism (sometimes referred to as liberal individualism) is what Eduardo Bonilla-Silva (2001, 2003) refers to as a "rhetorical strategy" often utilized by whites in the post–civil rights era to disregard group-based racial inequality ("rights and responsibilities are attributes of individuals not groups") and thereby deny individual and/or societal responsibility for the social-structural consequences of racism ("I have no responsibility for the suffering that was caused by slavery"). Bonilla-Silva suggests that in the post–civil rights era, the more explicit racism of the Jim Crow era has taken a back stage to new discursive techniques: the employment of rhetorical strategies that individualize, minimize, and thereby reproduce systemic racism. Not only has this tacitly influenced popular discourse concerning race and racism, but it has permeated the discourse surrounding race, as is evident in Jonathan's comments, and has resulted in a contemporary body of case law that individualizes racism and minimizes or disregards deep racist structures.

Even a cursory examination of the history of race in U.S. law reveals the hypocrisy contained in the abstract individualist frame.[2] From the very founding of the U.S. government, the law was used to construct racial group boundaries in conjunction with racial hierarchy and, subsequently, to enforce the maintenance of that hierarchy.[3] In the pre–civil rights era, this took place explicitly, and the courts relied upon an overtly racist discourse. However, in the post–civil rights era, we see a discursive shift in the language of the courts with regard to cases dealing with issues of race. In the early 1970s, the courts began to eschew racial group–based reasoning, drawing upon the tenets of abstract individualism, settling matters of discrimination and racial inequality by looking for identifiable culprits acting with racial malice. Since then, courts have continued to draw upon notions of liberalism and individualism as a rhetorical tool to confine legal discussions about racial inequality and racism to the level of the individual. The effect of this move on the part of the courts has been a reproduction of the racial status quo, the continuation of a racist social structure, the formation of which deeply implicates U.S. law and the courts. The logical incongruity between abstract liberalism in contemporary law and the law school discourse, together with the realities of the sociolegal history of race in the United States, presents a contradiction that makes this discourse particularly problematic within the context of law schools.

In this chapter, I examine the U.S. race jurisprudence, or the body of case law concerning issues of race. These cases, which represent the basis for the curriculum in law schools, illustrate the ways in which group interests, as opposed to individual rights, have dominated legal analysis for the vast majority of this country's history. This chapter, then, represents a subtle departure from the rest of the book. Here, rather than focusing on the actors in law schools, I focus on a voice that, although powerfully authoritative, is rarely critically examined in the literature on law schools.[4] That voice is the voice of the Court.[5] Case law, which serves as the main educational tool in legal pedagogy, is also representative of the most authoritative discourse in law schools. The cases that students read in their classes imperiously convey a particular ideological frame, one that, with regard to race, has served as a tool in organizing the racial state (Omi and Winant 1994, Winant 1997). In their work examining medical schools, Howard Becker et al. (1961) assert that medical students draw upon the ideological tenets of the medical profession in the process of developing their new identities as doctors. In law schools, the implications of internalizing the dominant ideologies of the profession of law reach far beyond professional socialization. When law students interpret and internalize legal principles, they simultaneously develop a relationship with one of the most powerful tools of the state. This chapter serves two purposes. First, I illuminate, for the nonlegally trained audience, the group-based legal frame from which the U.S. racial hierarchy was constructed and enforced. Second, I connect that legal history to contemporary assertions of legal individualism explicating the way in which these assertions operate as a mechanism through which law students are enabled to reproduce white group-based interests.

Legally Constructed Racial Boundaries and Racial Hierarchy

The United States was founded upon a Constitution that contains at least eight identifiable accommodations for the institution of racialized slavery, yet the word "slavery" never appears in the document (see Bell 1987, Feagin 2000). The framers of the Constitution, all propertied white men, recognized the hypocrisy inherent in creating a document that asserted the fundamental freedom of all individuals to form a government for a society whose economy was dependent upon the institution of race-based slavery. Yet, while not explicitly mentioning slavery, they acquiesced in this sham by creating protections for the institution without naming it. Hence, the foundational document of U.S. government, and the laws that followed from it, facilitated the construction of deep structures of racial hierarchy, the result of imperial conquest, the institution of racialized slavery, and notions of manifest destiny, all of which rested upon a belief in white racial superiority (Takaki 1993, McClintock 1995, Bell 2000).

The race-based case law that followed from the U.S. Constitution abandoned the attempts of the framers to conceal violent racial oppression in favor of an explicit legal recognition of race and racial subjugation. Thus, an explicitly racist discourse characterized the analyses of U.S. courts for the vast majority of this country's history. Racism was utilized as a justification for providing access to material, political, and social resources for whites, while subsequently denying this access to those who were determined to be non-white. As a part of this process, U.S. courts faced the somewhat daunting task of constructing and solidifying the racial boundaries from which to confer or deny access to resources.

In 1806, the Virginia Supreme Court decided the case of *Hudgins v. Wright*.[6] At issue in the case was whether two women, Hannah and her daughter, who asserted that they were free, were in fact the slaves of a white man who claimed to own them. Before the substantive question of these women's freedom could be reached, however, the court needed to establish which party (the two women of color or the white man) had the burden of proof in the case. The Virginia Supreme Court discussed the way in which this decision was to be made:

> From the first settlement of the colony of Virginia to the year 1778 . . . all negroes . . . brought into this country by sea, or by land, were slaves. And by the uniform declarations of our laws, the descendants of the females remain slaves, to this day, unless they can prove a right to freedom, by actual emancipation, or by descent in the maternal line from an emancipated female.[7]

This passage referred to a U.S. common law principle holding that any person legally found to be "black" was presumed to be enslaved unless he or she could prove otherwise. In other words, if Hannah and her daughter were found by the court to be "black," they would have the burden of proving either that Hannah's mother had been free or that they had documentation of emancipation. If, on the other hand, the court found that they were not "black," the burden of proof would shift to the white man who claimed to own them.[8] Thus, their racial classification became the single most important issue in their fight to gain freedom over their own bodies.

In the United States, unlike other societies in which slavery has existed, slavery was a fundamentally racialized institution (Franklin 1967). Blackness thus became legally associated with an enslaved status.[9] During the antebellum period, this meant that when legal controversies arose as to whether or not an individual could be legally enslaved, the court's construction of that individual's race became a central issue in the determination. This white racist presumption, of course, raised issues for the courts concerning how to define who was or was not "Negro" in the language of the time. State laws that attempted to define racial boundaries legally were based entirely upon the group interests of elite white slave owners and were absurd in their arbitrariness. In Arkansas, for example, a person who was "less than one-fourth negro" was presumed to be not black and therefore free.[10] But in other Southern states, like Louisiana, a person found to have "one-drop" of "Negro blood" was considered legally black (see Bell 2000). The logical (or perhaps illogical) conclusion was that a person's race could change, as could the presumption of slavery that attached to racial status, merely upon that person's crossing state lines. This reveals both the power of the courts (and the state more broadly) to define racial boundaries and the arbitrariness with which this process occurred. In the legal controversies that arose as a result of the common law presumption that African Americans were slaves, the subjugation the court was knowingly conferring upon those who were construed as black was the actual loss of human recognition—a legal status that equated a group of human beings with property, certainly not individuality.

Toni Morrison (1992) has suggested that whiteness and blackness are implicitly connected in that both become necessary in order to define the other. Through processes of legal reasoning, blackness came to signify subjugation, and the process of racialization in which the court engaged became the foundational rationale upon which U.S. courts drew to justify the denial of human—individual—rights. Whiteness, however, often contrasted with blackness in the law, signified power and superiority. Because of this, whiteness marked status, status that carried with it an acknowledgement of both individuality and human dignity. And the boundaries of this privileged status required legal protection. As a result, just as the courts participated in the construction of "blackness" with regard to determining human subjugation, they also engaged in the construction of the legal boundaries of "whiteness." This process took place explicitly in the law involving U.S. citizenship.

In 1790, the Congress of the United States restricted naturalization to "free white persons"—while many changes in immigration law occurred over the years, the white racial restriction remained in place until 1952. So, until that time, only those immigrants to the United States who were considered "white persons" were permitted to naturalize and become citizens.[11] This, however, was complicated by the fact that the boundaries of whiteness were not at all clear, and in fact, throughout history, the boundaries shifted and changed (Ignatiev 1995, Brodkin 1998, Jacobson 1998). The courts, then, were left to decipher the boundaries of whiteness, and the process of defining these boundaries became an exercise in exclusion rather than inclusion. In other words, rather than determining who was legally "white," the courts engaged in a process of defining who was not white (Lopez 1996).[12]

In 1914, Takao Ozawa, who was born in Japan, applied for naturalization. Ozawa and his legal counsel must have known that a plea to the U.S. courts that explicitly challenged the white racial restriction as ethically or morally wrong would have no supporting legal precedent and, so, would not have succeeded. Thus, instead of arguing against the "white-only" naturalization legislation, he argued that he was, in fact, a "white person" under the proper meaning of the term. Ozawa argued that the Court should interpret the term "white person" literally in terms of the color of one's skin. He suggested that the physical skin color of Japanese people was actually as white as that of other groups who were legally considered white. He said,

[I]n Japan the uncovered parts of the body are . . . white. . . . [T]he Japanese are of lighter color than other Eastern Asiatics, not rarely showing the transparent tint which whites assume as their own privilege. . . . [I]n the typical Japanese city of Kyoto, those not exposed to the heat of summer are particularly white skinned. They are whiter than the average Italian, Spaniard, or Portuguese.[13]

In 1928, however, the Supreme Court framed the question as such:

Is appellant, therefore, a "free white person," within the meaning of that phrase as found in the statute? . . . The provision is not that Negroes and Indians shall be excluded but it is, in effect, that only free white persons shall be *included*. The intention was to confer the privilege of citizenship upon that *class of persons* whom *the fathers* knew as white, and to deny it to all who could not be so classified. (Emphasis added.)[14]

In setting up the question this way, the Court both repeated that only whites, as a racial group, were entitled to the privilege of citizenship and that the racial classification of "whites" was intended to be defined as those "whom the fathers knew as white." Of course, these "fathers," not to mention all of the justices on the Court in 1928, were exclusively elite white men. So, not only were the privileges of citizenship connected to whiteness, but the privilege to confer whiteness was left to elite whites.

In Ozawa's case, the Court determined that he was not to be included within the boundaries of whiteness, regardless of the color of his skin. The Court said,

Manifestly, the test afforded by the mere color of the skin of each individual is impracticable in that it differs greatly among persons of the same race, even among Anglo-Saxons, ranging by imperceptible gradations from the fair blond to the swarthy brunette, the latter being darker than many of the lighter hued persons of the brown or yellow races. Hence to adopt the color test alone would result in a confused overlapping of races and a gradual merging of one into the other, without any practical line of separation. . . . [T]he federal and state courts, in an almost unbroken line, have held that the words "white person" were meant to indicate only a person of what is popularly known as the Caucasian race.[15]

In an effort to create a doctrine that lower courts could follow, the Supreme Court rejected skin color as the determinant of race and instead relied upon the pseudoscience of the time, which defined "white" as synonymous with "Caucasian," a racial classification asserted by racial anthropologists that was purportedly based upon geographical origination as well as phenotypical characteristics (see Gould 1996, Lopez 1996). However, just three months after holding that Japanese persons were not "Caucasian" and were therefore not white, the Court's doctrine was again challenged on its own terms.

Bhagat Singh Thind was a migrant to the United States who had been born in India. According to all of the anthropological classification schemes of the time, South Asian Indians were then considered "Caucasian" (see Gould 1996, Lopez 1996). Thus, Thind applied for citizenship, and based upon the Ozawa ruling that white was to be equated with the "scientific" racial category "Caucasian," his citizenship was granted at the district court level.[16] Appalled by this outcome, the United States appealed the case to the Supreme Court. Predictably, the Court reversed Thind's award of citizenship and backpedaled from its reliance upon racial pseudoscience. The Court said,

> It may be true that the blond Scandinavian and the brown Hindu have a common ancestor in the dim reaches of antiquity, but the average man knows perfectly well that there are unmistakable and profound differences between them today.[17]

The court also said, with the same type of dismissive sarcasm employed by contemporary law professors,

> We venture to think that the average well informed white American would learn with some degree of astonishment that the race to which he belongs is made up of such heterogeneous elements. . . . What we now hold is that the words "free white persons" are words of common speech, to be interpreted in accordance with the understanding of the common man, synonymous with the word "Caucasian" only as the word is popularly understood.[18]

As a legal holding, the notion that the boundaries of whiteness would be defined by the "common man" was misleading, as the judges knew that these decisions would be made by fellow judges who were certainly not "common" in the classed sense of the word. Still, the court reiterated that white people would be in charge of determining who would be included in the class of "white persons."

In constructing and patrolling the racial boundaries of blackness and whiteness, the courts simultaneously marked race as the determinant of subjugation and privilege. In doing so, the courts operated as both constructor and protector of white supremacy, as well as the arbiter of the boundaries of racial oppression. Moreover, when African American individuals attempted to utilize the courts to tap into the privileges the courts reserved for whites only, the courts responded with a more forceful racist discourse, solidifying the boundaries of race as also the boundaries of racial oppression and racial hierarchy.

Dred Scott and *Plessy*: African American Subjugation in Two Legal Eras

Perhaps the most infamous case in U.S. history with regard to the "individual rights" of African Americans was the 1857 *Dred Scott v. Sandford* case in which the Supreme Court said,

> The question is simply this: Can a negro whose ancestors were imported into this country, and sold as slaves, become a member of the political community formed and brought into existence by the Constitution of the United States, and as such become entitled to all the rights, privileges, and immunities, guaranteed by that instrument to the citizen? . . . It will be observed, that the plea applies to *that class of persons only* whose ancestors were negroes of the African race. . . . We think they are not, and that they are not included, and were not intended to be included, under the word "citizens" in the Constitution, and can therefore claim none of the rights and privileges which the instrument provides for. . . . On the contrary, they were at that time considered a *subordinate and inferior class of beings*. (Emphasis added)[19]

The Court's language and reasoning was not ambiguous: African American people were regarded as a "class of persons," not as individuals, and that class of persons was legally held to be inferior to white people—so inferior, in fact, that members of the "class" were not even entitled to *ask* the Court to be treated as individuals with individual legal rights.

Some scholars have suggested that the severity of the holding in the *Dred Scott* case pushed the nation into civil war (see, for example, Urofsky 1988). Whether this was the case or not, however, the oppression of African Americans did not come to an end after emancipation. After the Civil War, Congress proposed and pushed through a constitutional amendment designed specifically to nullify the decision in *Dred Scott*. The Fourteenth Amendment made citizenship a right of birth so that, thereafter, all those born within the United States automatically received citizenship, with all of the rights that confer to that status. Furthermore, the amendment stated explicitly that all citizens were to be guaranteed the "equal protection" of the law without regard to race. With the ratification of the Fourteenth Amendment (as well as the Thirteenth Amendment, which prohibited slavery and all "badges and incidents" of slavery, and the Fifteenth Amendment, which guaranteed the right to vote to all citizens without regard to race), a true possibility arose that notions of legal individual rights and freedoms could become more than just rhetoric. However, the Courts acted swiftly to solidify the permanence of white group-based interests.

In *Plessy v. Ferguson* the Supreme Court was asked to determine the constitutionality of a Louisiana law requiring trains traveling in the state of Louisiana to have separate railway cars for "the white and colored races."[20] Extending racial group-based reasoning into the postbellum period, the Court said,

> A statute which implies merely a legal distinction between the white and colored races—a distinction which is founded in the color of the two races, and which must always exist so long as white men are distinguished from other race [*sic*] by color—has no tendency to destroy the legal equality of the two races, or re-establish a state of involuntary servitude.[21]

Hence, the *Plessy* case established the legal doctrine of "separate but equal" that ushered in the era of Jim Crow racism. Equality, according to the reasoning of the Court, did not mean that racial groups could not be separated, only that the railway cars into which they were separated had to be equal in their facilities. But, as legal scholar john powell suggests, the construction of boundaries is rarely a neutral process:

> Boundaries are designed to keep something in, or out, or both. There needs to be some differential between who or what is inside and who or what is outside with a different valuation between them. If there is no differentiation, or if this differentiation is too weak, the boundaries will become meaningless. Boundaries and borders are not simply markers between equal spaces. They are put in place for the benefit of one group in opposition to another group. (2000, 435)

Racial group boundaries were constructed to separate and denote substantive difference, and the construction and maintenance of racial difference in the United States was at no time separate from the enforcement of racial oppression. The "separate-but-equal" doctrine was, from its inception, a lie. The facilities created to keep African Americans separate from whites were never "equal" in any sense of the word, as the courts and the state were well aware. And in fact, just moments after suggesting that the legal differentiation between whites and African Americans did not have the effect of denying legal equality, the Court recognized that it was perpetuating racial subjugation saying,

> The object of the [Fourteenth] [A]mendment was undoubtedly to enforce the absolute equality of the two races before the law, but in the nature of things, it

could not have been intended to abolish distinctions based upon color, or to enforce social, as distinguished from political, equality, or a commingling of the two races.[22]

Thus, the Court suggested that the equality of which the justices spoke was restricted to "political equality" and certainly did not include "social" equality; as such, it recognized the legally protected right of white people to engage in racism. Furthermore, the lone dissenter in the case, Justice John Marshall Harlan, who disagreed with the "separate-but-equal" doctrine and was the first Supreme Court justice to suggest in a court opinion that "our Constitution is color-blind," simultaneously said,

> The white race deems itself to be the dominant race in this country. And so it is, in prestige, in achievements, in education, in wealth and in power. So, I doubt not, it will continue to be for all time, if it remains true to its great heritage and holds fast to the principles of constitutional liberty.[23]

Thus, the Court justices knew at the time of their holding that they were conferring upon African Americans an inferior racial status openly supported by a white racist ideology. *Plessy* resulted in the continuation of the state-sanctioned subjugation of, and violence enacted upon, African Americans into the postbellum era (Feagin 2000, Thompson-Miller and Feagin, 2007; Katznelson 2005).[24]

Through a variety of legal analytical tactics, all of which were presented in an explicitly white racist frame, U.S. courts constructed African Americans as the consummate other in order to justify both racial exploitation and the preservation of societal resources for whites. The legal matrix of race, however, was complicated by the presence of other "racial groups," groups that did not fit neatly into the categories of "black" and "white." This left the courts with the problem of both legally defining these peoples (as was illustrated in the *Ozawa* and *Thind* cases) and legally situating them within the racial hierarchy of the state.

The Racial State: White and Nonwhite

As Joe Feagin (2000) has noted, the concept of whiteness and the superiority of the white race developed largely through the lens of racialized slavery and the process of creating a black "other" in order to justify the existence of slavery in a nation allegedly founded upon the principles of freedom, equality, and individualism (see also Roediger 1991, Morrison 1992, and Mutua 1999). Yet, in the process of maintaining this rigidly controlled racial hierarchy, the courts were also faced with decisions about where to place other people of color. As Athena Mutua (1999) has suggested, the process of racialization and the enforcement of a racial hierarchy based upon white supremacist ideology meant that the "white gaze," that is, the power structures (like the courts) that protected and reproduced white supremacy, could shift from African Americans to other groups of people when whites felt that their racial privileges might be threatened. In the case law related to slavery, the legal analysis functioned to distinguish between black and nonblack in order to keep subjugation behind the boundary lines of "blackness." But more often, like in the citizenship cases, the process was designed to distinguish white from nonwhite, to deny those whom the white-controlled courts deemed as racial "others" the privileges associated with whiteness.

In the state of California in 1854, the court faced a criminal case in which a Chinese person was called to testify against a white defendant. The state at the time had a law stating, "No Indian or Negro shall be allowed to testify as a witness in an action in which a white person is party."[25] The question that came before the California Supreme Court was how this statute applied to people of Chinese ethnicity. As was consistent with the legal frame, the court utilized a racial group–based rationale to come to the conclusion that the statute prohibited people of Chinese ancestry from testifying as witnesses in cases in which white people were parties. The court said,

> It will not be disputed that "White" and "Negro" are generic terms, and refer to two of the great types of mankind. . . . In using the words "no black or mulatto person, or Indian shall be allowed to give evidence for or against a white person," the Legislature . . . adopted the most comprehensive terms to embrace every known *class or shade of color*, as the apparent design was to *protect the white person* from the influence of all testimony other than that of persons of the same caste. . . . The word "white" has a distinct signification, which . . . excludes black, yellow, and all other colors. (Emphasis added)

The court clearly racially classified the Chinese as "yellow," a "shade of color" that distinguished them from whites, specifically for the purpose of "protecting" the privileges of citizenship and individual treatment that white persons received from the state. Effectively, the court created a white/nonwhite test, just as they had in the citizenship cases, to signify what the court describes as "caste" and, as a result, relegated all people of color ("all other colors") to a subordinate position without regard to national, cultural, or individual characteristics.

Similarly, the Supreme Court of Mississippi in 1925 relegated a young woman of Chinese ancestry, Martha Gum, to what the court termed the "Mongolian race" and suggested that, as a member of that racial group, she

was not intended to attend school with white school children.[26] Noting that
the legislature had previously prohibited intermarriage between "the white
and Mongolian race," in the same legislative vein as their prohibition of intermarriage between whites and "negroes," the court said,

> To all persons acquainted with the social conditions of this state and of the South-
> ern states generally it is well known that it is the earnest desire of the white race
> to preserve its racial integrity and purity, and to maintain the purity of the social
> relations as far as it can be done by law. . . . [The court then concluded,] [r]ace
> amalgamation has been frowned upon by Southern civilization always. . . . [T]he
> segregation laws have been so shaped as to show by their terms that it was the
> white race that was intended to be separated from other races. . . . [Martha Gum]
> is not entitled to attend a white public school.[27]

Just as in California, the clear goal of the court was to delineate the boundaries
of whiteness, a category legally associated with "purity," and to exclude those
whom the court found to be outside those boundaries in order to prevent
racial "amalgamation," which might threaten the boundary lines of white
privilege and power. In the legal reasoning of both the California and Mississippi courts, the nonwhite status of people of Chinese ancestry was racialized
in conjunction with that of African Americans, and the Chinese were defined
as racially nonwhite by the courts.

In the state of Texas, the courts proved ready to deny the rights of Mexicans
to attend schools that were white only, and, again, the legal reasoning of the
court hinged upon the racialization of Mexicans and Mexican Americans. In
the case of *Independent School District et al. v. Salvatierra et al.*, the Texas
Court of Appeals held that the city of Del Rio could properly segregate children of the "Mexican race." The court said,

> [T]he population of this section [of the state] is in many communities and coun-
> ties largely of Spanish and Mexican descent, *who may be designated . . . as the
> Mexican race, as distinguished . . . from all other white races.* (Emphasis added)[28]

So, while the histories and experiences of people of "Mexican ancestry" and
"Chinese ancestry" were distinct—both from those of each other and from
that of African Americans—when the "white gaze" of the courts turned upon
people of color who were asserting the right to be treated by the courts as individuals entitled to the privileges accorded to white individuals, the courts
rejected their entry into that privileged "class," analogized them to African
Americans, and classified them all as racial groups legally identified as distinct
and inferior.

In the case of American Indians, their treatment by the courts of the United States was slightly different because, at various moments in time, they were treated interchangeably as members of sovereign nations, "domestic dependents" entitled to political classification (as opposed to racial classification), and/or a racial group distinguishable from whites (see Wilkins 2007 and Clinton, Newton, and Price 1991). While the institution of slavery led to the racialization of African Americans as part of the project to legally construct a racially designated group as not people but property, it was the imperial quest to associate the physical property of this nation with whiteness that led to the legal racialization of American Indians (Takaki 1993, McClintock 1995). In the 1823 landmark case *Johnson v. M'Intosh*, the Supreme Court ruled that individual American Indian people, supposedly recognized as citizens of sovereign nations, did not have the legal authority to transfer *their own lands* to other individuals.[29] In justifying this decision, the Court said explicitly,

> According to every theory of property, the Indians had no individual rights to land, nor had they any collectively, or in their national capacity; for lands occupied by each tribe were not used by them in such a manner as to prevent their being appropriated by a people of cultivators.[30]

Although in *M'Intosh* the Court did suggest a political classification based upon white imperial rationalizations concerning the appropriation of land and land use, the language of the Court in *M'Intosh* also drew explicitly upon racialized notions to justify the removal of Native American property rights. Failing even to attempt to differentiate between the distinct cultures and political structures that distinguished the many different Native American nations in the territories at the time, the Court said,

> But the tribes of Indians inhabiting this country were *fierce savages*, whose occupation was war, and whose subsistence was drawn chiefly from the forest. To leave them in possession of their country, was to leave the country a wilderness; *to govern them as a distinct people, was impossible*, because *they were as brave and as high spirited as they were fierce*, and ready to repel by arms every attempt on their independence. (Emphasis added)[31]

Through the language of race, for example designations like "fierce" and "savage," thus utilizing the process of racialization, the Court justified the withdrawal of Native American lands and individual rights to own and dispose of property.

As all of the cases cited above reveal, U.S. legal history was deeply and extensively framed by the desire of elite white men to protect their status as superior and to construct and enforce a white racist society in which the lands and bodies of people of color could be exploited and denigrated. The process of racialization and racial "reasoning" employed by the courts often situated African Americans as the archetypal "other" against which to measure both whites and other racialized groups. When the "white gaze" turned upon people of color who attempted to assert their individuality within the U.S. legal frame, the courts repeatedly confirmed that the language of individualism was merely rhetorical and that group-based concerns, specifically the protection of white power and privilege, were the primary focus of the courts. Individuality under the law was an entitlement of white people, and the courts proved that they would consistently protect the exclusion of those deemed not "white."

It is hard to imagine how the rhetoric of freedom and individuality could have survived the first two hundred years of U.S. history. The pre–civil rights discourse concerning individual rights consciously disregarded people of color through racial group–based legal analyses that denied the basic humanity of people of color. Individual rights, and the determination as to who could claim such rights, were the domain of whites only. This racist legal reasoning was a fundamental mechanism by which the state organized and controlled racial hierarchy and white racial privilege and power. Yet, the ideological framework of individual rights, racialized as it was, also provided African Americans with a rhetorical tool, one that enabled them to challenge racial inequality based upon the very principles that were said to be at the heart of American democracy. African American leaders in the civil rights movement drew upon this rhetoric, challenging the state to live up to the ideology it asserted (Branch 1988, Morris 1999).

Racial Reform and Retrenchment in the Civil Rights Era

During the civil rights movement, from the mid-1950s until the early 1970s, a legal shift took place, and laws that were explicitly racist were challenged and began to be dismantled.[32] For the second time in U.S. history, the first being the post–Civil War era of Reconstruction, the possibility arose that the notion of a legal system based upon individual rights might approach social reality. In the 1954 *Brown v. Board of Education* case, the Supreme Court ruled that legally imposed racial segregation in education violated the guarantee of equal protection under the law found in the Fourteenth Amendment to the Constitution.[33] In the *Brown* case, the Supreme Court formally rejected the notion that legally sanctioned racial segregation could be benign, as the "separate-but-equal" doctrine of *Plessy v. Ferguson* suggested.[34] The Court was constrained by a long history of white racist precedent and was still embedded in a society characterized by open and extreme white racism. Still, the Court acknowledged, albeit in diluted language, that the racial group–based legal frame was fundamentally connected to oppression and inequality.[35]

> We come then to the question presented: Does segregation of children in public schools solely on the basis of race, even though the physical facilities and other "tangible" factors may be equal, deprive the children of the minority group of equal educational opportunities? We believe that it does. . . . We conclude that in the field of public education the doctrine of "separate but equal" has no place. Separate educational facilities are inherently unequal.[36]

Although the Court stopped short of acknowledging that the inherent inequality of racial segregation was the result of the legacy of systemic racism in the legal structure, the Court did recognize the connection between the construction of racial group boundaries and the maintenance of racial oppression.

The Court's analysis in *Brown* contained within it the seed of a process of legal reasoning that focused upon the actual consequences of structural racial oppression in the United States. That is to say, the Court formally recognized that the history of race and racism in the United States was connected to the reality of subjugation and oppression conferred by segregating children in separate educational facilities. The case laid the foundation for a series of cases and legislation, including the 1964 Civil Rights Act, in which the Court rejected explicit legal support for structures perpetuating white supremacy. And this line of reasoning opened the possibility for a jurisprudential shift, one that could have included a straightforward assessment of racial oppression and white racism. Unfortunately, white resistance to the dictates of the *Brown* decision was overwhelming, and the Court retreated from this possibility more quickly than it had come to it. Only one year later, in the case that came to be known as *Brown II*, the Court realigned itself with white interests.[37]

After deciding the *Brown* case, the Supreme Court asked that counsel in the case return the following year to reargue the issue of remedies to segregation in education. In *Brown II*, the Court balked at the opportunity to require immediate redress by ordering all school districts to desegregate immediately. In fact, the Courts decision was framed within a lens that disregarded the newly announced constitutional rights of African American school children and instead focused upon the needs and desires of the white elites who operated the school districts and the white racist citizenry who opposed desegregation. Leaving the process of enforcing the desegregation mandate to local district courts, the Court merely asked that school districts act "with all deliberate speed" to dismantle legally enforced segregation in schools. With this vague and cautious decision, the Court revealed that its attention to the structural consequences of white racism and racial hierarchy would be short-lived. And despite a period of progressive reforms with regard to explicitly racist law,

Brown II signaled the beginning of white retrenchment, moving to curtail any potential for real racial reform offered by the analyses in the *Brown* case. U.S. courts would not act to dismantle white racial supremacy; instead, they would draw upon the rhetoric of abstract individualism to create a discursive shift in legal reasoning that would perpetuate structural racial inequality and white supremacy.

Post–Civil Rights Retreat and the Law School Discourse

In a constitutional law class at Midstate Law School, Professor McDonald asked his class to consider the legal issues involved in remedying contemporary racial segregation in schools, an exercise in evaluating the post-*Brown* series of cases on educational segregation. Professor McDonald drew two diagrams on the class blackboard, each a box with a dotted line drawn horizontally across it. He explained to the class that both of these boxes represented school districts that were racially segregated. But, he explained, in one of the districts the segregation was the result of state and local laws that segregated the schools prior to the *Brown* decision. In contrast, in the other district, no laws had been passed concerning race or racial segregation in education. Discussing this second district, the professor said,

> Originally students in the North were all Norwegian and students in the South were all Swedes, but that changed over time. After the dividing line [a train track] was put in place, you had minority communities begin to move in. The school district line required that everyone north of the line goes to North school, which today is 90 percent black. Everyone south of the line goes to South school . . . and it is all white. Okay? So, is [this district] unconstitutional?

Edward, a white man in the class said, "It's tough to do anything about it because that's not created by state action." Professor McDonald then asked, "What is it about state action [that's relevant]?" Edward responded, "It's more difficult to get at because it's a natural border. . . . [For a Fourteenth Amendment challenge,] it has to be state action."[38] Professor McDonald then asked Edward how the neighborhoods became racially segregated. Edward said that it was "probably related to housing costs or choices about neighborhoods where people wanted to live," but he reiterated, it was not the state's action. Then Edward asked Professor McDonald whether issues of residential zoning might be relevant. Professor McDonald responded, "Did the particular named defendant zone? The school district did not zone. . . . You've got to show that the *named* defendant did it. . . . In [the second school district], the school board did not do it . . . but the thing I'm [also] after is you have to find some element of *intent.*"

This class discussion was designed to set the students up for another discussion about the Supreme Court case *Milliken v. Bradley.*[39] In the *Milliken* case, the district court in Michigan found that the Detroit Board of Education and the state of Michigan had acted intentionally to create a system of racial segregation in the Detroit schools. In other words, the Detroit school district was unconstitutionally segregated by law, and so, the district court was charged with overseeing a remedy in the form of a desegregation plan. Because the city of Detroit was overwhelmingly African American, the court determined that the *only* effective remedy would be a desegregation plan that included the entire Detroit metropolitan area; in other words, one that included the predominantly white suburban districts. The district court reasoned as follows:

> Governmental actions and inaction at all levels, federal, state and local, have combined, with those of private organizations, such as loaning institutions and real estate associations and brokerage firms, to establish and to maintain the pattern of residential segregation throughout the Detroit metropolitan area. . . . While it would be unfair to charge the present defendants with what other governmental officers or agencies have done, it can be said that the actions or the failure to act by the responsible school authorities, both city and state, were linked to that of these other governmental units. When we speak of governmental action we should not view the different agencies as a collection of unrelated units. Perhaps the most that can be said is that all of them, including the school authorities, are, in part, responsible for the segregated condition which exists.

Indeed, racial segregation in housing and white flight to sprawling suburban areas was the result of many policies and practices of state entities, for example, the Department of Housing and Urban Development, in many northern metropolitan areas like Detroit (Massey and Denton 1993). Thus, as a result of this broad, systemic analysis, the district court authorized a desegregation plan that included bussing between Detroit-area schools and the schools in the surrounding suburbs. The legal reasoning of the district court made sense, particularly if the goal of the court was to evaluate the multiple mechanisms through which systemic racism gets reproduced in the post–civil rights era in order to fashion an effective remedy for desegregating schools. However, when the *Milliken* case reached the Supreme Court, the framing changed dramatically. The Supreme Court rejected the structural analysis presented by the district court and held that the district court did not have the authority to order the school districts outside of Detroit to desegregate with the Detroit schools, absent a finding of *intentional discrimination* on the part of the suburban school boards. In other words, the interdistrict remedy was only legal if individual actors or a group of actors in the suburban school districts had acted in a manner that they knew would produce racial segregation in their schools. This, of course, was not necessary in order for the suburban districts to produce all-white schools because the populations in these suburban districts were nearly exclusively white.[40]

Although, as the district court in the *Milliken* case pointed out, housing segregation and school segregation are connected, and both of these are the result of broad state-constructed and state-enforced systemic racism. The Supreme Court rejected any form of structural analysis. The effect of the Court's decision was to ensure that Detroit schools would remain racially segregated. Similarly, Professor McDonald rejected a structural analysis in his class in so much as he never raised the issue of systemic racism and never discussed the relevant argument put forth by the Michigan District Court. When asked by a student explicitly about zoning, he responded as if the holding of the Supreme Court represented unadulterated truth. Both the *Milliken* case and Professor McDonald's class exercise generated an individualistic assessment of a systemic structural social problem that resulted in the perpetuation of racially isolated school districts. The protection of white interests—white parents who did not want their children bussed to predominantly black schools—outweighed the more realistic approach of acknowledging the mechanisms by which segregation and racial inequality are perpetuated in the post–civil rights era.

Milliken was not the final word from the Supreme Court on the individualistic interpretation of cases concerning racial inequality; in fact, it was only a beginning. In 1970, African American police officers brought a class action suit against the District of Columbia and its metropolitan police department, alleging discrimination against African Americans in hiring and promotion through the use of a personnel test, called "Test 21," that was said to measure verbal skills. The plaintiffs in the case of *Washington v. Davis* argued that Test 21 "bore no relationship to job performance," and it had a discriminatory impact on African American candidates in that four times as many African American applicants as white applicants failed to pass the test.[41] By the time the *Davis* case got to the Supreme Court in 1976, however, the issue of whether this test was actually a valid measure of police performance had faded into the background. Instead, the central issue for the Court became proof of intent to discriminate on the basis of race. Justice Byron White, speaking for the majority of the Court, said,

> [T]he central purpose of the Equal Protection Clause of the Fourteenth Amendment is the prevention of official conduct discriminating on the basis of race. . . . [O]ur cases have not embraced the proposition that a law, or other official act,

without regard to whether it reflects a racially discriminatory purpose, is unconstitutional solely because it has a racially disproportionate impact.[42]

Legal scholar Barbara Flagg (1993) has pointed out that the discriminatory-
intent requirement in *Davis* sets up a legal frame concerning race based upon
a definition of racism that assumes that individuals act with conscious racial
malice, precluding the possibility of evaluating the dynamics of institutional
racism or of individuals acting with unconscious racial biases. The Court in
Davis also acknowledged its unwillingness to examine structural racism. The
Court admitted that a significantly higher number of blacks failed Test 21, but
they said that this racial disparity, without proof of a person or persons intentionally acting to discriminate, did not trigger constitutional protection.
The most salient rationale for this conclusion was the fear of the far-reaching
nature of a decision to consider disparate racial impact in evaluating claims of
discrimination. Again, speaking for the Court, Justice White said,

> A rule that a statute designed to serve neutral ends is nevertheless invalid, absent
> compelling justification, if in practice it benefits one race more than another
> would be far reaching and would raise serious questions about, and perhaps in-
> validate, a whole range of tax, welfare, public service, regulatory, and licensing
> statutes that may be more burdensome to the poor and to the average black than
> to the more affluent white.[43]

In effect, the Court suggested that finding discrimination in the case presented
in *Davis* might lead to systemic social-structural change, or at least the need
to examine the entire legal structure for racial bias. The Court rejected this
possibility, in essence holding that legal analyses that considered structural
racial disparities might lead to *too much* justice.[44] Rather than acting to dismantle systemic white racial privilege and power, the Court acted to protect it
by drawing upon the rhetoric of individualism to dismiss the legal relevance
of embedded structural racism. And recall that when Professor McDonald set
up the discussion for the *Milliken* case, he had already planted the truth of the
analysis in his students' heads by saying, "[T]he thing I'm [also] after is you
have to find some element of *intent*." Cases like *Milliken* and *Davis*, and many
others since, have further entrenched an abstract individualist ideology into
contemporary race jurisprudence. Worse, this ideology gets inserted insidiously in the legal training of law students. And despite the striking contradiction between the long history of racial group–based legal reasoning and the
rigid individualist contemporary case law, the frame of abstract individualism, which reproduces white power and privilege by failing to assess honestly
the structural consequences of historical racism and the manifestations of
present day racism, gets presented as legal truth.

Conclusion

The legal framework of the post–civil rights era effectively renders the long history of explicit, legally imposed and enforced white supremacy irrelevant. As a result, U.S. law provides, as Cheryl Harris (1993) suggests, a legal entitlement for whites to the structural and ideological privilege that they receive as a result of years of legally created and enforced racial exclusion and oppression (see also Feagin 2006). The abstract individualist discursive frame employed by the courts in contemporary race-related cases resonates with broader social rhetoric concerning individual rights and "equality of opportunity." An adherence to abstract individualism becomes a rhetorical strategy that is a central component of what Bonilla-Silva calls "color-blind racism." Color-blind racism operates as an ideological framework that allows whites to espouse views that normalize systemic racism, minimize the relevance of racism, and denigrate the cultures of communities of color, while at the same time denying that they, themselves, are racist or responsible for racism.

In law schools, students like Jonathan, whose comments open this chapter, are able to openly disavow their responsibility for racism, while participating in, and benefiting from, the white racial privilege that stems from racist structures and racialized everyday practices. And despite the long history of explicitly racist case law, of which most law students are aware, the contemporary legal frame relies upon similar tenets of abstract individualism, empowering this discourse by giving it legal authority. So, in law schools the discursive naturalization of structural racial inequality is reified by the law's requirement of proof of invidious purpose or intent. The process of reification often manifests itself insidiously when law faculty teach post–civil rights cases like *Davis* and *Milliken* as though the individualist frame employed by the courts is presumptively correct. Beyond that, however, this color-blind racist frame operates as an unstated presumption informing the vast majority of educational and social interactions in the law school. In chapter 4, I explore the dominant discourse at Midstate and Presidential, which draws heavily upon the tenets of abstract individualism and other color-blind racist frames. I then examine the way in which the story lines that make up the color-blind racist discourse assist in normalizing and minimizing the everyday racialized practices that occur within the space of elite law schools, thereby justifying and reproducing the attributes of white institutional space.

Notes

1. See also Alexis De Tocqueville, *Democracy in America*, ed. Bowen (1876).
2. A full review of American race jurisprudence would comprise a book in itself. For example, see Derrick Bell, *Race, Racism and American Law*, 4th ed. (New York:

Aspen Press, 2000). Here, I draw upon cases that came up while I was doing my research at Midstate and Presidential, either in classes I observed or in discussions with professors and students.

3. In other words, the court has historically engaged in racial formation. This concept, developed by Michael Omi and Howard Winant (*Racial Formation in the United States from the 1960s to the 1990s*, 2nd ed. [New York: Routledge, 1994], 59), links the construction of racial meanings, or the connection between phenotypical characteristics and human capacities, to the distribution of material goods, such as land, for example.

4. Major studies on law school education have not examined the law as a relevant discourse in law schools. As I discuss in chapter 1, Robert Granfield, in *Making Elite Lawyers: Visions of Law at Harvard and Beyond* (New York: Routledge, 1992), has conducted research on the class dynamics of law schools, and Lani Guinier, Michelle Fine, and Jane Balin, in *Becoming Gentlemen: Women, Law School, and Institutional Change* (Boston: Beacon Press, 1997), have looked at gender. Elizabeth Mertz has conducted research on race in legal education, looking at classroom treatment and participation, but, similarly, does not examine the law as relevant to these issues. None of these scholars systematically examines the classed and gendered legal structure that students must engage in their law school education. This leaves perhaps the most authoritative voice in the law school unexamined in their research.

5. Throughout this chapter, I refer to "the Court" as a body with the power to speak, as legal scholars are trained to do. In doing so, I do not mean to suggest that I buy into the notion that when "the Court" speaks, it is above the subjective partialities of those individuals who are the judges on the court. Clearly, the individuals who sit as judges on the courts that I quote have subscribed to a blatantly racist ideology. However, I utilize the notion of "the Court" speaking in order to illustrate the discursive patterns that occur in this particular voice of the state, patterns that come from different courts and different judges but all draw upon elements of a white racist frame.

6. *Hudgins v. Wright*, 11 Va. 134 (1806).

7. *Hudgins v. Wright*, 11 Va. 134 (1806).

8. In the *Hudgins* case, Hannah and her daughter were held to be of "Indian" ancestry and, thus, not black; therefore, they were presumptively held not to be slaves.

9. Howard Winant has argued that slavery in the United States, coupled with the racist ideologies that justified it and the power of the United States in the world financial and political economy, has meant that blackness has come to signify subjugated status globally.

10. See *Daniel v. Guy*, 19 Ark. 121 (1857).

11. After the Civil War, the act was changed to include "people of African descent."

12. For a more detailed discussion of the legal construction of whiteness, see Ian Haney Lopez, *White by Law: The Legal Construction of Race* (New York: New York University Press, 1996).

13. Brief for Petitioner at 55, 57, 71, *Takao Ozawa v. United States*, 260 U.S. 178 (1922). Quoted in Ian Haney Lopez, *White by Law: The Legal Construction of Race* (New York: New York University Press, 1996), 81.

14. *Takao Ozawa v. United States*, 260 U.S. 178, 207, 208 (1922).

15. *Takao Ozawa v. United States*, 260 U.S. 208 (1922).

16. *United States v. Thind*, 261 U.S 204 (1923).

17. *United States v. Thind*, 261 U.S 211, 212.

18. *United States v. Thind*, 261 U.S 212.

19. *Dred Scott v. Sandford*, 60 U.S. (19 How) 393, 400 (1857).

20. *Plessy v. Ferguson*, 163 U.S. 537, 539 (1896).

21. *Plessy v. Ferguson*, 163 U.S. 542.

22. *Plessy v. Ferguson*, 163 U.S. 544.

23. *Plessy v. Ferguson*, 163 U.S. 559.

24. Some have argued that the racial violence and racial oppression that occurred during this historical period were extralegal and, thus, not state sanctioned. However, despite the Supreme Court's disingenuous insistence that separate could, in fact, be equal, legal entities at the state level were more than happy with unequal segregation. In fact, agents of the state, such as governors and the police, acted openly to enforce inequality and racial oppression. See Taylor Branch, *Parting the Waters: America in the King Years, 1954–1963* (New York: Simon and Schuster. 1988); Katznelson 2005. The "equal" in "separate but equal" was never a social reality; thus, the refusal of legal entities like the Supreme Court to acknowledge this was pragmatically the same as verbally sanctioning racism.

25. *People v. Hall*, 4 Cal. 399 (1854).

26. *Rice v. Gong Lum*, 104 So. 105 (1925).

27. *Rice v. Gong Lum*, 104 So. 108, 110.

28. *Independent School District et al. v. Salvatierra et al.*, 33 S.W. 2d 790, 794 (1930).

29. *Johnson v. M'Intosh*, 21 U.S. 543 (1823).

30. *Johnson v. M'Intosh*, 21 U.S. 570.

31. *Johnson v. M'Intosh*, 21 U.S. 570.

32. From a legal perspective, the civil rights movement probably began before 1954, with the pre-*Brown* attacks on racial segregation in education. However, most social-movements literature views the start of the movement as corresponding with *Brown* around 1954, the same year that Chief Justice Earl Warren was appointed to the Supreme Court, and the court decided *Brown v. Board of Education* (infra at note 33), holding that legally enforced racial segregation in education violated the Constitution. After this decision, other statutory and judicial case law follows in a similar vein. However, by the early 1970s, the Court had begun to retreat from these earlier progressive decisions. By 1976, the Court's discursive frame had shifted and we saw decisions like *Washington v. Davis* (supra, at note 41), which solidified the ideology of individualism rights in race jurisprudence. Social-movements scholars typically define the boundaries as beginning in 1954 and ending with the rise of black nationalism near the end of the 1960s. See Aldon Morris, "A Retrospective on the Civil Rights Movement: Political and Intellectual Landmarks," *Annual Review of Sociology* 25 (1999): 517–39. But while progressive legal reform with regard to race was never uncontested in the courts, the Supreme Court did consider structural and group-based aspects of racial inequality in several key legal cases until the shifting ideological frame of individualism took hold in cases like *Davis* in the early to mid 1970s. For this reason, I begin with the perspective of social-movements scholars'

identifying the start of the movement in 1954, but I do not identify the post–civil rights era as beginning until the early to mid 1970s.

33. *Brown v. Board of Education of Topeka*, 347 U.S. 483 (1954).

34. Infra at note 18.

35. Derrick Bell suggests that the decision in *Brown* was much more related to the convergence of interests between African Americans and the white power elite than it was about racial equity. At the end of a war, in which black Americans had fought, which directly challenged tyranny and racial/ethnic violence, and at a moment when the United States wanted to organize the world against communism, the fact of violent racial oppression and inequality in the United States became uncomfortable for state interests and the interests of elite whites. The hypocrisy between the ideals that the United States espoused in separating themselves from communist nations and the fact of racial oppression and intolerance was having an impact on the worldview of this nation. As a result, many political powers wanted to see the Court bring an end to legal segregation in education in order to upgrade the world's perception of American democracy. See Derrick Bell, *Silent Covenants: Brown v. Board of Education and the Unfulfilled Hopes for Racial Reform* (New York: Oxford University Press, 2004).

36. Infra note 20 at 492.

37. *Brown v. Board of Education of Topeka II*, 349 U.S. 294 (1955).

38. The protections guaranteed by the Constitution and the Reconstruction amendments, including the Fourteenth Amendment, are protections for citizens resulting from actions by the state government. A school board, for example, is a state-run government body, thus bound by these amendments. The actions of private individuals are not covered by these constitutional amendments. There has since been legislation designed to prohibit some actors that were previously considered private from discriminating. One example is Title VII of the 1964 Civil Rights Act.

39. *Milliken v. Bradley*, 418 U.S. 171 (1974).

40. *Bradley v. Milliken*, 338 F.Supp. 582, 587 (1971).

41. *Washington v. Davis*, 426 U.S. 229 (1976).

42. *Washington v. Davis*, 426 U.S. 239.

43. *Washington v. Davis*, 426 U.S. 248.

44. See also *McClesky v. Kemp*, 481 U.S. 279 (1987), where the court finds valid statistical indications that the state of Georgia disproportionately sentenced African Americans to the death penalty and disproportionately sentenced individuals convicted of killing whites to the death penalty; but without proof of an identifiable actor, or group of actors who were acting with intent to discriminate, the court could not find legal discrimination.

4

We Give Them the Moon,
but Still They Complain

Color-blind Racism in the Law Schools

W HEN I BEGAN MY RESEARCH at Presidential School of Law, a senior white
male professor, Professor Morgan, asked to speak to me about the nature of my research. When I went to meet with Professor Morgan, he was not
there, but his secretary, a middle-aged white woman, showed me into his office. She asked me whether I would like to have a cappuccino. When I said
no, she told me that she would just make one for Professor Morgan because
he liked to have one waiting for him when he came in. Professor Morgan's
office was large, and on his very large desk, he had a cappuccino machine.
His secretary made the drink and left it on the desk. She then left me, saying
that Professor Morgan would be in soon. Approximately five minutes later,
Professor Morgan arrived. He came in and walked to the other side of his
desk, looked down at the drink and asked, "Is this for you?" I said that it was
not, that it was for him, and he said, "Oh, good." Then he sat down, folded
his hands under his chin and stared at me without speaking. After a moment
of silence, I began to explain the broad picture of my research to him. After
I had explained, he asked "What is the relevance of your research?" I made
an effort to explain my theoretical framework and the contributions I saw
my research making. He then asked, "So, what difference does it make if you
interview a black student, and he says that he is discriminated against, as
they so often do, when there is no objective reality to support his claims?" I
answered carefully by explaining that how individuals perceive their experience is just as important and relevant to me as what others may view as the
"objective reality." He responded by saying that "the objective reality is that
we give them the moon, but they still complain."

"*So what difference does it make if you interview a black student, and he says that he is discriminated against, as they so often do, when there is no objective reality to support his claims?*" In the same question in which he asks for "objective reality" to support an assertion of discrimination, Professor Morgan stereotypically characterized black people (in this case, black students) as frequently perceiving discrimination that is not real. An ironic juxtaposition between "objectivity" and a color-blind racist discourse minimizes the relevance of racism. Possibly when he requested "objective reality," Professor Morgan was asking for evidence of specific differential treatment of people of color that suggested identifiable racial animus. As Eduardo Bonilla-Silva (2001) suggests, however, gone are the days of Jim Crow racism, where racial animosity was openly expressed, admitted, and justified. The subtler dynamics of color-blind racism occur within a structural framework of racial hierarchy in which white people can rely upon a white discursive frame to disavow racism while engaging in practices that reproduce white power and privilege (see also Feagin 2006). In fact, requests like Professor Morgan's for "objective reality" within the context of a white discursive frame serve to silently center a normatively white position by forcing people of color into a defensive posture from which they have to "prove" that they have a basis for perceiving discrimination or racism.

"*The objective reality is that we give them the moon, but still they complain.*" After relying upon a notion of objectivity that is actually a mechanism for constraining discussions about racism and discrimination into a white frame, Professor Morgan then asserted, in language that sounded closer to traditional Jim Crow racism, that students of color are *given* the "moon," but *they* still complain. His statement clearly indicates that the law school is composed of a racialized, presumptively white "we." The members of "we" are entitled to decipher objective reality. "We" also have the ability to "give" the "moon" to "them." "Them," then, are the students of color, who are clearly ungrateful outsiders who complain because they cannot objectively see that they are being given preferential treatment. It is important to note that Professor Morgan's comments rely upon the unstated assumption that the law school is a white space and that the fact of its being a white space is appropriate and not a form of racism or discrimination. Professor Morgan's comments, though more explicit than most, are part of a broader discourse that draws upon a white frame to silently reproduce and naturalize white space in the law schools. However, the reproduction of white space is not a result of discourse alone but also of the interaction between discourse and everyday racialized practices.

As Bonilla-Silva (1997) has pointed out, contemporary race discourse represents an ideological framework situated within a racialized social structure, a structure of white supremacy. He suggests that discourse does not maintain

white space in and of itself; rather, it works in concert with a racialized structure and everyday racialized practices that function to reproduce white privilege and black subjugation. In the two previous chapters, I discussed the deep
normative structures in the law school and in the law, and I examined how
these deep structures get presented as objective and neutral truth when, in
fact, they are insidiously enforcing and reproducing white space. In this chapter, I look at another important aspect of the enforcement of white space, the
everyday racialized practices and the color-blind racist discourse that justifies
and normalizes these practices. To do this, we must understand color-blind
racism as more than a discourse or an ideology; we must examine the ways in
which discourse interacts with practice.

The Practice of Color-Blind Racism

Bonilla-Silva (2001, 2003) suggests that in the post–civil rights United States,
whites have developed certain "story lines" or "frames" to create an ideology
that supports a racialized structure based upon white privilege and power
(2003, 138). These frames include an effort by whites to naturalize structural
racial inequality by, for example, reducing structural processes like housing
segregation to personal choices and intentions about where individuals want
to live. In addition, color-blind racist discourse gets utilized to minimize the
existence and impact of racism and discrimination, like we see in Professor
Morgan's comments above. Notions of the biologization or naturalization of
race or, alternately, notions of the cultural inferiority of communities of color
also come up in the story lines of color-blind racist discourse, and they are
often the basis, either explicitly or subtly, for the minimization of racism and
the justification of white privilege. Drawing upon these frames or story lines,
Bonilla-Silva suggests that whites create a discourse that ignores structural inequality while justifying and perpetuating the racial structure.[1]

The central aspect of the discursive process of color-blind racism, as discussed in the previous chapter, is the reliance upon notions of abstract or liberal individualism. Contemporary abstract individualistic ideology decontex-
tualizes notions of fairness and equality from social structures and patterns.
In doing so, systemic racism gets excluded from discussions about race, creating a very limited framework within which to understand racial inequality. As
Jackman points out, "Such a view falls considerably short of an abandonment
of the racial *status quo*" (1996, 762). Through liberal individualism, whites can
make claims about fairness by asserting that equality simply means treating all
individuals the same, while ignoring the structural disadvantage from which
minorities suffer. The discourse, as illustrated in the previous chapter, renders

the long history of explicit, legally imposed and enforced white supremacy ir-relevant.[2] Not only do these racial ideologies become the organizational map for maintaining racial hierarchy in society at large, but they also work within institutions, like law schools, to support the tacit norms that sustain white privilege. Furthermore, I suggest that the discursive aspect of color-blind racist ideology must be connected to the everyday racialized practices of ac-tors within these institutions.

Bonilla-Silva does not explicitly articulate the relationship between dis-course and practice in his color-blind racism framework (2001, 2003). Jen-nifer Pierce, however, extends the notion of color-blind racism as an ideology by delineating the manner in which whiteness is "constituted and reconsti-tuted in daily life" through the recursive interaction between practice and dis-course (2003, 53). In her studies of the racial dynamics within law firms, she argues that white people engage in everyday *practices* that form racialized pat-terns; for example, in the case of law firms, white partners invite white associ-ates to lunch for mentoring purposes much more frequently than they invite African American associates. Yet, in their explanations of their practices, white attorneys draw upon individualistic perspectives, dismissing the relevance of these patterns by minimizing them to distinct individual events. Through this discursive tactic, which Pierce terms "racing for innocence," white attorneys maintain white privilege while disavowing any responsibility for doing such. Pierce's work illustrates one of the ways in which liberal individualist dis-course becomes the "organizational map," discussed by Bonilla-Silva (1997), that guides racial actors in the practice of preserving white racial privilege. Color-blind racism in this construction is a discourse that interacts with prac-tice to reinforce racial social structure.

As I have discussed, in law schools, appeals to abstract individualism in re-sponse to racialized practices are particularly powerful because of the legal au-thority that supports this frame. The very subject matter taught to law stu-dents resonates with the dominant discourse in the schools. Law schools, as sites, represent a space in which the dominant ideology of abstract individu-alism, as well as other aspects of color-blind racism, gets reproduced through discourse and practice, as well as being held up as having legal force. It is im-portant to emphasize that the racialized practices and discourses in the law schools are not always covert, which is an assumption in color-blind racist frames. In fact, racism is sometimes explicit and overt, looking very much like traditional Jim Crow racism. It is often difficult, however, to tease out where color blindness begins and ends, particularly because even racism that looks overt is diminished by the suggestion that it was a joke or misunderstanding or that it was unintentional. The point is that color-blind racism frames are often used in concert with, and employed to disregard, more overt racism.

Sometimes this occurs through discursive tactics that minimize explicitly racist actions or comments; at other times, it is more subtly invasive in that the color-blind discourse can be utilized to reject overt racist sentiment, enabling people to assert, by comparison, that color blindness is an egalitarian, nonracist frame. In either case, the dominance of color-blind racism serves as a mechanism for racial reproduction.

Systemic Racism in Practice and Discourse

Geoffrey Stone et al.'s *Constitutional Law* (1996) is a very popular book utilized by many law professors in many law schools to teach constitutional law (or "Con Law," as law students call it) (see Perea 1997). Several Con Law professors at Midstate used the third edition of this text while I was there. Constitutional law is a massive body of law (the book is 1,766 pages long, not including the table of cases or bibliography), which covers many areas. The Constitution, in particular the Fourteenth Amendment, has been the legal basis for many of the civil rights challenges to racial inequality in the United States, so this area of law is particularly significant to the racial discourse in law schools. In Stone et al.'s textbook, chapter 5 is titled "Equality and the Constitution." The first section of that chapter is entitled "Race and the Constitution," and this section begins as follows:

> This section traces the evolution of constitutional doctrine concerning discrimination against African Americans. There are several reasons for beginning the study of constitutionally protected individual rights with this issue. First, in one form or another, the controversy about the legal status of African-Americans has been central to U.S. politics since the founding of the Republic. . . . Second, the Court's analysis of discrimination against African-Americans has served as a prototype for the development of other constitutional doctrines. (p. 495)

Several tacit assumptions in this opening paragraph reveal a white frame. First, the authors equate "race" with being "African American." This draws attention away from the more central "race" issue in constitutional law—the fact that the Constitution is a white racist document that provided legal protection for the enslavement of black people and became the foundation for an entire body of law constructing and enforcing white supremacy (see Harris 1993, Lopez 1996).[3] For Stone et al., whiteness is considered a nonproblematic norm. It is the fact of blackness and the "controversy" about the legal status of black people that raises a problem in constitutional jurisprudence. As part of this framing, the authors situate the issue of race as one of "constitutionally protected individual rights," as opposed to the oppression of groups based

upon racial constructions (or racial projects, as Omi and Winant [1994]
would argue). The tacit assumptions built into this explanation of "race and
the Constitution" insert an individualistic perspective and a normatively
white frame into the jurisprudence of constitutional law.

The above excerpt from a popular Constitutional law textbook used in
many law schools, including Midstate, illustrates the racialized practices and
discourses within the law school. It represents racial discourse in that it insti-
tutionalizes a discourse based upon a white frame. It becomes a racialized
practice, however, when law professors use their power as teachers of the law
to select and assign textbooks and materials that set up a normatively white
framework for law and jurisprudence. As I have discussed previously, this
power is even more significant in law schools than in other fields because, in
law schools, the hegemonic process of teaching from a normatively white perspective is further entrenched by the hegemonic force of law.

The framework represented in the Stone et al. *Constitutional Law* textbook—the presentation of race as a problem concerning people of color—
was an aspect of the white frame deeply internalized by many white students
at both Presidential and Midstate. As one result, white students often felt they
did not need to participate in discussions about race in the law school. They
felt as though race was not about them. In an interview with Nathaniel, a
third-year white man, I asked whether he was comfortable raising issues about
race in the classroom. He said,

> No—'cause I'm a white guy. . . . I was raised poor and I'm, I'm always comfort-
> able to raise my hand and be like, "Well you know, let's, let's look at the disad-
> vantages inherent in not having any fuckin' money," you know, . . .but I wouldn't
> wanna ever stand up and say, "Well, what would happen if I was black" . . . be-
> cause I'm not black. . . . I don't feel comfortable trying to pretend that I am.

The underlying assumption in Nathaniel's comments, like that in Stone's textbook, is that conversations about race are about and for people of color (or,
more specifically, African American people). In fact, he equates race with
blackness, making whiteness and the tacit white frame invisible (see Frankenberg 1993). Furthermore, when the "problem" of race is tacitly presented as a
problem about people of color, white students are never put in a position of
having to justify the privilege that they have within the law school space or society writ large (see DuBois 1903).

Another example of the willingness, or rather unwillingness, of white people in the law school to engage in discussions about race was revealed by a
white woman law professor at Midstate who explained to me that she often
avoided discussions about race in her classes. Professor Skally informed me

that she was more comfortable talking about gender than race. When I questioned her about this, she said, "If you're a woman, you can make fun of or invoke stereotypes about women and men, um, and everyone has a gender so everyone's involved in that discussion." It may be that she felt entitled to make jokes about gender inequality and stereotypes because she herself had experienced gender inequality, so subjectively she felt entitled to talk about gender issues. Yet, as she articulated it, she felt comfortable because "everyone has a gender," so women and men can participate in the discussion. The fact that everyone has a race, thus everyone should be required to participate in a race-related discussion as well, did not occur to her. Her comments, like Nathaniel's, illustrate the invisibility of whiteness, and her choice not to talk about race in the classroom reveals the way tacit white norms impact the practice of teaching the law.

One African American second-year student, Marcia, discussed why she felt that white students (and this may apply to white faculty as well) did not want to discuss race:

[White students] don't think [race is] an issue that they have to deal with, simply because they haven't had to deal with it. Nobody that they know has had to deal with an issue of discrimination, or being excluded. . . . I mean, it's just like [a] disease . . . health care problems. [Y]ou know, people are like, "Oh that doesn't affect me because I'm not sick, nobody I know is sick, therefore it has no relation to me, so let them do whatever they want with the laws with respect to those types of diseases."

In this powerful analogy, Marcia likens race, or racism/discrimination, to a disease. White people don't have to deal with that disease, so they see it as having no relation to them. But the practical consequence of this is that, although white people are the beneficiaries of privileges as a result of the "disease" of racism, as Marcia puts it, whiteness goes completely uninterrogated. Structural racial dynamics in law and society, and white privilege more broadly, are rarely critically examined in law classes. But when they are discussed, there is an expectation that people of color will carry those discussions.

The often unspoken requirement that students of color are responsible for leading discussions about race results in a heavy burden for students of color. If students of color choose to speak about race, they are confined within a white frame that organizes the discussions, the very same frame that puts them in the position of being responsible for these discussions. But there is an even more disturbing consequence. Discussions about race and the law become subjectified, in opposition to the normative presentation of law and legal issues as objective. Kimberle Crenshaw suggests that "subjectification" is the process by which students of color are asked to speak in class (or, as she says, "testify") about the impact of law or policy on communities of color (1994, 7). The normative "objective" and "neutral" stance required in law school discussions gets abandoned momentarily. Thus, when fellow students or professors break from the "objective" stance, when the issue being discussed is race, they put students of color in a position of opposition to the normal classroom context. This forces students of color into the uncomfortable role of expert on issues of race and the law, which they may know very little about. Further, it places students of color in a position to be viewed as biased, emotionally involved, or "unobjective" about issues of race. White students, on the other hand, retain their normatively "objective" position with regard to the law, as well as legal analysis and argumentation. By way of analogy, no one would ever argue that one would have to have been audited by the Internal Revenue Service in order to make a legal argument about tax law and the practice of auditing. Such an argument would seem utterly absurd in law schools where people are being trained to make legal arguments from many different perspectives.

Whether white people are not comfortable engaging issues of race because they are fearful or because they do not see race as relevant to their lives or the law, the result is racialized practices that reify white space. Another example of this occurs in the manner in which professors choose to teach their courses. For example, one white male constitutional law professor at Presidential, Professor Bradley, did not cover any Fourteenth Amendment or equal-protection law in his constitutional law course. Students in this course left his Con Law class having never read *Brown v. Board of Education* or any other case law that examined racial inequality in the United States. When I discussed this omission with administrators and faculty at Presidential, many pointed out that the law school offered an entire class on the Fourteenth Amendment that students could take if they were interested in race and the law. However, this class was an elective taught once per year (by only one faculty member), and it was capped at fifty students. Several students mentioned to me that they had been unable to get into the class as first-year students because it filled so quickly, and because first-year students received preference for admittance to the class, they could not get in as second- or third-year students either. As a result, these students were never taught the "equal-protection" doctrine of the Constitution in law school, a major area of law affecting the rights of people of color.

When I discussed the omission of Fourteenth Amendment jurisprudence with Professor Bradley, he told me that he tended to keep his class content confined to original constitutionalism. Since the 1950s, with the pre-*Brown* racial segregation cases and the holding in *Brown*, Fourteenth Amendment jurisprudence has become one of the most prolific areas of constitutional law. In fact, during the time that I was conducting my research, the Supreme Court was deciding upon two cases that would impact this area of law, the *Grutter* and *Gratz* cases.[4] Furthermore, both of these cases were directly relevant both to constitutional law and to law schools as institutions that make choices about the process of student admission. Professor Bradley's focus on "original constitutionalism," whether he intended it or not, was an explicit indication of white space. The original constitution was a slaveholder's document, and the Fourteenth Amendment was an (unfortunately ineffective) attempt to ameliorate the devastation of the institution of slavery. His omission and the reaction of many law school faculty and administrators who justified the decision because there was a Fourteenth Amendment elective course sent a message about what was viewed important and relevant to legal education.

The white frame that organizes discourse in law schools and white students' and faculty's practice of avoiding race-related discussions are components of the maintenance of white space within the law school. When students of color do something to challenge this white space, for example, organizing and joining student-of-color associations in the law school, there are attempts to disrupt this challenge. For example, during orientation at Midstate each year, the student-of-color organizations, like the other law student organizations, set up tables to make all incoming students aware of their organization and to recruit new students. Often, the student-of-color organizations also attempt to contact students who they know are students of color; for example, the Black Law Students Association (BLSA) contacts incoming African American students. Yet, none of the student-of-color organizations at either Midstate or Presidential claims to be racially exclusive, and the tables at orientation carry information for all incoming law students about each of the organizations. But a few weeks into the first semester of the year I conducted my research at Midstate, the Law Student Council sent out an e-mail to all student-of-color organization presidents, telling them that no "exclusive" groups could receive funding from the law school funds, which the Law Student Council distributed among all student organizations. Thus, they required that these organizations have one person who advertised the meetings, and those advertisements, generally in the form of e-mails, had to go out to the entire student body. This was not the normal practice for law student organizations because it would result in a vast amount of e-mail unwanted by most students, so e-mail announcements about organization meetings generally only went out to those individuals who had signed up as members.

The student-of-color organizations complied with this requirement, and although two white students who had connections with Native American communities joined the American Indian Law Students Association (AILSA), no white students joined any other student-of-color organization. After that, the Law Student Council went one step further. Several weeks after the e-mail requiring student-of-color organizations to advertise meetings and events to all students, the Law Student Council sent out a second e-mail to all student organizations. This message discussed how law school funds could and could not be spent. It said, in part, "It's okay to spend money on things like apple picking if you're going to share the apples with the whole student body." Just two weeks before this e-mail was sent out, the Asian American Law Students Association (AALSA) had used organization funds to go apple picking as a so-cial event to welcome incoming students who had become members. The AALSA had a large number of new members who were from out of state, so this activity was designed to get members together to help students socialize, get familiar with the city in which Midstate was located, and form networks with other AALSA members. Clearly this message was targeted at AALSA, and very likely other student-of-color organizations, because these organizations often hosted social events, like the apple-picking event, to help create a social space in which students of color felt supported.

The Law Student Council's policy requiring student groups to share any-thing they spent funds on with the entire student body entailed obvious im-practicalities. For example, many student organizations regularly had lunchtime events; they sent out invitations to the whole school and bought food for those who attended. Would they now be required to buy enough food for the entire student body and offer the food to people who did not come to the event? This scenario seems absurd, but the requirement that AALSA share their apples with the entire student body was equally absurd. They had not held themselves out as an exclusive organization; they had complied with the Law Student Council's requirement that they advertise meetings and invite the entire student body to join. Yet, the council still imposed an additional burden that was plainly targeted at socializing events held by student-of-color organizations. Not only were AALSA and other student-of-color organiza-tions required to *invite* the entire student body to their organization func-tions, but they were further required to provide accommodations for students who did not become members even after invited.

This action by the Law Student Council revealed that its members did not see any legitimate reason for students of color to socialize in a space that they could construct for themselves, a space safe from the tacit assumptions of whiteness that objectify (or subjectify) students of color and disregard their experiences. They were either unaware of, or unconcerned about, the fact that students of color may want to discuss their experiences without being forced to construct these experiences within a white frame.

While the Law Student Council expected that students of color should go out of their way to make their organizations accessible to, and comfortable for, white students, social events held for the law school at large were nearly always held in white spaces. The discomfort of the students of color in these spaces was ironically ignored. At both Midstate and Presidential, the students have a social event on Thursday nights, which they call "Bar Review," in which a local bar is selected, and students meet to socialize.[5] At both schools, students of color consistently told me that they did not go or that they felt extremely uncomfortable when they went because they were always held at white bars. (One of the bars that became a site for Bar Review was actually called "Whitey's." This became a regular joke among many students of color.)

At Midstate, the location for Bar Review was selected by a particular first-year section, and it was generally selected by votes from a majority of interested students in that section. Midstate is 84 percent white, and so it is not surprising that the locations selected by white students were always the winners. At Presidential, the Law Student Council selected the locations for the event, and inevitably they also turned out to be white bars. Students of color at both schools complained. At Midstate, there was no serious response (some white students agreed, but no changes were made, and many ignored the entire discussion). At Presidential, several years before I did my research there, the Law Student Council responded, deciding that it would be equitable if each of the student organizations was allowed to pick a location for Bar Review during their "week," which is generally the week in which the student organization puts on programming on subjects related to its purpose. This meant that, for example, that the BLSA would get to choose a location during its week, and the Federalist Society would get to choose a location during its week, and so forth. However, the year before I got to Presidential, they had stopped this practice and returned to having the Law Student Council select the location each week. Two members of the Law Student Council told me that the change was made because there were not enough weeks for each student organization to have a chance to select a location. This did not make sense to me because there were not, in fact, more student organizations than there were weeks of the school year. There were organizations that had programming for more than one week; for example, BLSA planned events for the entire month of February, Black History Month. But this did not mean that they could not have been restricted to one week for selection of a Bar Review location. Even with this policy, however, students of color would get to pick locations only a small number of times as there were many more majority-white student organizations than there were student-of-color organizations. After this practice ended, the Law Student Council went back to selecting locations that were nearly always white bars.[6]

The experience for students of color that resulted from the selection of culturally white bars in which to hold the main law school social event was one of isolation. Many students of color made comments similar to those of Kimberly, a second-year Latina:

> Why is there never a Bar Review at places where there are minority people? . . . It's just exclusively geared toward white people, and I hate to say that, but it is. Look at the bars that they've gone to this whole year. . . . Why do we always have to go to their bars? It's not fair.

Kimberly's comments reveal the discomfort of students of color in the white spaces at which Bar Review was held, as well as her frustration with the unfairness of the practice of selecting locations for Bar Review. Despite many requests from students of color that those in charge make more of an effort to select racially mixed locations, the practice of selecting white bars continued. White law students assumed that white cultural social spaces would be acceptable to everyone, even in social situations that took place outside of the law school (see Lipsitz 1998). This stood in sharp contrast to the accusations of unfair exclusivity directed toward students of color who were involved in student-of-color organizations.

Another racial practice that occurs in the law school deals with the value that is placed on activities of students of color. When students of color were engaged in activities or received awards in programs that were designed specifically for racial minorities, these activities and awards were not valued as much as the traditional, usually white-dominated activities and awards. For example, the year before I conducted my research at Presidential, the Latino Law Students Association (LLSA) put together a team of first-year law students to compete in the Hispanic National Bar Association Moot Court Competition. In this competition, students compete with other law students from across the nation by presenting oral arguments on legal issues as if they were arguing before an appellate court. Presidential's team of first-year students received second place in the nation in the competition. Again, the sentiments of Kimberly, who was then the president of the LLSA and who had been on the team as a first-year student, represent the feelings of many involved in the competition:

> KIMBERLY: "Last year we went to the HNBA, the Hispanic National Bar Association Moot Court Competition, and placed second nationally out of thirty-two teams. We were the only 1Ls there; it was only our third year in the competition. You know, we . . . we came back with trophies, and like we tried many times to get—there's like a trophy kind of case thing up on the second floor—and nobody would respond to us about putting them in there. And I just thought . . . I guarantee you . . . if it was, like, a regular national moot court competition, I know they would have put that . . ."

ME: "Is it up there now?"

KIMBERLY: "No, it's still not. And we, our president last year . . . was the one e-mailing everyone, you know the dean, saying how can we get it in there, and everybody would say, "Talk to this person, talk to this person." Well those trophies are sitting at my house, and that really pisses me off, because they gave us the trophies, and my mom went out and paid to have our names put on them, because she thought they were gonna go in a trophy case. . . . It cost us over three thousand dollars to go, which we paid for from fund-raising and what not. We devoted so much of our second 1L semester to it, and I just feel like for everyone to point the finger and be like, "just talk to this person," it's like we had to beg to have it put in there, and it just never ended up getting done."

Despite the impressive achievement of the 1L members of LLSA in placing second in a national moot court competition, the school failed to recognize their achievement in any formal way, and a year later the school still had not responded to the members of LLSA who wanted to place their trophy in the law school trophy case. Ironically, several days after my discussion with Kimberly, a team of third-year students came back from a national moot court competition on issues of criminal law in which they had won third place. The dean of Presidential sent an e-mail of congratulations out to the entire school, which said in part, "Please join me in congratulating the outstanding members of our [moot court] team which placed third overall at the 2003 [national moot court competition]." The dean went on to name all of the members of the team, as well as the teams they had beat in the competition, and announced that they had received a plaque "to honor their achievement," ending with a URL to a Presidential website featuring pictures of the team and plaque. Kimberly forwarded the e-mail to me and said, "See how other teams get treated when they place in a 'national' competition. By contrast, we made it to the finals of our competition as 1Ls. I think this is shady." Although the LLSA team, a team of first-year students, had placed second in the Hispanic National Bar Association Moot Court Competition, they had received no such congratulations; nor could they find anyone who would put their trophy in the law school trophy case. This sent the message to those involved that clearly the achievements of students of color are not valued the way the achievements of white students are.

All of the above actions reveal the practices that maintain white space and normative assumptions of whiteness within that space. Actions like these are often viewed and discussed as individual incidents and, as such, are diminished. Sometimes these types of incidents are said to be unintentional and therefore not racially significant; sometimes they are dismissed as mere figments of the imagination. For example, Brent, a white man who was a second-year student, said,

> I hear about some students complaining about things that happen to them in the school, and I really think that a lot of it is crying wolf, you know. . . . I would be really shocked to hear that there was any sort of, you know, white supremacist sentiment or, you know, or any kind of feelings that, ah, I don't know that, that, that white students were making comments or sort of being derogatory. I would be really shocked.

Asserting that someone is "crying wolf" gives one the ability to dismiss a perspective and, at the same time, identifies the one with that perspective as an outsider, someone without a real understanding of the institutional context of which they are a part (Goodrich and Mills 2001). Brent rejected the idea that there was any "white supremacist sentiment," and in doing so, he was able to construct racism in a narrow way, as only white supremacist sentiment (probably akin to explicit Jim Crow racism). Thus, he was able to ignore structural patterns of racialized behavior. Focusing on narrow aspects of incidents and ignoring the larger social context are major aspects of learning to think like a lawyer, as discussed above; thus, law students, faculty, and administrators are skilled in their ability to trivialize and argue away these types of incidents. Yet, as Pierce points out when discussing the racially isolating activities of lawyers in law firms and the discourse they engage in to dismiss these activities, "By defining social life as the sum total of conscious and deliberate individual activities, these white lawyers are able to ignore the very systematic practices they themselves deploy, practices that exclude and marginalize African American lawyers" (2003, 98). The discourses that allow lawyers to dismiss the relevance of the practices they deploy, or "racing for innocence," exist also within the white space of elite law schools.

White Racial Discourse: The Discursive Support of White Space

Abstract individualism is a central aspect of post–Jim Crow law and legal structure, as the above example from a popular constitutional law text that speaks of "individual rights" reveals. An individualist framework assists lawyers, lawmakers, and courts in removing legal issues and controversies from their structural context to narrow the focus of arguments and decisions—in other words, thinking like a lawyer. This aspect of the law is connected to a broader societal ideology based upon abstract individualism, and the connection between this ideology and its effect in law combine to reify white structural advantage. Jackman notes, "[Whites] have developed ideologies in which individual rights have become the hallmark cry: such a stance offers a seemingly principled way of denying the moral legitimacy of egalitarian demands made on behalf of groups" (1996, 764). This discourse, which is asserted to be racially neutral, allows whites to disavow racism and racial animus while simultaneously engaging in racial ideologies and practices that support and maintain white privilege (Bobo, Kluegel, and Smith 1997; Bonilla-Silva 2001, 2003; Pierce 2003). Examining the dominant white discourse in law schools illustrates both how this discourse gets utilized with regard to race and how contradictory it is when set up against the everyday racialized practices that characterize these spaces.

Let me begin by noting, again, that the larger framework of color-blind racism in the law school does not mean that racism is exclusively covert. In fact, several white students told me stories of explicit racism in the law school.[7] For example, Pete, a white male first-year student, told me about an incident that occurred during a law school–sponsored diversity training session. With only three minutes left in the diversity session, everyone was eager to leave. The discussion was about modern-day consequences of slavery, and just as the session was wrapping up, another white student, Felix, said, "Well, you know, originally the blacks wanted [to be enslaved]." No one responded to Felix's comment, according to Pete, and he explained, "I think all of us were just like, 'No, we couldn't have actually heard that.' But time has shown [long pause], he's a character." Felix was known for making comments such as the one he made at the diversity training, and when I was conducting my research, I noticed that he always showed up at law school presentations and events. Although I never heard him say anything that explicitly racist, when I observed a debate about a constitutional ban on gay marriage, near the end he spoke directly to a white man who had identified himself as gay, saying, "But being gay is immoral. It is an offense to God, so shouldn't that be a consideration in the debate?" This explicitly homophobic comment, like the comment Pete told me about, occurred near the end of the discussion, and although there were responses, with several people talking at once, all very upset by his comments, there was no time for any structured response or consideration of what he had said. People's explanations for his behavior generally fell in line with what Pete had said—"He's a character"—and everyone disavowed his perspective. Yet, it was tolerated; at least, neither students nor administrators took formal action to stop him from making public comments like these or to publicly address the accurateness or the consequences of the things he said.

In another example, I was talking with Andrew, a white second-year student, and he told me that he had seen an example of racism that he wanted to tell me about. He was on a law school basketball team that played with other law school teams, as well as teams of undergraduate students. When he got to the gym to practice with his team, he told me,

> several of the people, who were all people who I have classes with and know, were talking about the competition from the undergrads. One of the guys said they were all going to beat us because they have all those "niggers" on their team, and then there was this whole discussion, and people were just using the word over and over again.

I asked Andrew whether he commented on their use of the racial epithet, and he said he had just ignored them and made a mental note not to hang around with them or study with them anymore. This conversation with Andrew was revealing of the fact that people in the law school who may not express overt racism while in school may in fact express their true racist feelings in smaller social settings in which they feel more comfortable (see Picca and Feagin 2007). The comments of these law students may not have been expressed in a law school class or in front of people of color, but in smaller social settings with fellow law students, they came out. And not only did this racism come out, but no one challenged it, and several people joined in. Even though Andrew was offended, he did nothing to indicate his disapproval.

Unlike the examples above, the vast majority of the discourse in the law school vehemently rejected these overtly racist comments, but examples like these still reveal a level of tolerance of racism. In both of these instances, people generally felt more comfortable ignoring the racist behavior than confronting it. And in Felix's case, when the racism was in open forums, including classrooms, lectures, and debate sessions, those with authority in the law school did not find it necessary to attempt to curb this behavior or to publicly condemn such sentiment. More importantly, these types of overt racist expression, which people are comfortable identifying as racism and therefore condemn, albeit not publicly, lend support to the notion that the frames of liberal individualism and color-blind racism are *not really* racism. In reality, the racism that is part of the everyday discourse and practice in the law school ranges from this overt behavior to very subtle assertions of individuality that do not take account of the racial social structure. But all of these manifestations of racism work together to create a white institutional space.

When I was conducting my research, color-blind racist discourse became strongest when the subject of discussion was affirmative action. This may have been a result of the legal challenges to the University of Michigan's affirmative action policies taking place at the time. This litigation meant that the topic of affirmative action was dominant in the law school discourse at the time. However, other research on racial attitudes has revealed similar patterns; when policies designed to remedy racial inequality arise as a topic of conversation, white racial attitudes become increasingly individualistic, and color-blind racist frames get used to explain away a lack of support for such remedial policies (see Bobo and Kluegel 1993; Wellman 1993; Bobo, Kluegel, and Smith 1997; Bonilla-Silva 2001, 2003).

The affirmative action discourse in the law schools revealed a shared narrative among many white students and faculty that subtly challenged the right of students of color to be in the space of the law school by invoking liberal individualist and color-blind racist frames. Within this shared narrative, the presence of students of color in the space was assumed to be because of a racial preference (as opposed to "merit"), and this resulted in a consistent scrutiny of these students. This scrutiny came not only from people who said they were opposed to affirmative action but also from students who said that they approved of the use of affirmative action to increase numbers of students of color. For example, Raymond, a second-year white man who said that he was in favor of affirmative action to increase diversity in the law school, noted that most white students critically assessed the ability of students of color because of affirmative action policies. I asked him whether he thought most white students made the assumption that students of color were in the law school because of affirmative action, and he said,

> I think that, that perception is there. If, if a minority student said something really stupid in class, and, like, a, like if a white student said that in class you'd be, like, "Well, it's a wonder they're in law school" or "What the hell is he doing here? He must have cheated on the LSAT," or something. But if a minority student comes up, they might instead be like, "Oh, he's here because he's a minority." And they—no one would say that out loud, but I think that would come into peoples' minds.

Because the law school is a white space, white students are free to answer questions poorly in class without indicting their entire race. Students of color, on the other hand, speak on behalf of all "minorities" when they speak. If a student of color answers a question poorly, an assumption about race and affirmative action exists as an explanation. These assumptions invoke an underlying belief that students of color as a group are not as intelligent as white students—individual white students may be unintelligent, but as a group they belong in the law school. Yet, Raymond also acknowledges that this opinion is unstated, or at least not spoken aloud in class or in the presence of students of color, because although white students hold that opinion, they do not want to voice it for fear of allegations of racism.

In a similar narrative, Judy, a second-year white woman, discussed what a friend told her about the affirmative action policy at Midstate Law School, and in the process, she revealed her contradictory feelings about race, racism, and affirmative action policy:

> See, well, I thought, I was told, and granted the source is from one of the real conservative people in the school, borderline racist, other than that not a bad guy. And I hate to even say that, normally I wouldn't even wonder if he was a good guy or not, but I don't know, he's a weird one. . . . I do need to talk to him about, he just needs to drop this whole racism thing, but anyways [*sic*], so he told me that the mean LSAT scores for women and minority groups are lower than it is for men. People are being admitted with lower scores. He said he read it somewhere. I don't know whether or not it's true, but I don't think he'd make it up. So that could be, I think, I actually I might have actually seen it in one of the blurbs they hand out. About how great we are. They hand out periodically little pamphlets about how great [Midstate] is and how proud we should be to be going there. So, I don't know, I think that's fine actually. I'm fine with that. I'm not super uncomfortable with affirmative action. I guess if they wanted to do more of it, that would be good, but then it's already . . . it would start to become an artificial environment then. It already is not the real world in law school at all, but if we started doing that, I don't know. Because we're already more diverse than [the state Midstate is in], and that's good. But do we need to, like, make a completely artificial environment of, like, so it reflects the general population of America? I don't know if that is such a good goal.

Judy began by noting that her information about the affirmative action policy came from someone who was "borderline racist" but then noted that, aside from the racism, he was a good guy. After saying this, she felt uncomfortable and began racing to make what she said sound less dismissive about the relevance of racism. As Pierce (2003) would suggest, she was "racing for innocence." She realized that her first response, dismissing the racist beliefs of this man as an important component of being a "good guy," might be inappropriate. So, she said that she hated to say that he was a good guy and returned to this "race for innocence" again, later saying that she really needed to tell him to "drop" the "racism thing."

Judy went on to note that she had heard from her friend, and perhaps read in some written materials at Midstate, that the mean Law School Admissions Test (LSAT) scores were lower for "minorities" and "women" than they were for "men." (Note here that both women and men are presumptively white.) When she continued, she revealed that she was not sure where the information came from, but she did not think that her "borderline racist" friend would make this up. The narrative became the reality upon which she made her decisions about the affirmative action policy; thus, the narrative shaped her understanding (see Chase 1995). Based upon this, Judy revealed her belief that minority students are less capable or prepared for law school. Note that

Judy did not reflect upon the fact that white women also benefit from affirmative action policies or that the scores of white women are lower than those of white men. She did not personalize the affirmative action discussion but made it about race alone.

Judy admitted that she viewed minority students as less capable and prepared for law school, but she said that she was not opposed to admitting them despite this fact. Right after that, however, she noted that she actually was opposed to it because it created an artificial environment as the state in which Midstate is located is not particularly diverse. However, Midstate is an elite law school drawing its population from across the nation. She recognized this when she questioned whether the law school population should mirror the U.S. population. Yet, Midstate does not even come close to mirroring the U.S. population, with only a 2 percent African American student body (furthermore, Midstate is not, in fact, more racially diverse than the state in which it is located). Judy's comments reveal assumptions about the abilities of students of color, drawing subtly on notions of cultural inferiority, another component of color-blind racism. There is a tacit assumption in Judy's narrative, as Raymond suggests exists in the broader narrative of the law schools, that minority students are less competent or prepared for law school than white students (or at least white men).

The perception of lack of capability was sometimes stated more explicitly. For example, Steve, a second-year white man, said that he "did not care one way or the other" whether the law school utilized affirmative action policies to increase the numbers of students of color. When I asked him whether white students tended to perceive that students of color were in the law school because of affirmative action, he said,

> STEVE: "I think many people think that. I think I think that."
>
> ME: "Can you say more about that? What makes you think that?"
>
> STEVE: "I think a disproportionate number of minority students underperform. And that's obvious, I think, by the participation in class. I guess that's the only criteria I use for making that assumption, I guess."

Steve was explicit about the fact that he perceived students of color to be less competent than white students based upon his perception of their participation in class. But later in our discussion, I asked him whether he felt that students of color had a different experience in the law school than white students. He replied that he thought the experience was only different for students of color (specifically black students) who did not do well in law school:

> I think, and I don't think it's because they're black, I think it's because they're not as smart. I think they shouldn't have been here in the first place. I think their

experience is that, "I'm not smart enough to do this," and they come to class ill-prepared; they do poorly in class; they're pissed off because they think everybody has it out for them when they're just not prepared and they're just not as smart as everybody else. And that's how life works. Some people aren't as smart. Some people don't belong in law school. I don't care.

Here, Steve clarified that he was not talking about all African American students, just those that he perceived to be "not as smart." Yet, his comments are clearly racialized because, above, he suggested that minority students "underperform," and here the suggestion is that this underperformance is because they are not smart enough to succeed. He also suggested that students of color misperceive their law school experience, thinking that "everybody has it out for them." The outsider status of students of color is confirmed in his comments both by his insinuation that students of color are disproportionately not as competent as white students and by his assertion that they are not capable of accurately perceiving their own experiences (I return to this topic in chapter 5). Implicit in his narrative is an individualist perspective—"some people aren't as smart"—yet, clearly, he is making a group-based claim founded upon an assumption about black intelligence. His comments also echo the rhetoric of a culture of poverty that often provides the basis for color-blind racism, particularly in reference to African Americans (Bonilla-Silva 2003).

In another interview, Larry, a white second-year student, did not specifically state that students of color were not as competent or intelligent as whites; instead, he drew upon a popular stereotype to make his point:

> I just don't understand how [he pauses and looks in his Con Law book for a moment] . . . I don't understand how not letting *me* in [his emphasis]—I think admissions to the university should be race blind. . . . I don't think [long pause] diversity in the racial sense is important enough to justify (a) the effect that I think it has on individuals, and on people as a group who are hurt by it, whether its males, or whites, or white males, and (b) I don't think it justifies, and this is what I guess my major concern when I think about affirmative action is, um, lowering standards, um, and, you know, I, do I watch, you know, do I watch Georgetown's college basketball games? Yes. But do I really wish that the standards would be the same, or even similar in those cases? . . . I don't think you do anyone any favors when you put people in situations that they cannot handle.

Larry drew upon a deeply racialized stereotype that black people get into college, despite their inferior intelligence, to play basketball. He struggled to make his point at the beginning, pausing to look into his constitutional law book for legal authority. Then, to make his essential, abstract, individualistic point, he said he opposed affirmative action because it would require lowering standards, and he evoked the racialized basketball player as an illustration of that point.

Gary, a second-year white man, asserted the same narrative of intellectual inferiority but also expressed another important aspect of the affirmative action narrative that is connected to the mythical, undeserving, unintelligent beneficiary. Gary talked about the idea that middle-class African Americans are unworthy beneficiaries of these policies:

> I'm for equality, I think everybody should play on a level playing field. I came from a small town and was raised by a single mother; she never made more than $20,000 a year. . . . But the son of a black doctor and lawyer could—I mean I'm sure you've looked at the University of Michigan stats [discussed in the legal documents of the affirmative action law suit] where I think it was between a 148 and a 152 LSAT with a 3.25 GPA to a 3.49 GPA—black students were 50 percent [more] likely to get in with those numbers. A 148 LSAT getting into the University of Michigan Law School—really [with a surprised and sarcastic tone]? Because of their color, a son of a black doctor and a black lawyer could'a [sic] gotten into the University of Michigan with a 148 LSAT. I mean, come on! I'm all for—it's all about merit. . . . I'm all for access regardless of age, race, creed, sexual identity, whatever. They should have every opportunity, and I'm all for that. But I don't think that people should be given, you know, *a 148 to 152 LSAT* [his emphasis]! You know, if it comes down to two people tied, and you've got one who's an Olympic athlete and one who's a white guy, or one who's a—you know, okay, I can see it, one is a black person—but other than that, I, I, and the University of Michigan case shows it's not just one little factor like extracurricular activity, but when you talk about these things, it's like, "Oh, well, you're racist."

In Gary's narrative, the hypothetical black son of two professionals will be given privileges he will not despite the fact that he comes from a poor background and succeeded despite struggling with poverty.[8] Aside from the farfetched *Cosby Show* image he invoked in his example, this type of narrative ignores the reality of racism and the racial struggle for African Americans who are middle or upper class (see Jhally and Lewis 1992, Feagin and Sikes 1994). In doing so, the narrative once again reveals both the narrow lens of racism and normatively white perspective that are the basis of abstract individualism. But Gary said that he was all for "equal access" and that the key was "merit." The terms "equal access" and "merit" are also both terms of abstract individualism. Utilizing this language, he could to claim that he was making an argument about fairness while disregarding social structure altogether—in this case by comparing his own class background with a fictional African American person from a professional class.

Another assumption in Gary's narrative was that the LSAT is a definitive measure of "merit." Given that much research has suggested that the LSAT is race-, class-, and gender-biased, this assumption is problematic (see Bowen and Bok 1998). Gary's narrative reveals the process by which normatively white measures of success become the unqualified definition of "merit." Nathaniel, a third-year white man, made a similar argument about law school grades when he discussed the ways in which he perceived students of color to have better access to jobs as a result of affirmative action; in this case, however, he took the argument further by directly challenging the competence of an African American woman classmate. He said,

> I went to OCI [an on-campus interviewing process that brings law firms to the school to do interviews for summer positions] with a 2.9 [GPA], which is a terrible GPA. I had twenty-three interviews and not a single callback. . . . I was talking to a friend of mine here, who's, ah, she's a black woman, ah, I think she's got some Asian or [laughs], I mean, she hits a lot of the minority buttons, um, you know. . . . [S]he went to OCI, and she can't sit down for all her callbacks. . . . And she stopped me and she was like, "My big problem is, I don't know if I want to go to [a large prestigious law firm]." I'm like, no, "Your big problem is that you," you know, I'm, I'm honest with her. I'm like, "I don't think you're smart enough to work at [that law firm]." [Laughs.] I'm like, "Nothing personal—I'm not either." You know, I'm like, you know, "I just want you to think about it, you know. You don't wanna go and get fired, you know, and you don't wanna go and have to work your ass off and have to do stuff that is not, you know."

Nathaniel argued that his friend got callbacks because she was a person of color. And his "problem" with that was not affirmative action but that she was not smart enough to go to a large, prestigious law firm. It is unlikely that Nathaniel actually knew his friend's grades because there is an unspoken rule in the law school about not comparing grades, even among friends. But even if he did, his assertion that law school grades are the most important measure of whether or not one will succeed in a law firm ignores all of the other components of legal education that go into getting a law degree and makes a questionable connection between law firm work and the ability to regurgitate legal principles in a three-to-four-hour law school exam (see Guinier, Fine, and Balin 1997).

In his narrative, Nathaniel asserted that he was looking out for his friend's best interest—her lack of intelligence was not *bad*; he was not intelligent enough to work at the firm either. In this way, he absolved himself, claiming innocence, of any responsibility for telling her that she was not smart enough to work in a prestigious law firm. Yet, this narrative, once again, makes a racialized claim about intelligence. While he was only talking about his friend, he was talking about her in the context of a larger affirmative action policy. The continuing theme that students of color, especially black students, are not as intelligent as their white counterparts flows through the narrative. This sometimes subtle, sometimes explicit assumption of the intellectual inferiority of students of color connects the affirmative action narrative to the rhetoric of the racialized "culture of poverty." There is something about people of color that makes them less intelligent, and since there is never any connection to structures of racial inequality, this must be about people of color in a biological sense, or in a cultural sense, or both (Bonilla-Silva 2003). These story lines parallel the culture-of-poverty arguments that social scientists have used to pathologize black culture.

Nathaniel identified himself as a liberal in our discussion, yet his comments also reveal many of the story lines of color-blind racism. In fact, he was not alone in that regard. Although it was true that conservative students utilized color-blind racist discourse to express opposition to affirmative action, white students who labeled themselves "liberal" or "progressive" also fell into that narrative. For example, in my interview with Rich, the chief editor for a law school journal that focused on issues of structural inequality and the law, he began by making some important points about race that indicated his progressive standpoint. When I asked him about discussions about race in the classroom, he said,

> Well, given that race is such an important topic, and it has, I mean, it's important to all of us. . . . [P]eople of any race are suffered [*sic*] when it isn't addressed. . . . So, in one sense, I think that we are all victimized by racism and the reticence to discuss it. But, ah, I can't, it has to affect people that have historically been the direct victims of it differently.

Here, Rich showed both an understanding that racism is detrimental to people of all races, then a sensitivity to the perspectives of people of color who have been the direct target of racist discourse and action. But when we began discussing affirmative action, Rich began to draw upon the story lines of color-blind racism. He said,

> To the extent that there is an affirmative action policy here, it's not achieving racial diversity. . . . But if, if the goal is to achieve diversity, then . . . I'm not sure how I wanna say it . . . then, then we should be lowering the bar even more, to, um, get more minorities here. But obviously you don't want to do that either because [long pause]. . . . Um, but I think that if you did have a more aggressive affirmative action policy, you would exacerbate the impression among white students that minorities are here because of affirmative action. And I think there is that perception. And, [long pause] who knows why people got admitted. I mean, you can't say that anybody, any particular person got admitted for such and such a reason. . . . I think it's a faulty conclusion to say that so and so is here because of affirmative action. 'Cause, you don't, you don't know. That's not fair. I will say

that, um, working with people on the journal, there have been some peoples' performance and [pause], let me think about what I'm saying here. . . . Not everyone has performed at the same level at this journal. . . . Some people are not as
prepared. And I don't think it's a large enough statistical sample to say whether
it falls along racial lines, um [pause]. . . .

When Rich began talking about affirmative action, he drew upon an unspoken assumption that there is not more racial diversity in the law school because the "bar" is not low enough for "minorities" to get in. He did not consider structural racism; in particular, he did not believe that the LSAT has any
racial bias, or preference for that matter, that impacts how students will perform on the test. Further, he assumed that the standard measures of GPA and
LSAT are definitive measures for how one will perform in law school. Even
Rich, a self-identified progressive and the editor of a journal that publishes
material on racial inequality, fell into the discourse of liberal individualism
and color-blind racism. Another interesting aspect of my interview with
Rich, and of those with many of the white students I talked to, was the hesitation and lack of articulation that surfaced when we began to talk about race
and affirmative action (see Bonilla-Silva 2001). He had been very confident
in his language and his ideas, and he had expressed his perspectives without
hesitation before we began to talk about race, but once the conversation
shifted to race and particularly affirmative action, he became hesitant, taking
long pauses, and making his points with less clarity.

Conclusion: Color-Blind Racism and White Space

Within the law schools, there are patterns of racialized practices, practices that
reinforce a normatively white frame and structure, which get minimized and
justified through color-blind racist discourse. Furthermore, an ideology that
assumes the white space of elite law schools comes out of the racial discourse
about affirmative action in law schools. There are also clear assertions of intellectual inadequacy on the part of people of color. Frequently, underlying
these assertions are notions of inferior culture, which echo the sentiments of
the racialized culture-of-poverty rhetoric. And, most importantly, there is a
silent assumption of a white space, in which white students belong without
question, and white students and faculty get to define the boundaries of the
frame within which all issues, particularly issues of race, are understood. The
racial discourse provides the "organizational map" that Bonilla-Silva (1997)
discusses, which allows students to discursively disavow racism as they maintain and continually reconstruct white space in the law schools. The interaction between practice and discourse becomes a mechanism, combined with

the racialized structure of the law and the law school, for reinforcing an entirely whitewashed space in the law schools.

The white institutional space of the law school creates a setting in which the perspectives of white people become the baseline for understanding the law, as well as racism. As a result, white students (and faculty) are able to assess and evaluate the behavior of outsiders, the "them" that represents students of color. For example, one white first-year student, Larry, said this when we talked:

> So, there's this, um, female black classmate of mine, Jane . . . and then there's this, like, um, really, like, federalist, state's rights white male . . . Jake. And Jake is, like, the person who . . . says, like, the Fourteenth Amendment is a terrible thing, and there's a lot of, like, head shaking and nodding. And then there's a lot, like from Jane, there's a lot of seeping anger, like she's angry about her life . . . and these are more like interpersonal, like, psychological aspects. . . . My response is, what are you so angry about? Please, fucking relax. Like, not everything is a personal affront to you.

Larry did not agree with Jake, the "really federalist, state's rights white male," but he did not characterize him as angry either. He did not suggest that Jake was angry about his life; nor did he attempt to evaluate his interpersonal or psychological traits. But with Jane, an African American woman, he did. He dismissed her perspective, saying she was "angry about her life," minimizing the impact of racism on her life (not to mention the effect of sitting in a class with a white man who asserts that the Fourteenth Amendment to the constitution was a bad thing) and he effectively negates her knowledge about race and the law. Within the white space of the law school, people shook their heads, some in agreement, some in disagreement, at Jake's perspectives. Jane's perspectives, however, were completely negated because she had interpersonal and psychological problems.

In chapter 5, I move on to discuss the experiences of students of color within the white space of the law school. Negotiating and contesting the kinds of racialized practices and discourses discussed in this chapter becomes a central aspect of the law school experience for students of color. The white frame that organizes the deep structures, as well as the everyday practice and discourse of the law school, puts students of color in the precarious position of having to battle to have their own assessment of their own life experiences recognized. This battle for mere recognition distracts attention from the real issue that is not being addressed, the systemic racism in the law school. Systemic racism, the primary feature of white space, never becomes the subject of a serious discussion about race in the law school. But examining the experiences of students of color with white space and color-blind racism reveals a great deal about how white space reproduces itself and what the consequences of that racial reproduction are for students of color trying to negotiate that space.

Notes

1. Bonilla-Silva identifies these frames as a component of what he terms "color-blind racism." Bonilla-Silva's conception of "color-blind racism" is very similar to Lawrence Bobo, James R. Kluegel, and Ryan Smith's conception of "laissez-faire racism" ("Laissez-Faire Racism: The Crystallization of a Kinder, Gentler Antiblack Ideology," in *Racial Attitudes in the 1990s: Continuity and Change*, ed. Steven A. Tuch and Jack K. Martin [Westport, CT: Praeger, 1997]); these authors suggest that racial attitudes in the 1990s are based upon "a sense among members of the dominant racial group of proprietary claim or entitlement to greater resources and status and . . . a perception of threat imposed by subordinate racial group members to those entitlements" ("Laissez-Faire Racism," 22). However, Bonilla-Silva indicates that he chooses the term "color-blind racism" because it better fits the language that is employed by whites themselves (2001, 12). In addition, Bonilla-Silva's framework differs from Bobo, Kluegel, and Smith's in that he has created a more specific delineation of the frames and semantic moves used by whites to construct the contemporary racial ideology. Further, Bonilla-Silva differs from these other scholars methodologically as he asserts that researchers cannot get at the frames and semantic moves involved in the ideology of color-blind racism with surveys alone. Bonilla-Silva and Forman (2000) suggest that frequently white people answer survey questions about race in one way, but then, when asked more detailed questions about their responses, they reveal that they feel very differently than their survey responses would indicate; for example, many white respondents indicated on surveys that they did not have a problem with interracial marriage, but when interviewed in depth, they gave many indications that they had serious problems with interracial marriages. Bonilla-Silva attempts to capture this phenomenon with the construction of these frames. In addition, he argues for a structural conceptualization of racism, critiquing other definitions of racism that tend to conceptualize racism as an irrational attitude (or ideology). David T. Wellman, in *Portraits of White Racism*. 2nd ed. (Cambridge: Cambridge University Press, 1993), has suggested a similar framework for understanding racism, arguing that the focus on attitudes, on the one hand, does not adequately take into account the actions of whites that serve to reproduce their material privilege and, on the other hand, results in class bias in work on racism because lower-class whites tend to be less savvy in answering questionnaires than upper-class whites. The focus of both Bonilla-Silva and Wellman is on white racism. Robert Miles, in *Racism* (London: Routledge, 1989) and *Racism after Race Relations* (London: Routledge, 1993), has seriously criticized the idea that only whites can be racist, suggesting that a sociological definition applying to only one group is not theoretically useful. On the other hand, Joe R. Feagin and Hernan Vera, in *White Racism: The Basics* (New York: Routledge, 1995), and Feagin, in *Racist America: Roots, Current Realities and Future*

Reparations (New York: Routledge, 2000), have suggested that racism is a phenomenon that should only apply to whites because of the structure of white supremacy and race privilege in the United States. These authors, like Bonilla-Silva and Wellman, suggest that given the history of race in the United States, only whites have the structural capacity for racism and the power of structural support. See also Beverly Tatum (*"Why Are All the Black Kids Sitting Together in the Cafeteria?" and Other Conversations about Race* [New York: Basic Books, 1997], who argues that power is a fundamental component for racism. I accept the position of these later scholars in my formation of the concept of racism in elite law schools.

2. See also Edward G. Carmines and W. Richard Merriman Jr., "The Changing American Dilemma: Liberal Values and Racial Policies," in *Prejudice, Politics, and the American Dilemma,* ed. Paul M. Sniderman, Philip E. Tetlock, and Edward G. Carmines, 237–55 (Stanford, CA: Stanford University Press, 1993); Mary Jackman. 1996. "Individualism, Self-Interest, and White Racism," *Social Science Quarterly* 77: 760–767; and Lawrence Bobo, James R. Kluegel, and Ryan Smith, "Laissez-Faire Racism: The Crystallization of a Kinder, Gentler Antiblack Ideology," in *Racial Attitudes in the 1990s: Continuity and Change,* ed. Steven A. Tuch and Jack K. Martin, 15–41 (Westport, CT: Praeger, 1997); for discussions of liberal individualism and white racial attitudes.

3. This opening construction also reifies "blackness" as the racial other, and ignores other racial minorities and the vast amount of legal history pertaining to white racism against minority groups other than African Americans. See Juan F. Perea, "The Black/White Binary Paradigm of Race: The 'Normal Science' of American Racial Thought," *California Law Review* 85 (1997): 1213–58.

4. *Gratz v. Bollinger,* 539 U.S. 244 (2003); *Grutter v. Bollinger,* 539 U.S. 306 (2003).

5. "Bar review" is an event held at many law schools that is designed to be a socializing experience for law students outside the law school. The term "Bar Review" is a play on words because the courses designed to help students prepare for the bar examination are also called "Bar Review."

6. This social event at the law schools brought the law school population in contact with the racial structures of society more broadly. When I say that the bars were white bars, this is a consequence of racial residential and social segregation (Douglas S. Massey and Nancy A. Denton, *American Apartheid: Segregation and the Making of the Underclass* [Cambridge, MA: Harvard University Press, 1993). Obviously, the bars selected for Bar Review were not excluding people of color, but by virtue of societal racial segregation, many bars were exclusively white and were also culturally white (George Lipsitz, *The Possessive Investment in Whiteness* [Philadelphia: Temple University Press, 1998]). Students of color wanted to go to bars that were in African American or Latino neighborhoods or that played R&B music, jazz music, or had salsa dancing, for example. Students at Presidential said that one reason they did not hold Bar Review at bars in black neighborhoods was that they were unable to get cabs back home from those neighborhoods. Several students took me to a bar where they had requested that a Bar Review be held. Not only was the crowd incredibly diverse, but we had no problem getting cabs back to the law school area after we left. Furthermore, the assertion that white people could not get a cab in black neighborhoods has a certain

amount of irony, given that African Americans are frequently unable to get cabs anywhere because of racial discrimination (Joe R. Feagin and Melvin Sikes, *Living with Racism: The Black Middle Class Experience* [Boston: Beacon Press, 1994]).

7. Several students of color also told me about incidents of explicit, overt racism, and I discuss these in chapter 5. In this chapter, I focus on the story lines of white students and their perspectives on the daily experiences of law school life. Then, I move on to discuss the experiences of students of color within the white space of the law school.

8. In fact, Gary may have received some preference for coming from a poor background as this is a diversity component that many law schools, including the University of Michigan Law School, often take into account.

5

"Wow, You Are Really Articulate!"

Law Students of Color Negotiating White Space

IN THE PREVIOUS CHAPTERS, I have discussed the way in which the deep normative structures of the law school, the everyday racialized practices, and
the dominant discourse interact in concert to reproduce and entrench white
institutional space. In this chapter, I take on a question that the literature on
"whiteness" has largely failed to ask (Andersen 2003): What are the consequences of "whiteness" or, more accurately here, white institutional power for
people of color who gain access to white institutional spaces? The failure of
the whiteness literature to include the perspectives of people of color reveals
a gap in this research, resulting in an incomplete framework for examining the
reproduction of white space and white privilege. Within the white institutional space of elite law schools, students of color are systematically faced with
hurdles that their white fellows do not encounter. Herein, I shift the focus to
examine the experiences of law students of color who must negotiate this
white space to succeed in elite law schools.

Law professor Linda Greene's (1997) comments about her experience as an
African American female law professor reveal the challenges for people of
color (particularly women of color) in elite law schools. She says,

> My early experiences were an intellectual version of a nighttime ride through the
> countryside in the deep South: I had a constant awareness of racist and sexist
> danger, both real and imagined. I never knew when a student's seemingly in-
> nocuous response to my questions would slide into a challenge to my right to
> profess. I came to fear this almost daily assault on my psyche. (Greene 1997, 88)

Professor Greene speaks about racist and sexist danger in the law school where she teaches as "both real and imagined." But in the post–civil rights era, because the liberal individualistic interpretations of racism do not account for racist structures, deciphering the "realness" of racism or racist danger becomes extremely problematic. Professor Greene discusses the ways in which her "tokenism," or her status as the only black woman professor at the law school where she taught, led to both subtle and overt challenges to her competence as a law professor in ways that white male law professors would never have experienced. Whether patterns such as the ones Greene experienced were "real" or "imagined," race- and gender-based treatment actually rests upon whose perspective is given priority in assessing her experiences in the space of the law school.

Recall the comments of Professor Morgan, which opened the previous chapter; he both asks for "objectivity" in the recognition of discrimination and invokes racist language to assert that his perception of events is more "objective" than the perceptions of students of color. An important aspect of the construction and maintenance of white institutional space is the normalization of white perspectives *about* the experiences of people of color. As Joe Feagin notes in *Racist America*, "[W]hite privilege . . . includes an entitlement to decipher a black person's reality and experience" (2000, 176). The comments of white students and faculty in the previous chapter illustrated that they felt entitled to decipher the experiences of students of color without considering how these students interpreted their own experiences. But it is important to make explicit that when this process occurred, white people in the law school often invoked the rhetoric of individualism and intent to challenge the perceptions of students of color.

Racism and the Entrenchment of Individualism and Intent

In order for the social narratives of color-blind racism and liberal individualism to be logically stable, not only does one have to ignore legally created structural racial inequality but white perspectives about the experiences of people of color must be normalized. With regard to defining what constitutes racism or discrimination, the process of enforcing a white-centered perspective includes the use of abstract individualistic constructions of racism. As discussed in chapter 3, this focus on individualism then leads to a legal construction of racism and discrimination that requires explicit racial animus—or intent. Thus, the discourses on individualism and intent become entrenched in the law school in a manner that assists white students in disregarding the perspectives of students (and sometimes faculty) of color. The discourse has the force of law, which gives explicit or implicit support to the white frame that allows white students and faculty to minimize racism by forcing students of color to defend their interpretations of their life experiences within the limited boundaries of this frame.

Toward the end of my research at Presidential, the Black Law Students Association (BLSA) held a forum on issues of race. During this forum, an interaction between two students illustrated the relationship between normalizing white perspectives and assumptions about intent. Carl, a second-year African American man, was discussing the ways in which race impacted his life and ability to function in the law school. He noted that when he came to law school, in his first year, he dated a white woman for the first time in his life. He recalled that as the holidays were approaching, the girl's parents were coming to visit her. Carl asked her when she wanted him to meet her parents, and she replied that she could not introduce him to her parents because they would not approve of her dating a black man. In response to Carl's story, Dave, a white man, responded by saying that he thought his story really illustrated racial progress because, although the girl's parents were racist, she was not because she was dating him. He went on to say that she must not have *meant* to hurt his feelings by refusing to introduce him to her parents, and then he asked Carl, "Right?" Carl was visibly upset by Dave's comments. He did not respond to Dave at that moment, but after the panel, as a group of us were discussing the event, he said that he felt that his girlfriend's denial of her relationship with him was clearly racism and that Dave had missed the point entirely, which was about the challenges of being a black man in the law school.

As Carl told his story in the forum, he relied on his interpretation of his experience, which included the assumption that his white girlfriend's actions were obviously a form of racism that highlighted his outsider status in the white space of the law school. In Dave's reconstruction of the story Carl told, however, he relied on an unstated assumption that racism only occurs when there is intent to do racial harm—she must not have meant to hurt Carl's feelings; after all, she was dating him. Thus, her actions could not be construed as racist. In this example, we see that Dave is reframing Carl's narrative, in effect telling Carl that he has misperceived the events of his own life. When individual intent to cause racial harm is used as the measure of racism, the perceptions of people of color can be disregarded.

As I discussed in chapter 3, in the *Washington v. Davis* case, the Supreme Court said that laws or policies that do not explicitly mention race must be shown to have been motivated by an "invidious discriminatory purpose" in order to prove discrimination.[1] As legal scholar Barbara Flagg (1993) has pointed out, the discriminatory intent requirement in *Washington v. Davis* and the body of law that followed in its wake set up a legal framework based upon an ideology of individualism that ignores structural and institutional racism. The result is the reproduction and entrenchment of structural racial inequality and white privilege and power. Moreover, in law schools, the white privilege to decipher the reality of people of color by demanding that they accept a white-centered construction of racism is further strengthened by the legal force of a Supreme Court decision that most first-year law students will read in constitutional law. This effectively provides legal authority for the reproduction of white institutional space. Dave's assumption that intent to harm was required in order for Carl's girlfriend's actions to be racist draws upon that unspoken, legally supported construction of racism. Carl's larger point about the difficulties of being a black man negotiating racism in the law school and the incident with his girlfriend as one manifestation of a broader structural phenomenon was dismissed, and the discussion turned into one about whether there was intent to cause him racial harm. Even in his law school discussions, Carl must establish invidious intent on the part of his girlfriend in order for his perception of events to be viewed as valid.

The requirement of invidious intent in evaluating the experiences of law students of color reaffirms that a normatively white perspective is the starting point for evaluating what is "objective reality." In addition, when Dave publicly forced Carl into this individualistic, white-framed construction of racism in order to minimize Carl's experience with racism, he engaged in both the practice and discourse of color-blind racism. Distilling "real" racial hostility or intent to cause race-related harm from that which is merely a reflection of the assumptions of an underlying white frame enforced through color-blind racism is functionally impossible. This is especially so in the complex negotiations of everyday life in an already challenging situation like law school. However, when we disregard this requirement of intent and place the perspectives and understandings of students of color in the central position, we find that students of color are constantly negotiating and contesting systemic racism in the law schools. Centering the experiences of students of color in elite law schools provides a valuable insight into white space and the process of reproducing racism.

Racism and White Institutional Space

The narratives of students of color at Midstate and Presidential reveal that they must overcome a wide variety of hurdles as a result of color-blind racism. Racism, in both overt and covert forms, becomes a defining component of their law school education. Their capabilities are often challenged, they bump up against white racist notions of cultural pathologies associated with culture-of-poverty theories, and their white fellow students challenge their right even to be present in elite law schools. The experience of Anthony, a second-year African American man, illustrates the color-blind racist frames often employed against people of color.[2] Anthony discussed an experience he had in class:

> ANTHONY: "I usually dress like this, which people might consider to be somewhat urban or something like that. . . . That day I wore a suit to class. I was late for class, and I stepped into class, and, my professor, she's usually a stickler about attendance . . . and being on time, and so, when I stepped in, she stopped. And I thought she was gonna, you know . . . ask me why I was late. But she was so amazed that I was in a suit, and then she says, '[Anthony], you look so—smart.' You know what I'm sayin', and I was just, like, 'Oh yeah, funny, funny, funny' . . . but that comment itself, I think is indicative of, you know, the perception that people have. Well, if I tell people what undergraduate institution I went to [Anthony graduated from Columbia University] . . . they might ask me, 'Are you talking about Columbia Missouri?' you know what I'm saying."
>
> ME: "Has that happened to you?"
>
> ANTHONY: "Yeah . . . it's happened a whole lot. . . . Little instances like that have come up . . . on a consistent basis, but, I mean, that's just a part of our being black. So I just shrug it off."

When Anthony went from wearing clothes that he felt signified black urban culture to wearing a suit, more indicative of white middle-class culture, his professor was so surprised that she stopped lecturing to tell him that he looked "smart" in front of the entire class. Her surprise registered her unstated assumption that middle-class white culture represents the "smart" whereas black urban culture does not. Whether or not she was consciously asserting this assumption, she was clearly powerfully moved by his change in dress because she stopped the class to comment. Similarly, his peers registered surprise when they find out that he graduated from Columbia University, an elite undergraduate institution, and suggested that maybe he meant the University of Missouri in Columbia, a much less prestigious public university from which they would expect to see a black man graduate. According to Anthony, incidents like these happened consistently. These actions subtly draw upon notions of black cultural inferiority, and Anthony recognized that. Thus, part of his law school experience entailed negotiating these color-blind racist insults.

Derrick, also a second-year black man, discussed a similar form of color-blind racism:

> [O]ne thing that drives me absolutely nuts is when I talk, or I do something, and somebody comes up to me and says, "Wow, great point. You are really articulate." What the hell does that mean? Do you know how much money I've put into my

education—damn right—you know what I mean. It's like, that is so condescending. Like, "Fine, great, I got your approval, but if I was a white male, that
shit would never come outta your mouth. There's no way you would ever say I'm
articulate." . . . Everyone says, "Oh, I'm not prejudiced." I see everyone sayin' it.
It's like, well, then why did you say those comments, because obviously if I'm articulate and I speak just the same as everyone else in the class, the bar is set lower
for me.

Later in our interview, Derrick discussed his experience with having white
people attempt to minimize racist incidents like the one above and the ways
in which they challenged his interpretations of his own experiences. He said,

I think racism, or any sort of form of discrimination, is like, basically, excuse my
language, but it's a mind fuck. It really is—because it's not something you can
grasp. It's like this intangible thing, because you don't know when somebody's
doing it, really what's happening. And so people can completely back out of it.
They're like, "Oh, you know"—a lot of it comes through humor. They're like, "I
was just kidding." And then it places the responsibility on the person who was offended, and I think . . . it's really tough.

Derrick's comments reveal the ways that white students can simultaneously
engage in racist practice by noting surprise when he, a black man, makes a
good legal argument, then draw upon color-blind racist discourse to deny that
their comments are racist by saying that they were only joking. As Jennifer
Pierce (2003) might suggest, they are "racing for innocence" by denying that
they hold any racist intent, and in doing so, they recenter the white perspective and dismiss Derrick's interpretation of events that are happening to him.
    Ashalata, a second-year South Asian woman, told a similar story about an
incident that she saw happen to a friend of hers, an African American woman,
in their first-year torts class. In Ashalata's narrative, the racialized conceptions
of African Americans presented by white students signify a connection between race, class, and criminal activity, echoing the color-blind racist notions
of inferior black culture. In the incident she related, the topic of discussion in
her torts class was whether a criminal defendant should have to "dress up" to
come to court. The case that the class was discussing happened to be a criminal case in which the defendant was black, and Ashalata's friend, an African
American woman, was arguing that the clothes defendants wear to court
should not reflect on their truthfulness or innocence. Ashalata told the story:

[My friend] said, "No, I really wish the defendant wouldn't have to get dressed
up, people would just take what they say. . . . I think people should be able to
wear what they want to wear. You should be able to wear jeans, and that's it,
and [the jury] shouldn't make their judgments off of that." And [another stu-

dent in the class] is like, "Well, don't you respect the court?" And she's like, "Yeah, but you should be able to wear whatever you were wearing that day. And I don't understand why people won't believe a black defendant unless they come in a suit." And so another student was like, "Well, what are you gonna put 'em in? The, ah, the mask and give them the shot gun they were using when they committed the crime?" And so [my friend] was like, "That's assuming that they committed the crime—you're doing it again." . . . And [then] other students were, like, getting up and yelling at her from across the room and saying . . . "Are you trying to say that no one's gonna believe a black defendant?" . . . And to my friend, I know a few students were telling her and saying stuff like, oh, you know, "Your assumption of white juries is too much" and things like that. And "not everyone goes by race."

When Ashalata's friend suggested that a criminal defendant should not be judged based upon clothing, a signifier of class and race, which we also saw in Anthony's experience above, a white student in the class suggested that clothing alone could mask the *presumed* guilt of the black defendant. Ashalata's friend challenged this racialized image, which assumed criminal activity on the part of the black defendant, and was attacked by other students in the class, some of them standing up and yelling at her. This experience is especially insidious in that the students in the discussion could rely upon a racialized image of the poor black man as a criminal, yet avoid a challenge that they were engaged in racism by suggesting that the issue was not one of race but of respect for the court. Utilizing the tenets of color-blind racism, white students could turn the tables on Ashalata's friend with hostility, shouting that "not everybody goes by race." Their own color-blind racist assumptions went unchallenged because they managed to reframe the issue and simultaneously suggest that Ashalata's friend was the one who was racially biased.

Maria, a second-year Mexican American woman, also dealt with white racism, but in her case the racism invoked her Mexican heritage and her citizenship. She said,

I'm in my immigration class, and I'm sitting there waiting to talk to the professor when this guy—he's a white guy—and he comes up to me, and he says . . . "Hey, you look very thoughtful—are you afraid that they're gonna deport you?" He said this to me, and I'm sittin' there, and I'm so stunned that I didn't have an answer. And I still hate myself for that, because I just sat there. I was like, "Oh my God . . . you're asking me that just because I look thoughtful, that I'm afraid of being deported." And I didn't do anything. And for God's sake, I'm a second-year law student, and I'm gonna be a lawyer, and I have all this huge resume, and somebody asks me if I'm gonna get deported. . . . This guy doesn't know me. I have never ever directed anything towards him. I didn't even know his name. . . . So, I think, why do I have to put up with this?

The comments of the student in Maria's class reveal a racist assumption that "Americanness" is equated with "whiteness" (see Morrison 1992). Because Maria is Mexican American, her Americanness and her citizenship rights became the object of ridicule, echoing a broader racialized discourse about Mexican immigration. The comment seems to be overtly racist, yet it was made as though it were a joke—as Derrick noted, this is one way in which whites can engage in racism, yet deny responsibility for it. Maria did not say anything, yet had she commented, her experience would likely have resembled the experiences of others. The white student would have denied intentional racial animus; then the problem would have been regarded as Maria's misperception of events. But Maria's shock and pain prevented her from saying anything, and her inability to respond became a secondary source of stress for her, and coping with this pain and stress thus became a central component of Maria's law school education.

Yoshimi, a second-year Asian American woman, discussed comments made by a professor that echo those of the student who insulted Maria, revealing the citizenship privilege associated with whiteness. In Yoshimi's case, however, the insult came not from a fellow student but from a professor. Her constitutional law class was discussing the case of *Korematsu v. United States*.[3] The year before the *Korematsu* case, the Supreme Court, in *Hirabayashi v. United States*, had upheld the constitutionality of an order to remove all persons of Japanese ancestry living on the West Coast and place them in internment camps (euphemistically called "relocation centers").[4] Mr. Korematsu, a U.S. citizen, had been arrested, tried, and convicted of failing to leave his home in California in conjunction with that order, and in the Supreme Court case, Korematsu was challenging the constitutionality of that conviction. The court upheld the conviction, based upon the ruling in *Hirabayashi* that the order to intern people of Japanese ancestry was constitutional. Yoshimi explained what happened when this case was discussed in her constitutional law class:

> [W]ell, we were discussing *Korematsu*, and [the professor], it was the very end of class . . . he's like, "and don't forget, this guy got screwed, and his name was Fred for crying out loud." As if . . . his first name Fred, as opposed to, like, a Japanese first name, like it made a difference to the case, you know. And it's just like, I don't think anyone noticed it except for me. Only because I was born here, you know, and I have a Japanese-sounding name . . . that comment just struck me because it was the type of comment that people hear, and they don't think anything of it . . . [I]t's one of those absorbing comments, you know. It's like, "Oh yeah, okay . . . like he was so American that his name was Fred," and that's why it's wrong . . . whereas you know, like a Japanese man . . . if his name was, you know, Ishiro, maybe that's not American enough [for him to have citizenship rights].

Through an off-the-cuff comment by a professor wrapping up a class, Yoshimi experienced a challenge to her own Americanness. Because her name is "Japanese sounding" and not a typically white Anglo-American name, there was a suggestion that this might justify differential treatment by the U.S. government with regard to citizenship rights. As Yoshimi pointed out, it was an "absorbing comment," one which people accept as true and relevant without ever having to examine the underlying racist assumption. These types of "absorbing comments" reassert the normality of the white frame and systemic racism, thereby reproducing white space in a seemingly innocuous manner. Furthermore, in this instance, the comment was made by a professor, a person in a position of power with regard to students in the law school.

The above incidents all occurred within the space of the law school and, in particular, in classroom settings. However, as I discussed in the previous chapter, both law schools where I conducted my research had a social tradition, called "Bar Review," of getting students together at local bars. Many students of color, including Tiffany, a first-year African American, told me that Bar Review was nearly always located at white bars, and when students of color attempted to suggest other locations, they were either ignored or turned down. The experience for students of color as a result of the selection of culturally white bars in which to hold the main law school social event was one of isolation. As Tiffany told me,

TIFFANY: "It's just awkward for us [going to Bar Review]."

ME: "What's awkward about it?"

TIFFANY: "Um, every time, it, it seems like, well, the two times I went, it seemed like there was the group of black people, and there was like five or six of us, and we were all congregated in the corner, and then there was, like, everybody else."

ME: "Everybody else in the bar?"

TIFFANY: "Yeah . . . and I don't think it was that we couldn't talk to each other but it was more like—we don't go to the bar and drink in excess all the time. So, it just, it was a different scene for us. It wasn't like something that we would do normally, and I think a lot of us were doing it forced—we were forced to go because we didn't want people to think we were antisocial or, you know, not trying to participate . . . ."

The white bar scene was not comfortable to Tiffany, and many other students expressed this sentiment. So, students of color stopped going to these social gatherings, which often serve to create connections with fellow students who will later become part of important professional networks. This practice revealed the social and cultural aspects of color-blind racism dominant in the law schools (see Lipsitz 1998). White law students assumed that white cultural social spaces would be acceptable to everyone, even in social situations that took place outside of the law school. This was a widely noted issue at both schools, and despite quite vocal criticisms from students of color, Bar Review continued to be held at white bars, and the requests of students of color were continually ignored.

Hypervisible, Yet Still Invisible

In their research examining race at a major university in the United States, Feagin, Hernan Vera, and Nikitah Imani (1997) point out that the perspectives and issues of African American students in universities are often ignored in a manner that denies these students full human recognition and effectively renders them invisible. As Elizabeth Higginbotham (2001) suggests, however, in her discussion of black women who entered white graduate and professional programs in the era of integration, these women were hypervisible because they were so underrepresented in these programs. As a result, every comment or action was viewed as much more than an individual comment or action. The experiences of students of color reveal that a major hurdle they encounter in negotiating the white space of the law school is living within a contradictory location of simultaneous invisibility and hypervisibility. In fact, negotiating this contradictory location becomes a major source of struggle for many students of color.

One mechanism of color-blind racism utilized to render people of color simultaneously invisible and hypervisible in the law schools was the dismissal of the perspectives of people of color based upon the assertion that they were either too emotional about issues of race or "biased." In one instance, a well-known critical race scholar, an Asian American woman, Professor Kim, was invited to one of the law schools to speak about critical race theory in the wake of the Supreme Court decisions in the Michigan affirmative action cases. In a meeting of the law school student council the day after the event, several students of color suggested that the law school needed to get someone like Professor Kim, who could teach critical race theory. Kevin, a third-year white man, said, "Not her. I'd hate to take a class with her. She's the type who would fail anyone who didn't agree with her."

The assumption in this statement, that Professor Kim was so biased that she could not be professional in her teaching, effectively rendered Professor Kim invisible: first, because Kevin was suggesting that Professor Kim's perspective on race was not legitimate because it was not "objective" in the sense that she would not evaluate students without regard to her opinions, and, second, because he literally suggested that she should be excluded from the law school, that she should not be the one to teach in that law school. But Professor Kim also became hypervisible as a woman of color who was expressing a particular perspective on legal issues. When law professors give presentations, as opposed to teaching classes, they nearly always present a perspective that represents their own personal opinions. Very often, they do so with intense emotion and/or with vigorous argumentation. This form of presentation and argumentation is quite often highly valued and considered an important aspect of being a good attorney, the zealous advocate. Yet, when a woman of color presented a legal issue with zeal, it was not regarded as professional prowess. To the contrary, it was considered biased to such an extent that there was an assertion that she could not give a fair grade to a student who did not agree with her views.[5] I never heard such an assertion made about a white male professor, even those who were very outspoken and had highly conservative opinions. Professor Kim's race (and likely her gender as well) rendered her simultaneously invisible and hypervisible.

Many students of color worry that they will be perceived and treated as Professor Kim was, particularly if they talk about issues of race. It often influenced their willingness to discuss race in the law school. For example, when I asked Yoshimi, whether she would feel comfortable bringing up race in the classroom, she said that she would not. I asked,

> ME: "If you were in, you know, one of your regular classes . . . and you felt like, um, there was an issue about race that needed to be brought up, how comfortable would you feel about bringing it up?"
>
> YOSHIMI: "Not very. Actually, not at all."
>
> ME: "How come?"
>
> YOSHIMI: "One, I don't want to look like the minority bitch by complaining. And two, I, I don't want to, I don't want to be the only one defending my view, if that's the case. You know, and I think that, I mean this is just my view, but I don't know that other, other nonminority people would feel comfortable speaking up for me."

Yoshimi feared being viewed as a "minority bitch" if she brought up issues of race in the classroom, and this prevented her from voicing her opinions in the law school. On an individual level, she became invisible because she did not contribute her thoughts or perspectives to classroom discussions. On a broader level, however, this represents widespread invisibility because, despite the fact that there are some students of color present in the classroom, many hesitate to contribute to the discussion, which facilitates a white-normative discussion (I discuss this phenomenon more in the following chapter). Of course, this is also a result of hypervisibility because their comments about race and racism are, ironically, labeled as biased or suggestive of "bitchiness" because they are not white. One can imagine a counternarrative suggesting that, in fact, white people may be biased when it comes to discussing race because they are the beneficiaries of white privilege; however, I never heard this counternarrative presented in the law school.

When students of color resisted being silenced by the white frame by consciously speaking up in class, they became acutely aware of their hypervisibility. For example, Kimberly, a second-year Latina, noted the ways in which students of color became the subject of extra scrutiny in the law school:

> I just feel like, for some reason, when a minority student raises their hand in class, I just feel like more ears are starting to go, "Oh, well, what are they gonna say."

Later in the interview, she reiterated her point:

> [L]ike I said, if you sit in on classes . . . you will notice that as soon as a minority raises their hand, everybody turns around. They're just lookin' a little harder, like "they're not gonna get [the right answer]," or if they say something really sharp, it's like they always have this troubled look on their face like, "Wow, that was pretty good," you know what I mean? Whereas they're not checking for it the same way with white students.

In fact, I did notice on more than one occasion that when students of color spoke, white students often perked up and turned in their chairs to watch them (this happened more frequently when the topic being discussed was explicitly about race). This hypervisibility put an extreme amount of pressure on students of color as a group. Ian, a third-year man of biracial Korean and white heritage, also talked about the pressure of hypervisibility on his perception of himself and other Asian students. He said,

> [Gary Chen] bothered me a lot [because he was often late for class]. . . . I don't like it when another Asian student does something like passes or looks . . . not prepared, is continually not prepared, because I think it looks bad for everybody who also is Asian.

Students "pass" when a professor calls on them and they are not prepared or don't want to answer, so here Ian was talking about his frustration when other Asian American students were not able or willing to answer questions in class. Ian's comments reveal the pressure that students of color face, even when it is other students of color who are speaking. Students of color are aware that their individual actions may be attributed to all other members of their race, or even all other students of color. Ian was not alone in his fear that incorrect comments, lateness, or failure to prepare on the part of one student of color would reflect poorly on all students of color. For example, Devon also said, "We used to get mad when a minority kid said something really stupid. We'd be like, 'Oh my God, you're hurting us all [laughs].'"

In one final example, Jen, a third-year biracial woman who described herself as half Korean and half black, explained the simultaneous hypervisibility and invisibility of students of color. The incident, ironically, occurred at a diversity training in which a white woman was struggling to get people to participate in discussing white privilege. Jen said that the woman was not making people feel comfortable enough to talk, and so, when she asked the group to identify which race is the privileged race, no one responded. Jen described what happened next:

> She actually finally said, "Well, fine, fine, fine, let's just do this. Raise your hand if you're white." We were like, "Oh my God, you're kidding. Oh my God, you're *kidding.*" . . . We didn't know what to do, and she's like, well, "I think it's very important to have this discussion," and she's talking about the diversity statement of the law school, [and she says] "I think it's very important because, you know, I'm looking around this room, and you know, even though we say there's diversity in our society, there are only two black students in here. What do you say to that?" And I raised my hand, and I said, "You know what I say, I say there are four people sitting in the front row." Nicole, who's obviously black, Gwen, she's obviously black, me and John who's mixed (his mother is white, his father black). "We're all sitting in the front row in front of you. Why did you say there were only two black people in here. Bias—what? Perception? You just looked at a whole row full of brown people and said that there are only two black people in this room. Am I not black? Which two of us don't count—I can guess, but which two of us don't count." . . . We were just like, this is bull----.

Here, a white woman leading a diversity training for new students racially designated two of these four students in the front row as black, despite the fact that the other two students self-identified as black. In pointing out the "black" students, she increased the hypervisibility of all the students of color for her own ends, without considering whether these students wanted to be singled out. In addition, she presumed that she was entitled, and able, to define Jen and her friends racially. In doing so, she ignored and dismissed not only their self-perception but essentially their presence.

Students of color are invisible because their perspectives, histories, and life experiences are not represented or respected in the law school curriculum or discourse. But they are simultaneously hypervisible in their presence in the classroom because there are so few students of color in each classroom and because the relevance of race in their life experience is either diminished or essentialized. The words and actions of individual students of color become representative of all students of color. Through this process, their full humanity, as well as their unique individuality, is not recognized (Feagin, Vera, and Imani 1997). As such, the process tends to reproduce itself. As Derrick says, "The more you talk, the less people listen. . . . [I]f you're the one spear-heading it a couple times, people are just like, 'Oh, he's off on a tangent.' There's been times where sometimes I don't talk for specifically that reason." In other words, it's not *what* Derrick says, but *whatever* he says that gets dismissed. This contradictory space is another example of racism with which students of color must contend in order to negotiate the white space of the law school.

The Collective Experience of Racism

When law students of color discuss racism in the law school, they note that these types of incidents happen to them on a regular basis. In other words, the racism in the law schools is systematic. Not only do these incidents impact the individuals who experience them, but they become the basis for a shared narrative among law students of color (see Chase 1995, Feagin 2006). As students discuss the racism they face with one another, a broader narrative about these experiences comes to represent the collective experiences of students of color (Feagin and Sikes 1994). In my conversations with Derrick, for example, he discussed not only his own experiences (see above) but also several experiences that fellow law students had told him about. He described a particularly personal story shared with him by a close friend that impacted his law school experience. At the end of his first semester of law school, his good friend, who was an African American woman (and a first-year student at the time), went out to dinner with a group of students to celebrate finishing their first round of final exams. She was the only person of color at the dinner, and Derrick explained what happened to her, noting that she called him as soon as she got home from the dinner:

> For some reason . . . I don't know what they were doing—or maybe they felt really comfortable with her, they started talking about the different ways you can call blacks "niggers" without getting caught . . . and one woman was from Africa, and she's like, "Oh, you can call them kaffirs," and like the whole conversation was all about how you can talk to blacks without being caught and say the word "nigger" by using different terms from around the world. . . . These are all my classmates. . . . I know all the students who were at the table, so it's very strange to, like, work with them in these groups in classes where, like, I just want to sit there and say, "You think I'm a nigger, let's stop talking." I don't want to be like, "Oh, what did you think about my brief?" [He laughs.][6]

Although this example seems much less like color-blind racism and more like the explicit racism of the Jim Crow South, in fact, Derrick again suggests that these types of actions can be dismissed as merely a joke and not representative of these students' true feelings about black people. They had no racial animus, no intent to cause racial harm; it was merely a hypothetical conversation. But Derrick and his friend felt the incident to be harmful and something that continued to prevent their ability to work on law school activities with these people. Notably, this incident had an impact on both Derrick and his friend, although Derrick was not at the dinner. The racism law students of color experience in the law school becomes part of a shared narrative, a collective consciousness that causes individual students to view their own experiences as part of a larger structural problem (Feagin 2006). This shared narrative can be healing because it often serves as a way for students of color to avoid internalizing these incidents as individual experiences and provides them with experiential knowledge with which to challenge the white frame of individualism and intent. However, it also adds to the pain of racism experienced by these students because they become aware of how frequent and common racism is in the law school when they learn of the stories of their peers.

While conducting my research at both law schools, I frequently heard the same stories about incidents of racism from many different students. One particular example at one of the schools stood out because I heard the story from so many different students, students of color and white students, and several faculty members and administrators also discussed the event with me. The story remained consistent: one of the professors at the law school, a senior white man, was walking into the law school building late at night, and two students of color were attempting to walk in behind him. The law school buildings were locked at night, and only faculty and students had the key card to open the building doors. Before the students could get in, the professor shut the door on them so it would lock. The students were very upset, especially because one of the students was actually in the professor's class at the time. This story was widely shared among students of color as a cautionary tale, and some students noted that they had shared the story with others to make students aware of this professor's racial biases and to prepare them in case they had a similar experience with him so that it would be less personally painful. All of the students of color I spoke with saw this incident as a clear example of racism in the law school.

During my conversations with several white students, two white faculty members, and one administrator who was a woman of color, this story also came up when I asked them whether they had heard about or experienced incidents of racism in the law school. Yet, their analysis of the incident was different and was punctuated by discomfort, as opposed to the anger that had been expressed by students of color. While all of these people told the story in response to a question about racism, they quickly qualified the story. They all suggested, in one way or another, that they did not think it was an act of racism but that the professor was merely following the policy of the law school, which was not to let in anyone whom you did not know. They also all pointed out that this particular professor was not very socially connected and, so, sometimes did things that were not socially conscious.

While students of color clearly shared this story as a cautionary tale of racism, and all of them viewed the shared narrative as part of their own law school experience, white students, as well as faculty and administrators with the power to respond to the incident, uncomfortably dismissed the relevance of the incident. White students and faculty and one administrator of color seemed to be rushing to qualify the event as not racist, clearly uncomfortable with the idea of racism in the law school or of attributing racist intent to this professor. And the notion that racism must be equated with conscious invidious intent was the underlying assumption of their story lines as they explained away the professor's actions. As a result, the interpretation of students of color, that his act was an example of racism, did not become the dominant interpretation. (Even though, as some students of color pointed out, one of the students the professor shut out was in his class and was one of the few students of color in the class, which should have given him the opportunity to "know" her, thus allow her entry.) In the case of this incident, the dismissal of the perspective of students of color came from faculty and administrators, those in a position to take action, but because the dominant interpretation rejected the perspectives of students of color, no action of any kind was taken.

In another shared narrative about racism, told to me by many students and a few faculty members at one of the law schools, several confounding incidents occurred in a legislation class that students of color perceived as evidence of systemic racism. The professor of the class, Professor Skally, was a white woman, and many students who shared the story with me noted that she seemed very insecure when she was teaching. Near the beginning of the semester, in the second or third week of class, Professor Skally called on a student, Brett, to answer a question. Brett said, "Pass," indicating that he did not want to answer her. She responded that he needn't have done the readings to answer the question and should be able to answer if he was listening to the class discussion. Brett responded, "Well, I haven't been paying attention. I've been ignoring you." He went on to say that he hated the class, thought that it should not be a required course, and did not appreciate that Professor Skally required attendance. Professor Skally became very flustered and attempted to engage in a debate with Brett about the relevance of the legislation course.

After several minutes of uncomfortable debate with Brett, she moved on to another case that was assigned that day. Students who were in the class reported that she seemed very rattled and unable to concentrate after her debate with Brett. In the case that followed, the issue for discussion was about racial and gender bias in the LSAT, and she asked whether the tests should be differentially scored so that points were added for minorities and for women. Alex, a white man, responded by saying, "I think it should be. The LSAT is really hard. . . . [B]lack people can't pass the LSAT. . . . I even had trouble with the LSAT." Professor Skally responded, "Okay, okay," and students said it appeared she had not even been paying attention to what Alex said. But after Professor Skally failed to respond to Alex's comments, Karna, an African American woman, got up and walked out of the class. And she never went back to the class after that. That incident became the basis of much conversation about Professor Skally's racial bias, as well as her incompetence as a teacher. After this incident, the classroom climate reportedly became more uncomfortable than it had already been.

This was not, however, the final incident in the class. Several weeks after that class, Professor Skally was discussing sexual harassment, and she asked the class whether, if a situation arose where only one man was harassing only one woman, this action would rise to the level of a sexual-harassment action under Title VII of the 1964 Civil Rights Act. A student in the class was arguing that it did not because it was only between the two of them, and thus was not a workplace-climate issue. Naheed, a first-year South Asian woman, shook her head, illustrating that she disagreed with the man, so Professor Skally called on her and asked her to respond. Naheed explained to me what happened next:

> I said, "I think that's ridiculous, and maybe it doesn't sound so ridiculous because it's gender, but I think that when people talk about race, they understand it much more, for whatever reason. Even though neither form is acceptable, um, so if there were a bunch of white guys in an office, or if there were a lot of white men and a lot of black men, um, and one white guy was constantly going up to one of the black guys, just one of them, not the rest of them, and saying, 'Hey nigger, what's up?' um, no one would question that it's because of race, even though he's not doing it to all the rest of the people. So why for gender would you question it?"

Professor Skally then cut Naheed off, and she responded angrily, "I'd prefer if you did not use that kind of language in my classroom. I can't have that language in my classroom." Naheed was shocked and upset by this reaction, so she said that she went home for the rest of the day.

That afternoon Professor Skally phoned Naheed at her home to tell her that she wanted Naheed to know that because of the "three incidents" in the class, she was planning to send out an e-mail to the entire class about how she expected the class members to conduct themselves. Naheed asked her what three incidents she was referring to, and Professor Skally told her she meant the incidents with Brett and Alex and Naheed's comments in class that day. Naheed said, "Well, I hope you're not lumping my comment together with the other two. . . . [M]y comment was made in a certain context [to make a point]." And she told me that Professor Skally responded, "There's just no excuse for that in the classroom. . . . [T]here is just no excuse. That's a horrible word. You just can't just go using that word. . . . [Y]ou don't know how bad that word is." Naheed was furious, and when she told me about it, she said,

> I'm like, excuse me? What do you know about what I know, first of all, and how dare you say that. . . . It just it pissed me off on so many levels. . . . And maybe I feel that I'm okay to use [that term] because it's been directed at me. . . . Um, and, but how are we gonna talk about racism in there. I mean if we have a case where someone is called a nigger, are we just not gonna discuss that case because it might upset someone? The other thing is, um, she immediately addressed my comment in the classroom, um, you know, "I would prefer that you did not use that language in my classroom," kind of thing, um, and I'm a woman of color. Whereas the other two men who did these incidents were white men, and she didn't address what they did specifically in the classroom, which she really should have.

After talking with Naheed, Professor Skally sent an e-mail to the entire class apologizing for the "three incidents." In response, Alex, who had made the comments about black people being unable to pass the LSAT, complained to Professor Skally that he had apologized after making the comments, and he resented her including his comments in the e-mail. In response, Professor Skally sent out a second e-mail retracting her earlier e-mail, noting that one of the incidents (Alex's comments) was accidental.

The reaction from students of color to this incident, and the narrative that formed as a result of it, focused on the fact that Professor Skally did not properly handle race-related matters (or conflict) that came up in her classroom. Many students of color were angry that she did not respond critically to Alex's comments, even after Karna walked out of class. They were further upset by the fact that she then let him off the hook by retracting her inclusion of Alex's comment as one of the classroom "incidents," saying it was "accidental." This sharply contrasted with the fact that she had singled out Naheed, a woman of color, in class, and she never swayed from her position that Naheed's comments were offensive, despite Naheed's continual assertion that she did not intend to offend anyone. Naheed was very dark in complexion and had very dark black hair and eyes, and she had herself been the victim of racial epithets, including being called a nigger (see Herring 2002 for a discussion of "colorism" and race). Under these circumstances, many students of color were offended that a white woman would lecture a woman of color and suggest that she did not understand how horrible such a racial epithet was. Many students of color also told me that they had recommended that fellow students not take a class from Professor Skally. Naheed said that after the incidents, she was very hesitant to go back to Professor Skally's class and went only rarely. As a consequence of Professor Skally's mismanagement of the situations that arose in her classroom, two of the students of color in her classroom were never again comfortable in her class (Karna actually said she never returned to class), and other students of color in the law school were cautious about taking classes taught by her.

When white students and several faculty discussed these events with me, they described them with the same apprehension with which white students and faculty had discussed the professor's closing the law school door on two students of color. Many made the point of saying things like, "I don't think [Professor Skally] is a racist" and "I think she is just insecure and does not handle issues of race well." Again, the underlying assumption individualizes racism and disregards the complex analysis students of color presented when explaining the events. More importantly, despite the widespread conversation about the events that took place in Professor Skally's class, there was no action taken at the administrative level to respond to the events or to acknowledge the widespread anger among students of color.

Institutional (Non)Response to Racial Indignities

At the end of the fall semester of his third year of law school, Joseph Jackson, an African American, went in to take his criminal procedure final exam. He had been the only African American person in the class of over eighty-five people, and there were many times that he had been frustrated by discussions (or lack of discussion) about issues of race and criminal procedure in the class. Like many African American men, however, he had chosen to ignore these issues most of the time because he was just interested in finishing his final year of law school. He entered the exam room, sat down, and began to read the hypothetical situation that was the basis for the exam. In the first paragraph, he read that the criminal defendant in the hypothetical case, a major drug dealer, was named Joseph Jackson. He was not the only one who noticed that the name of the drug dealer in the exam was also *his* name, *the only black man in the class,* but he alone was personally impacted. He sat embarrassed for a moment, then attempted to forget about the name and focus on the exam.

When Joseph finished the exam, as he was leaving several students who had been in the class commented apologetically to him about the name. Over the winter break, he talked with several friends and fellow members of the BLSA, and many of them pointed out that the situation must have had an impact upon his ability to do his best on the exam. He decided that he would talk with the dean of students. As it turned out, several other students had talked with the dean of students about it before Joseph, and many students suggested that the incident was distracting. The dean of students had spoken with Professor Espin, who had written the exam, and he said that he had not realized that the name of the hypothetical drug dealer was also the name of the one black man in the class. He did not know many of the students' names and had not even realized that there was a Joseph Jackson in the classroom. When Joseph went to talk with the dean of students, he told her that he felt that it had impacted his ability to do his best on the exam, and she replied that he should wait to see how he did on the exam. She noted that it would not be fair to *other students* to allow him to retake the exam. After that, the only response from the administration came several weeks into spring semester when the dean sent out an e-mail noting that there had been "unfortunate incidents" that some students found offensive. He wanted the student body to know that the law school was committed to diversity and that he wanted students and faculty to work to create a friendly and cooperative law school community.

Like many of the incidents discussed in the previous section, this incident was part of a shared law school narrative at the school where it took place. The incident was discussed with me in many interviews and informal conversations. (I talked with Joseph about it, though I did not interview him because this incident had taken place the year before I began my research, and he had graduated.) A major aspect of this law school narrative, like the ones above, was criticism about the response of the law school administration. Most of the students of color (though not all) who talked about the incident believed that Professor Espin had not realized that the name he'd chosen for the drug dealer in the hypothetical case was the name of a black man in his class. Despite Professor Espin's lack of intention, however, these students felt that the response did not do enough to remedy the impact of his mistake. The comments of many students echoed the sentiments of Devon, a South Asian second-year student:

DEVON: "Most minority students were upset not so much about the fact that he used the name, but the way the school went about fixing things. They sent a general e-mail out to all the students saying, 'Sorry, didn't mean to do that.' They didn't talk to the student personally, the school didn't say, 'Hey, you can retake the exam to the student,' and we all thought . . . well, I think they should have done something a little bit different because, in my opinion, it would have been really distracting and very upsetting to see such a thing like that. . . . [T]he school tried to pretend like, 'Oh, it was a mistake,' which it could have been, okay, no big deal. . . . It could have been an innocent mistake. I don't think that was the issue. . . . [It was the way the professor handled it], and so, I know a lot of minority students now won't take [classes with that professor]."

ME: "That's really interesting. Do you think that the faculty or administration know that?"

DEVON: "I don't think they care. You know, I think that in a lot of instances, it seems like the school would rather just sweep things under and pretend like nothing happened, not take student input into it."

The perception of students that the administration had failed to address this situation contributed to a general feeling that the administration did not really care about remedying racist practices and discourses in the law school. More broadly, students of color felt that the administration was unconcerned about issues of racial inequality and the unique challenges faced by students of color in the law school. The administration failed to see this incident as one of racism because Professor Espin did not intend to harm Joseph, but as Devon made clear, his intention was not relevant to the outcomes that resulted from his actions, and that was what students of color wanted the administration to address.

In another incident, the law school administration failed to respond to racism experienced by a law student in a law firm that recruited heavily from the law school. Tyson, an African American third-year student, had had a very bad experience during his summer job with this law firm during the summer of his first year. He got a summer job at the reputable firm through the law school recruitment program ("On-Campus Interviews," or OCI, a program through which law firms come to the law schools to recruit and interview law students for summer positions). Toward the end of his summer with the law firm, Tyson commented to his attorney mentor (law student interns are generally paired up with attorneys at the firm who act as their mentors during the summer employment) that he had noticed that he had not been taken out to lunch much. Another student intern from his law school was a white man, and Tyson had learned that this intern had been asked to lunch several times each week throughout the summer.[7] After this conversation, one of the partners at the firm, an older white man, asked Tyson, along with another intern who was a white woman, to lunch.

During the lunch, the partner turned to Tyson and said, "The problem with the black community is that all the urban blacks smoke crack, and there's such a high rate of illegitimate children, and the moms and dads don't take care of them, so they have to be raised by their grandparents." Tyson was shocked by the comment because they had not been talking about race, the black community, or the family. So, he responded by simply saying, "That's not true." The partner responded, "Oh yes it is. I know because my wife works in an urban school teaching the fifth grade." Tyson responded, "Even if every kid in her class is illegitimate and smokes crack, that still does not mean all urban black people smoke crack." The partner then said that he knew because he grew up in a black community, so Tyson asked him where he grew up. The partner responded, "Well, it was a white street in the black neighborhood." The partner then turned and began a new conversation with the other intern.

The next day when Tyson was at work, his mentor came into his office. Evidently, word had gotten out about what had happened at the lunch (Tyson assumed that the other intern had told people about the conversation). Tyson explained what happened next:

> He sits down and tells me that the partner is not representative of the firm and that he understands that he said some offensive things, but what he really wants to talk to me about is what he had said about the firm's history of corporate law. [The partner had also made comments about this during the lunch.] So, he proceeds to give me a history of the firm's corporate law practice. So, I asked, "Well, what about the racist things he said to me?" So, he goes, "Well, that was wrong, but the real issue is about the firm and the work we do." Then he says to me, "You should really take a look at whether you think this firm is a good fit for you," and he tells me I'm very articulate, and I may want to go somewhere where I can do litigation work.

A group of students were with us when Tyson told me the story, and they laughed and joked that between the firm partner and Tyson's mentor, the lawyers had managed to hit the whole spectrum of racial insults.

When Tyson got back to the law school in the fall, he went to talk to people in the career services office to tell them about his experience at the firm. Because the firm did a lot of recruiting from the law school, he felt that people should be aware of the racism he had faced there. When he talked to people in the career services office, they told him that there was a complaint process. He tried to pursue the process, but after several people were unable to explain the process to him, he finally talked with a senior person in the career services office, who told him that the office did not support that complaint process anymore. He asked that person what he should do, and the person said, "I don't know." He then talked with several other administrators, including two associate deans, and while all of them condemned the comments of the partner, none was willing to take any action to reprimand the law firm or to make other students in the law school aware of what had happened at the firm. All of the students who were present when Tyson told me the story agreed that Tyson's experience was not important enough for the law school to risk jeopardizing its relationship with the law firm. It seemed that the law school wanted to minimize the incident, to view it as the unfortunate act of a misinformed individual and not a systemic problem that should be addressed formally in any manner.

These incidents of racism faced by Tyson and Joseph illustrate the fact that racism takes place not only in the everyday interactions between students, or even between students and faculty, but at the institutional level as well. When I conducted my research, I learned of at least six incidents like these that students of color brought to the administration to request action. In none of these cases did the administration act at the institutional level (with the exception of the school-wide e-mail sent out in response to Joseph's experience, and this response was not perceived as institutional *action* by students of color). Each incident was treated as an individual occurrence or as a series of unrelated individual occurrences and was minimized and/or explained away as not racist. Administrators employed the practices and discourses of color-blind racism in the same manner as students and faculty.

Conclusion

A central mechanism of color-blind racism that reinforces white institutional space in the law schools is the confounding rhetoric of individualism and intent, which allows white students, faculty, and administrators to suggest that students of color are misperceiving their own experiences. By interpreting the kinds of experiences students in this chapter discussed within the limits of this white frame, we see that people in the law school minimize racism, making it more challenging for students of color to openly challenge or even discuss the systematic racism they face in the law schools. Students of color face daily challenges to their abilities, including open and registered surprise from faculty and students when they appear well dressed, have exceptional credentials, or make thoughtful and knowledgeable comments in class. Yet, through a constant reassertion of the white frame, these incidents are dismissed, and even when comments or actions are explicitly racist, they are diminished by whites who assert that it was all a joke or the actions of a misguided or socially incompetent individual.

It is not only students, or even faculty, who engage in a white frame to diminish the realities of racism that students of color face in the law school. Because the faculty and administration treat incidents of racism that are brought to their attention as individual, isolated events, there is no institutional response to racism in the law schools. The administration often denies that racism is the cause of the experiences of students of color. Again, the underlying assumption is that racism requires intentional racial animus, and the administration's refusal to view racism as systemic lends institutional power to the reproduction of white space. Despite this lack of institutional support, however, students of color do devise strategies of resistance that enable them to cope with, and contest, the white frame and white space that define the law school. In chapter 6, I discuss the strategies students of color employ in resistance, as well as the invisible mental and emotional labor expended in the process.

Notes

1. *Washington v. Davis*, 426 U.S. 229 (1976).
2. The experiences of students that I discuss in this chapter come from both interviews and observations. I do sometimes quote students more than once because some students had a lot to say about their experiences with racism in the law school. However, I want to note that of the thirty-one students I interviewed, twenty-two shared explicit stories of racist experiences. Furthermore, in my informal conversations and participant observations, many students of color expressed agreement with the sentiments of the students of color that I interviewed about the general racial climate of the school. Thus, I am comfortable suggesting that the quotes and experiences of students of color I present in this and the following chapter are widely shared by the majority of students of color in the law schools where I conducted my research.
3. *Korematsu v. United States*, 323 U.S. 214 (1944).
4. *Hirabayashi v. United States*, 320 U.S. 81 (1943).
5. See Jennifer Pierce, "Racing for Innocence: Whiteness, Corporate Culture, and the Backlash against Affirmative Action," *Qualitative Sociology* 26, no. 1 (2003): 53–70, for a discussion of similar assumptions aimed at attorneys of color by white partners in law firms.
6. I did not speak with Derrick's friend directly about this incident because she had left the law school by the time I was conducting my research.
7. See Jennifer Pierce, "Racing for Innocence: Whiteness, Corporate Culture, and the Backlash against Affirmative Action," *Qualitative Sociology* 26, no. 1 (2003): 53–70, for a discussion of this phenomenon in law firms more generally.

6

Still Asking Too Much

I N *Too Much to Ask: Black Women in the Era of Integration*, Elizabeth Higgin-botham (2001) discusses the emotional costs that black women faced in the 1960s and early 1970s when they entered graduate and professional programs that had been exclusively white. She suggests that the emotional costs of ne-gotiating the racial ideologies and structures in white educational institutions was "too much to ask" of these black women. She explains that for people of color entering white institutions, "membership in an oppressed racial group [meant] confronting ideological and structural limitations throughout their lives to achieve specific goals" (Higginbotham 2001, 232). The experiences of students of color in contemporary law schools reveal that, decades later, these students still face the high costs of racism while pursuing educational goals. The daily racialized practices, as well as racial insults students of color must negotiate and contest, their simultaneously invisible and hypervisible pres-ence in the contradictory space they occupy, and the failure of institutions to recognize color-blind racism and respond to it in a manner that gives students of color full human recognition—all of these dynamics in elite law schools suggest that these institutions are still asking too much of students of color.

One of the most challenging contradictions for students of color in law schools is the presence of an institutional norm that tacitly defines "objec-tivity" and "neutrality" as the absence of anger, frustration, or sadness, con-tinuously enforced within a space that is characterized by color-blind racism that normalizes racial subjugation. Law professor Patricia Williams (1991) has argued that when students of color are faced with the emotional pain of racism, while being constrained by a dominant discourse that requires so-called objectivity, they must choose either to violate that institutional norm or to participate in their own dehumanization and objectification. She illustrates the perverse consequence of this when she examines law school exams that engage issues of race. The exams she found included

- a tax exam in which students were asked to calculate the tax implications for Kunta Kinte's master when the slave catchers cut off his foot.
- a securities-regulation exam in which the professor muses about whether white-collar defendants should go to jail, since, "unlike ghetto kids," they are not equipped to fare in that environment.
- a constitutional-law exam in which students are given the lengthy text of a hate-filled polemic entitled "How to Be a Jew-Nigger" and then told to use the First Amendment to defend it. (Williams 1991, 84)

As Professor Williams notes,

[S]tudents are required to take the perspective of "everybody"; for black students this requires their taking a stance in which they objectify themselves with reference to the interrogatories. (I use the word "objectify" in the literal, grammatical sense of the subject-verb-object: the removing of oneself from the subject position of power, control, and direction over the verb-action. "We," blacks, become "them.") The law becomes less than universally accessible or participatory. The point of view assumes a community of "everybody's" that is, in fact, exclusionary. (1991, 89)

The inaccurate assumption of an inclusive community in the law schools places law students of color (and often faculty of color) in an emotional quagmire. If students choose to participate unquestioningly in this so-called community, they must essentially objectify themselves, removing their personal life experiences and the recognition of the histories of their communities from the law school discourse in which they engage. However, to reject this dehumanizing white frame, they must either attempt to disengage from their law school experiences or choose to fight an ongoing daily battle against the power of an institutional space with deeply racialized norms. The mental and emotional consequences of these paradoxical choices represent an extremely high cost that only students of color are required to pay in their pursuit of a legal education.

In her study of airline attendants, Arlie Hochschild suggests that emotional labor occurs when individuals manage their feelings to create an outward public display of emotion that is given value as a part of the work for which they are compensated (2003, 7). Jennifer Pierce (1995) has extended this definition beyond the area of service work, arguing that in law firms, paralegals and litigators perform gendered forms of emotional labor, including the work of presenting particular emotions in their work roles and acting in ways that signify these emotions; for example, paralegals (who are most often female) are expected to be nurturing toward the litigators (who are most often male) for whom they work.[1] I suggest that law students of color must perform emotional labor, meaning they must manage their emotions and the ways in which they choose to express them in order to negotiate the contradictions between their experiences in a racialized space and the institutional norms that equate objectivity with calm, disconnected emotive responses (discussed in more detail in chapter 2). Unfortunately, however, neither law schools nor the profession of law more broadly recognize the emotional labor that students of color perform. As a result, it is merely, as Higginbotham points out, a *cost* of their law school experience, which goes unrecognized and unrewarded.

Emotional labor is not the only form of unrecognized labor that students of color perform but is connected to other forms of labor that correspond to resisting white institutional space. In fact, students of color become active in resisting the white space of the law school in a variety of ways, including membership in student-of-color organizations, like the Black Law Students Association (BLSA), the Latino Law Students Association (LLSA), and the like; representation on various law school and universitywide committees; and involvement in programs that connect the law school to communities of color in the cities in which the law schools are located. Involvement in student organizations, committees, and community work is by no means unique to students of color. However, involvement by white students in these types of activities is based upon individual choice and does not carry with it the need or responsibility to create a space in which people of color are recognized in their full humanity. While the histories and perspectives of white students are represented in the law school, when these students enter the institution, law students of color (and law faculty of color) are themselves responsible for bringing the histories and perspectives of people of color into the law school. *To resist white institutional space, students and faculty of color are forced to carry the load of creating the institutional conditions by which they may be successful in these spaces.*[2] Furthermore, within a white institutional space, white students, faculty, and staff often view as problematic the activities that students of color pursue to resist the white normative frames they encounter.

In this chapter, I discuss the ways in which students of color resist white institutional space, the labor they must perform to accomplish this resistance, and the personal and educational costs they incur as a result.[3] The invisible and unrecognized labor of law students of color becomes especially clear when situated within the broader discourse of affirmative action in the law schools. This is true for three reasons. First, the issue of affirmative action is directly connected to the long history of racial oppression in the United States, but as I have discussed in previous chapters, the topic rarely gets discussed within this context. Second, a huge amount of emotional labor is performed by students of color in negotiating and contesting white students' perception that students of color do not deserve to be in elite law schools (these perceptions of white students are discussed in chapter 4). And third, because the rhetoric of "merit," which becomes a baseline assumption for discussions about affirmative action, fails to account for the labor students of color must perform in negotiating and contesting white space, labor that is not required of their white counterparts.

Emotional Costs of Affirmative Action Rhetoric

The lawsuits challenging the University of Michigan's affirmative action policies that the Supreme Court reviewed while I was conducting my research led to a great many discussions, presentations, and debates in the law schools when I was there. I observed one such panel debate organized jointly by the LLSA and the Federalist Society. As the debate opened, a representative for the Federalist Society, James Ferell, said, "No matter how good a thing diversity might be, it does not, under any circumstances, justify the use of race in any admissions decision. . . . [T]here's an injustice to any student who is not admitted . . . but an even more damaging message is sent to the beneficiaries of affirmative action . . . that as a group, they simply can't compete with majority students." After he spoke, Carmen, a Latina woman and a recent law school graduate working in the law school clinic and the panel representative for the LLSA, did not immediately respond. When she spoke, she began in a slow measured tone, saying, "Because I went to Michigan . . . that felt a little personal. I know that was not Mr. Ferell's intention, but . . . it brought back memories of being at Michigan . . . so forgive me if I start out a little angry." I looked up at Carmen and realized that she was tearing up and was attempting to choke back her tears. After asking the audience to "forgive" her for responding with emotion, she paused again, took a deep breath and then began to discuss the arguments in support of affirmative action.

As this example illustrates, a central issue for students of color as they negotiate and contest the perception that they do not belong in the law school stems from the widely asserted criticism of affirmative action that posits that if institutions like law schools admit people of color through affirmative action policies, these students will suffer stigmatization because they will not be viewed as competent.[4] This argument is extremely insidious because when students of color respond with anger or frustration to the indignity of having their competence or merit challenged, they actually provide fodder for proponents of this argument. But the logic of this argument requires the acceptance of a normatively white standpoint. We have to accept the assertion of incompetence or lack of merit in order to get to the issue of stigma. In other words, the argument that African Americans and other people of color suffer stigma as a result of affirmative action requires a passive agreement with the notion that people of color are not competent or meritorious. This narrative necessitates several underlying propositions: (1) that we are all starting from the same structural location; (2) that measures of competence or "merit," developed by white elite institutions, are valid and complete measures of ability; and (3) that the pain and indignity suffered by people of color who are the target of the assertion of incompetence logically lead to the result of ending the policy of affirmative action.

If this narrative were removed from the white normative frame, one could easily construct a counternarrative that would support the use of affirmative action as necessary for *white* people. This narrative would begin from the position that the history of legally constructed and supported white supremacy has resulted in unequal distribution of material and ideological resources. As a result, white people benefit from unearned privilege, which is not related to competence or merit. This racial preference properly stigmatizes white people, not people of color, in a social structure in which "merit" is valued over "group preferences." Thus, we should institute systematic affirmative action for people of color in order to equalize resources among racial groups to reduce the stigma for white people who have received positions in elite white institutions as a result of race privilege and not "merit."

I use this counternarrative to illustrate the pervasiveness of the white frame and the way this frame gets insidiously presented as nonracialized. An argument positing that it is in African Americans' best interest to end affirmative action seems racially neutral, even empathic. Yet, when we expose the white normative assumptions in the argument, we see that it is by no means racially neutral. And the damage this argument does goes beyond normalizing a perspective that naturalizes white privilege and power. It also creates a climate in which students of color cannot openly discuss and challenge the stigma of affirmative action, a stigma that is created not by affirmative action policies but by a dominant white narrative. I suggest that this argument becomes a background narrative, which gets pulled to the foreground at moments when affirmative action opponents want to aggressively assert the white frame to constrain the affirmative action debate. As a result of this argument, in combination with the rest of the anti–affirmative action rhetoric, students of color must perform a tremendous amount of emotional labor managing a white narrative that problematizes their right even to be in the space of the law school.

I discussed the ways in which white students perceive and discuss students of color in relation to affirmative action in chapter 4. As I noted there, the dominant white narrative in the law schools contains the assumption that students of color are in the law school because of affirmative action rather than "merit." While this is not always viewed as a *bad* thing (i.e., some white students are in support of affirmative action despite the perception that it "lowers the bar" of "merit"), it does reinforce a notion that the law school is a *white* space, a space where your legitimacy to be there will not be challenged if you are white. But if you are a student of color, you will find your presence in the law school consistently challenged. One of the most visceral emotional issues for students of color in the law schools I examined was battling the rhetoric of affirmative action and its less-than-subtle reification of the law school as a white space.

As students of color begin their law school experience, just as they are becoming acquainted with law school, they are met with a narrative that questions their presence. As Marcia, a second-year African American, described,

> First year, I think [it is] a negative experience, because it's this, like, it's sort of this climate that you're an affirmative action admit . . . like you're an affirmative action admit and that you don't really belong there, and I mean, they pair you up with one other . . . and thank goodness they pair you up with one or two other [African Americans] so you're like, "Okay, you guys, let's huddle together, let's stay tough" [laughs]. So, but I think that has a negative effect, not only on the African Americans that are there, but I think the rest of the people [of color].

As Marcia described it, the *climate* of the law school is colored by a feeling that students of color are only admitted into the school because of affirmative action. Thus, just as students arrive in the school, they feel a need to "huddle together," to begin to form a resistance to a narrative so strong that it is felt without anything being directly stated.

The affirmative action discourse, however, is not subtle or silent. In fact, it is often stated openly to students of color. And, as Devon, a second-year South Asian student, suggests, this narrative often feels like an attack:

> [W]ell, you get some strange comments about—well, some kids who come from [a rural area in a Midwestern state] . . . saying things like "Wow," you know, "I've never seen so many minority kids before. I wonder if they have affirmative action here" . . . and so . . . I think part of that is again these myths of affirmative action so kids automatically assume that if you're a minority you might be here because of affirmative action. And so, that's an extra attack, verbal attack on, you know, minority students.

This verbal attack is painful for students of color, and it adds to the already overwhelming everyday pressures of law school

The challenge to the rights of students of color to be in elite law schools has an impact upon even the most confident students. Maria, a first-year Mexican American student, explained how a white man she had thought of as a friend made her doubt her own abilities utilizing the affirmative action rhetoric:

> I have a good friend . . . and he straight up just told me, he goes, "You know what I'm so pissed about, because you got in here with a free ride and you probably have lower scores than I have, but you're still here with me." Well, I thought he was my friend. . . . [And then later when this white "friend" learned that an Asian American woman had received a summer internship, he said,] "I hate that minorities get special jobs. . . . [Y]ou know why they got that job" [her emphasis]. . . . It is a horrible ordeal. . . . [I]t's just very difficult to wake up thinking, "Oh my God, did I really get in here because I deserve to be here, or did I really get in because of affirmative action?"

One ironic consequence of this white narrative is that, as a result of the painful challenge to their right to be in that space, when students of color are successful, they often do not share that information with white students because they fear these verbal attacks. Maria continued,

> MARIA: "[When white students make comments like that,] it hurts your pride; you know, everybody wants to think that they're there because they're very smart and very talented. But I don't think anybody but minorities have to deal with that. Questioning yourself, you know, 'Am I really smart? Do I really belong here? Or did they just let me in here to fill a quota?' . . . Stuff like that, you know, it bothers you. I'm sorry I can't tell people my accomplishments because . . . [She pauses and looks upset.]"

> ME: "They think you got them because of affirmative action?"

> MARIA: "Exactly—all the time. I mean, anybody else could show off the fact that they got a kick-ass job. I don't feel free to do that. So it's just—it's hard."

Despite her success in law school and the job market, success that precisely indicated her ability to succeed within the structure of law school and the legal profession, she did not share these successes for fear that they would be minimized by the white affirmative action narrative.

The white affirmative action narrative, which sometimes takes the form of a silent, tacit issue of "climate" and sometimes becomes an explicit "attack," leads some students to feel more self-conscious about race than ever before. For example, Emma, a third-year African American woman who grew up in a wealthy, predominantly white community, explained to me that she became very cognizant of race for the first time in her life in law school. She said,

> I think probably being here, I'm more aware of being black than I ever have been in my entire life. . . . [W]hen you have a pack of four black women or something, people notice that, and you *know* they notice that, and I'm aware of that.

Despite growing up black in a white community, when Emma came to an elite law school, she experienced for the first time the feeling that she was the "other" whom white people noticed in that space.

Being the "other" in the law school space and feeling as though they must constantly prove themselves requires a great deal of emotional and mental energy on the part of students of color. In addition, students of color reported that they felt a responsibility to their entire racial community to succeed and perform their best in law school so that they could challenge racist stereotypes. As Marta, a second-year Mexican American woman with a fairly light complexion and reddish-brown hair, explained, the need to prove oneself extends beyond just a personal need:

> [W]e have the baggage of people doubting that we are capable. And, ah . . . but for me, most people . . . people don't know I am [Mexican American], and . . . I think, unless they know me personally, I don't think I get that so much. But I do feel a responsibility to do well, because I'm representin' . . . you see what I'm saying. And so, I think that, even if they're not looking at me, at my color, I feel like I'm showcasing what my people can do. Because affirmative action is . . . whatever it is, we're still living with that baggage—the expectation, you know, the challenge that we're not good enough.

Despite the fact that Marta was not often the target of the white affirmative action narrative herself, she felt the need to challenge the narrative and to "represent" for Mexican Americans and other people of color (Marta was involved with the LLSA, but also with several other student-of-color organizations). This constant feeling of needing to prove not only oneself but the worthiness of one's community puts an overwhelming amount of pressure on students of color.

Yet another paradox for students of color results from the extremely individualistic frame of the white affirmative action narrative dominant in the law school. Several programs were designed to assist students of color who had to overcome the barriers created by systemic racism on their path to elite law schools through their law school careers. These programs existed both to provide these students access to the social and cultural capital that white students had before coming to the law school, particularly with professional networking, and to assist them with the process of negotiating white institutional space. Yet, these programs were also viewed as a form of affirmative action and an "unfair advantage" by whites in the law schools. Kimberly, a second-year Latina student, explained,

I find . . . you know . . . just little things, about minority jobs fairs, or like. . . . [T]hey have this mentorship program for minority affairs, and I had a great mentor at [a law firm in the city], who's awesome, a Puerto Rican girl. . . . I know [white] people are like . . . "Oh, why do you get a mentor at [that law firm]." You know what I mean, like stuff like that, "Oh, cause you're a minority.". . . Or, like, we have our LLSAs, BLSAs . . . and I think that for them, they don't understand. It's like, you know, "Why shouldn't I have a mentor" . . . [but] I know that there is a difference in the way that we've grown up and that we haven't always been on equal footing . . . and these little things that we're getting now, they're all like a drop in the bucket. So, I feel like some of these little [minority] mixers, you know, or whatever, that's just a drop in the bucket. I'd trade it all for me to go to a school, or for people in my community to go to a school where, you know, teachers want to teach, and you have books. You know, where you have a college advisor.

The white affirmative action narrative ignores systemic racism, and as a result of the individualistic framing, whites are able to attack programs that, as Kimberly noted, are actually only "a drop in the bucket" with regard to attending to racial inequality in American society. But, as I noted, this framing leads to yet another paradox for students of color. If they participate in the very programs designed to provide minor compensation for systemic structural inequalities, like mentor programs, they are told, both subtly and explicitly, that they are receiving an unfair advantage. If they do not participate, they face the daunting task of independently overcoming the structural barriers of a racist society and institution, while competing academically with white students who face no such hurdles.

The white narrative of affirmative action that places continual scrutiny upon the presence of people of color in the law school causes students of color to question their own abilities, to downplay their educational and professional achievements, and sometimes even to avoid the programs and institutional supports designed to assist students of color in overcoming systemic racism so that they can be successful law students and lawyers. Coping with this color-blind racist narrative is often emotionally challenging, and negotiating that emotion can be time-consuming, taking the focus of students of color away from their legal education. Within white institutional space, students of color face the pain of being constructed as outsiders by the dominant narratives in the schools. And they are forced to contend with this "other" status within a space characterized by an institutional logic that rejects expressions of emotion and actually utilizes the expression of anger and frustration as evidence of nonbelonging. As a result, managing emotion becomes one of the most difficult aspects of resisting white space.

Emotional Labor and Resistance within White Space

At the end of a long day of observing at one of my law school sites, I ran into Michael, a first-year African American man, and he looked frustrated. I had seen him earlier that morning while observing his constitutional law class, which had been discussing affirmative action. I had noticed that he left class that morning about fifteen minutes early, and so I asked him whether the class topic had upset him. In a disgusted tone, he said that the discussion "was just like we were discussing Washington apples." Michael was referring to a case in which the Supreme Court held that North Carolina could not enact a law that restricted the grading of apples to the U.S. Department of Agriculture standards because the state of Washington had a higher standard of grading apples, and the North Carolina law therefore unconstitutionally burdened Washington's right to advertise their higher standard.[5] Michael's point was that in law school, discussions about affirmative action concerning the legal rights and remedies of human beings who have been violently oppressed through force of law get presented in a manner that is not substantively different from discussions about the economic rights of a business or state. This frustrated Michael, but he told me that he just wanted to forget about his frustration because he knew that he could neither change the law nor the opinions of others in the law school. In other words, Michael disengaged from a legal discussion because he knew that he could neither discuss the topic with the institutionally required "emotion-free" distance nor produce any desirable legal or institutional outcome if he introduced the idea that this discussion required emotional connection because it related to the violent history of African American subjugation. Unfortunately, despite his desire to disengage from the discussion about affirmative action, Michael carried the frustration he experienced from that classroom discussion with him for the rest of the day.

I encountered students who had experienced anger during a classroom discussion concerning issues of race on a regular basis during my two years of research at both law schools. Yet, they, like Michael, all expressed that they knew that this anger would not be accepted as a legitimate response in that space, so many of them chose to disengage from a legal issue that was socially important and personally relevant. And just as Michael was unable to focus on the learning that took place in his constitutional law class or any other class he attended that day, they too carried with them their initial emotion of anger, as well as the frustration of trying to shut off that emotion. Still, students of color attempted to reduce their anger and frustration and resist the white frame by disengaging in a variety of ways.

When I talked with Tiffany, a first-year African American student, she explained to me how she and her friend and classmate Sean, also an African American in his first year, had stopped speaking up in their criminal law class. The class was discussing a case in which a black man had been following a white woman. Although he never got close enough to touch the woman, she called the police, and he was arrested and charged with attempted rape. Tiffany explained that several white students in the class (men and women) made comments rationalizing the white woman's fear of the black man and her assumption that he intended to rape her, despite the fact that he never touched her. She said that because she was frustrated by the discussion, she said nothing, and when she looked over at her classmate Sean, one of the two African American men in the class, she could tell he was angry as well. Tiffany recalled, "I looked at [Sean], and I could just tell he was pissed. I could see it in him. But he didn't say anything, which was really surprising because I thought he was just gonna explode." Tiffany and Sean both reacted with anger to a discussion framed by racist stereotyping, yet both of them stifled their reaction by not responding. After that, Tiffany told me that she and Sean both decided that they would just not speak in that class anymore.

Similarly, Devon, a second-year South Asian student, explained why she often chose to avoid discussions about race in the law school. She said,

> [Y]ou know, you don't rock the boat, you don't have to worry about getting into large arguments. Um, you know, I think it could be a good strategy [for minority students to ignore issues of race] because you don't have to deal with a lot of issues, and you don't have to deal with a lot of problems. And if you just pretend like you don't hear it, you don't get upset by it.

If, as Devon put it, minority students speak their mind about race, they are "rocking the boat," and she felt that this would lead to upsetting racist comments from white people. In order to avoid hurtful discussions about race, Devon attempted to make *herself* invisible by pretending as if she did not hear comments about race.

When I asked Lisette, a third-year Latina student, whether she felt comfortable bringing up issues of race in the classroom, she discussed the connection between legal issues concerning race, broadly speaking, and the white affirmative action narrative. She said,

> [Race] is a delicate subject because the first question we often get faced with is, "Are you here because you are whatever fill-in-the-blank minority?" And, I mean, that was, like, constantly coming up, and so, it was a constant battle to,

like, prove yourself on different levels to say, like, "I deserve to be here, regardless of what race I am."

As a result of the pressure she felt from the affirmative action rhetoric employed against her, Lisette had to manage whether and how she would engage in other conversations about race in the law school. The white frame, as a rhetorical tool, becomes a powerful means by which race-related discussions get limited. Not only does this preclude students of color from informing classroom discussions with their knowledge, but it also has serious consequences for their ability to develop, through critical discourse, well-constructed arguments about race and the law.

For some students of color, disengaging from discussions about race in the law school was only the beginning. These students suggested that they also tended to avoid allowing white students into their peer groups. Kimmi, a second-year South Asian student, explained,

> It's funny. In undergraduate, I had a broad range of friends. I had Asian American friends; I had white friends. Um, I mean, I'm in an interracial relationship, I—and now more than ever, I feel like I, I'm becoming more narrow in scope, only because of the atmosphere. . . . [L]ike first of all, why is it my job to reach out to people I don't feel want to reach out to me? Okay, so that you can say that you have an Asian American friend.

This sentiment was shared by Regina, a first-year Asian American student, who also said that her peer group at her undergraduate university was racially diverse, but when she came to law school, that changed. Regina said it most strikingly when she said, "My other friends in the law school are people of color, you know—it's us and them." In addition, I carried on a long interview with Benjamin, a soft-spoken Asian American first-year student. Throughout the first half of the interview, he said that he never had any problems with race in the law school, but as we continued to talk, he explained that a major reason he did not have problems was because he avoided spending time with white students, and all of his friends were Asian.

Although white students, as well as faculty and administrators, often suggested that students of color self-segregated in the law school, they failed to understand that many students of color segregated themselves as a form of resistance to the emotional challenge of coping with a white racist discourse. (see Tatum 1997). While this form of resistance often worked to help students of color manage the pain of coping with racism and the white frame, it had the unfortunate consequence of assisting the reproduction of the white frame within the institution more broadly.[6] The consequences for the legal education of students of color are clear when these students either leave class physically or stop talking and engaging in class. But this also impacts the law school institution more subtly because the disengagement of students of color has the effect of assisting the reproduction of white institutional space by silencing the possible public resistance of white norms and white discursive frames that students might express.

Attempts to Manage Emotion and the White Frame

Ample evidence reveals that, in general, the experience of law school is emotionally difficult (see Krieger 2002). In addition to the general stresses of law school, the ideological and structural challenges for students of color in this white space create a context in which they must constantly negotiate and contest various expressions of racism. As Joe Feagin and Karyn McKinny (2003) have discussed, the process of coping with racism can produce a large range of emotional and mental consequences for people of color, including frustration, anger, sadness, and depression, as well as physical reactions like headaches and high blood pressure. Yet, as I have discussed previously, within the institutional space of law schools, expressions of the types of emotions that are attached to coping with racism are viewed as inappropriate; "emotional" arguments are not "lawyerly" arguments.[7] As a result, students of color find themselves, once again, in a contradictory space. Every facet of this elite white space challenges their dignity and humanity, yet they must suppress emotional response or risk being further alienated from the space because they are dismissed as overly emotional.

The dismissal of the perspectives of students of color as overly emotional represents a powerful mechanism by which their voices are removed from the law school discussion, even when they speak. In the law schools where I conducted my research, even when students attempted to negotiate their own emotions and express themselves within the institutional frame of calm "rationality," their criticism of whiteness was dismissed through this tactic. Recall that in the previous chapter, Anthony, an second-year African American student, said that when he faced racist stereotyping, he just shrugged it off. But later in our interview, he explained why:

ANTHONY: "I always try to think of whether or not I should respond or whether I should just sit back, you know."

ME: "If you respond or raise issues of race, what is the reaction?"

ANTHONY: "[M]aybe people might be, like, this angry black man is at it again . . . and that is one of the reasons why I, I'm cognizant of when I, you know, participate and when I don't. . . . [I]n undergrad, you know, I raised my hand every time, and that's how I was in high school. Every single time my professor said something that was . . . remotely racist, I was like 'Yo, this is racist' . . . but here, it just, you're just too tired, like, I'm too, it's too tiring to go through it again."

Anthony felt tired of having his resistance to racism dismissed by the assertion that he was an "angry black man," so he decided to "shrug it off" when he encountered racism. In my observations, I saw Anthony challenge racism in many situations in the law school. He was also very active in both BLSA and law school programs that connected the law school with nearby communities of color. But I did observe that he was always careful about his demeanor when he spoke about race, and he made a conscious decision to manage his emotions so that he did not express anger or frustration publicly.

It is ironic about Anthony's attempts to manage his emotion, something that took a great deal of energy on his part, that a shared white narrative in the law school still characterized him as both angry and hypersensitive about race issues. When I was beginning my research at Anthony's law school, I was introduced to an administrator at the school who suggested that I should talk to Anthony during my initial visit (before I was actually recruiting interview participants). She told me that she would introduce me to him the following day. When I went back to her the next day to be introduced, she told me that an associate dean had told her not to introduce me to Anthony; the associate dean had said that eventually I would meet him, but she did not want him to be the first student I met because it might skew my perspective. This foreshadowed the narrative about Anthony that I would encounter when I did get involved in my research.

In one interview, a second-year white woman told me that many students dismissed Anthony when he spoke in class and at law school events because he was "so angry." Another white student, a third-year man, said that "lots of students" perceived Anthony as "angry." In addition, when I was discussing comments Anthony made in a law school forum on race with another law school administrator who had attended the forum, she dismissed his perspective, saying, "You know—race is his thing." In addition to these explicit comments, on many occasions, white students and students of color made comments like, "Oh, you know Anthony," again in a condescending and dismissive manner.

Anthony was not the only black man I watched being characterized as "angry." In fact, this form of racialization as a means of rendering the perspectives of black men irrelevant revealed an interesting phenomenon in the law schools that exposed a particular mode of operation in white institutional space. During my research, I observed two very different black men, with very different presentation styles, and both of their perspectives were dismissed because they were labeled as angry and irrational about issues of race. At one law school, Anthony was described as the "angry black man"; at the other, Jason, also a second-year African American student, was characterized in a very similar manner. Anthony and Jason, however, were very different people who made very different arguments about race.

When Anthony discussed race—in our interview, in casual discussions, and in law school classes and at events that I observed—his arguments were very sophisticated. He was clearly better read than most law students, and he always contextualized his arguments within the social and historical, as well as legal, aspects of racial hierarchy (occasionally even providing citations for his comments). I never saw him raise his voice or get visibly upset. In contrast, Jason often became openly frustrated by discussions about race. He rarely advanced social-structural or legal arguments, instead relying upon personal experiences. And he often expressed anger by yelling. On two occasions, I observed Jason in a yelling match with other law students in the halls of the law school; these incidents were very public and thereafter often became the subject of discussion among students. Both of these incidents were with students of color (and both happened to be women of color). In one instance, he was berating a South Asian woman because she was dating a white man, and in the other instance, he was yelling at an African American woman for not being critical enough in her comments about race in the classroom. He generally refused to speak to white people (although there were some exceptions, and he and I did talk on several occasions, though I did not interview him).

I call attention to these differences not to criticize Jason's way of expressing his perspectives on race; as I have discussed, given the kinds of racism revealed in my research, as well as the systemic racism that characterizes U.S. society, anger seems the appropriate reaction.[8] Rather, I point to these differences to note that despite Anthony and Jason's very different responses to racism and racial inequality, as well as their completely different presentation styles, the narratives that developed about these two men were remarkably similar. Students and some administrators characterized both of them as "angry." Others in the law school dismissed both of their arguments and perspectives because of this perceived anger, and both were said to be too focused on issues of race. This characterization of Anthony and Jason denied aspects of their lives and their experiences in the law school that occurred because they were black men. It also reveals an important aspect of white institutional space. These men managed their emotions in the law school in very distinct ways, but because both were openly critical of the white frame, both were labeled as the "angry black man."

Jason and Anthony were not the only African American men labeled as "angry" in the law schools. In fact, one of the students whom I talked with, but did not formally interview, Aaron, a third-year African American student, was very quiet and rarely spoke to anyone other than the people in his peer network. He was a member of the BLSA, but I never heard him speak about race in any class or at any public BLSA event. However, Aaron had on his computer screen background a picture of the Black Panthers. Two white students, on separate occasions, suggested to me that although they did not know Aaron, they had seen his screen background and assumed that he was an "angry black man" (in those words). Thus, any challenge to white power and privilege, even an unspoken, personal expression of support for the Black Panthers illustrated on one's own computer, could make a student of color vulnerable to the label of "angry." This being the case, it is not surprising that many students of color chose to disengage from law school discussions about race or to select peer groups that were nonwhite.

Attempts to manage and control normal human emotions in order to conform to the expectations of the institutional space require a great deal of emotional labor. Students must continuously negotiate or contest racialized discourses and racial indignities, and they must meet this challenge without expressing emotion. Yet, unfortunately, even when students attempt to manipulate and suppress their emotions when they challenge the white frame, they still get labeled as "angry" or "emotional." Lisette, a third-year Latina student, noted that, over time, all of the emotional labor required in negotiating the white space of the law school takes its toll on law students of color. She said, "In the long run, I think [law school] beats a person down. . . . [I]t definitely was out of balance for what is a healthy lifestyle." Yet despite being beaten down, students continue to succeed in the law school by creating support networks as outlets for emotion.

Resistance through Community Building

Despite the prevalence of mechanisms of white institutional space that dismissed students of color and criticisms of the white frame, students of color continued to resist white space by forming networks in which they could resist without the risk of white interference. Students came to rely upon the community of students of color for support in coping with racism. Tiffany explained it as such:

> We have kind of a, you could call it a clique among the first-year students of color. . . . [W]e'll sit and talk for a while, and there's always discussions about ignorant comments that are made in class, and how you can't believe some of the things that come out of [white] students' mouths, you know, and you wanna retaliate and say something back, but then, you know you have to pick your battles, and you just sit quietly.

For Tiffany and other students of color, although they chose not to engage comments about race in their classes, they did resist the white color-blind racist frames by talking with one another to confirm both that these comments were "ignorant" and to confirm that they were not alone in their experiences. Discussing racial indignities with one another reveals the patterns of racialized behaviors and discourses in the law schools. While sharing these stories can be painful, it also gives students an outlet to discuss their emotions without being challenged or having their perspectives negated. These conversations develop the broader narratives about the racial dynamics of the law school space, which is emotionally sustaining in the sense that it helps students of color see a broader structural picture that prevents them from individualizing, thus internalizing, what is happening to them. These forms of alliances and shared narratives can assuage the "mind fuck" of racism described by Derrick in the previous chapter, in which students begin to doubt their own perspectives and realities.

Roshni, a second-year South Asian woman, noted that she got through classes in which racially offensive comments were made through nonverbal communication with other students of color. As she explained,

> It's nice, just during class, someone can say something completely wild, just, you know, like "What?" And then, you know, to have someone in that class to make eye contact with, and you can both be like [rolls her eyes].

So, even when students choose to not speak up in class, this does not mean that they are not responding in the classroom. But to avoid having the white frame employed against them in the classroom, students of color merely look to each other, literally, to acknowledge their resistance to one another. Thus, while students may feel too angry or uncomfortable to speak, they receive support from one another by maintaining eye contact, smiling, shaking their head, or rolling their eyes at racialized comments.

Students of color thus develop tacit knowledge about how to maneuver within this white elite space so that they may be successful despite the challenges added onto the already cumbersome task of completing the work of law school. Although this requires emotional labor, a cost that law students of color have to pay for their legal education, they develop a range of strategies to cope with this additional cost. The invisible emotional labor, as well as the necessity of developing the tacit knowledge to get through law school, is unrecognized and unrewarded within the structure of the law school and the larger legal profession. However, emotional labor is not the only form of unrewarded labor that students of color perform in the law school. In order to survive within the white space of the law school, many students of color feel they must also take on the responsibility of creating for themselves a space in which their histories and perspectives are represented and respected.

The Invisible Labor of Deconstructing White Space

When students of color resist the white color-blind racist frame that dominates the law school discourse, they challenge the institutional logic of the law schools (Goodrich and Mills 2001). In doing so, they get dismissed through a variety of techniques, including the use of the rhetoric of affirmative action and the manipulation of the concept of emotion in order to label students as overly emotional and, therefore, outside the appropriate frame of legal discourse. From this outsider status, students of color must attempt to bring in the perspectives and histories of people of color, and this makes the involvement of students of color in law school organizations, on law school committees, and in activities in communities of color substantively different from similar activities performed by white students.

In my ethnographic research at both law schools, I was continually amazed by the amount of work that students of color were doing to create a space in which issues of race, racial inequality, and positive representations of people of color were presented. This took the form of involvement in what they referred to as the "LSAs" (the student-of-color law student associations like the BLSA, LLSA, and so on). Throughout my field notes, I have entries like the following:

> I went to the BLSA meeting today, and once again my reaction is shock at how much work they are doing. At this meeting they talked about several projects. They are going to do a book rally to collect books and money for the Books for Africa program. They are starting a new mentor program to have it in place for fall so that all the African American incoming 1Ls can have an upper-class mentor. They have also organized a meeting to talk about how to make contacts to get legal jobs. [Melanie,] the president, said, "You all have to work very hard. Don't rely on CSO [the Career Services Office] to get you a job." Then she went on to discuss the routes to making contacts with black lawyers in the area, and she said, "When you talk to them, you have to be confident, but not arrogant." They also talked about getting support from faculty for presentations that they wanted to suggest for the following academic year (which they have to make preliminary plans for now so that they can put together a budget to request funding). They divided up the work, but it seemed as if everyone had a lot to do.

The LSAs served as organizational support for students of color (organizational support that, I note, students of color had to supply for themselves), but they also served as the major source of education about racially inclusive history, racial inequality, and nuanced presentations about communities of color for the law school. These organizations would do the work of seeking out funding, contacting and recruiting people to come and talk about various issues related to race, and putting on presentations (generally over the lunch hour) in the law school. This type of work was done by all of the law student organizations, but for the LSAs, their work served to fill a void in the presentation of race-related matters. Over the course of my observations, I saw events organized by the LSAs that included bringing in a prominent professor of American Indian law to discuss problems with contemporary American Indian law; no less than four panels put together to present perspectives on affirmative action and the Michigan affirmative action cases; a presentation by a prominent law professor detailing the racial disparities in the criminal justice system; presentations by minority elected officials, including a presentation by former congresswoman and current ambassador Carol Moseley Braun; a presentation by local elected officials discussing underrepresentation of Latinos in the legal system; and a full-day symposium on the legal and political implications of genocide in Rwanda.

This list of activities represents less than a quarter of the presentations and educational forums put on by the LSAs during the time that I was observing (over the course of two academic years). And the law student community recognized the role of student-of-color organizations in presenting issues of race to the larger law school community. As Nathan, a third-year white man and an officer in law student government, said, "Everyone knows [the LSAs] put on some of the best programming in the law school." The work involved in bringing this programming to the law school was widely recognized by students of color as being the only way that they could feel comfortable within the space, but being responsible for that programming could be overwhelming, as Marta, a second-year Mexican American student, suggested:

MARTA: "I really feel that all of us people of color have a role to play in the larger schemes of things, to set an example. I mean, I really, I really believe that. And, you know, some people say, 'Oh, I, I have all these other things to worry about'—everyone has all these things to worry about; *next*. That's life. [Laughs.] . . . Because you can make excuses until you're blue in the face, but I think that it's really important, especially in our case, to give back. I mean, ah, for instance, Latinos are the, I mean, Latinos are the largest majority minority, and, ah, but we're not represented as such in law schools, and not as such in any law schools . . . and it's because, and there's a lot of factors to that, and I think, even more so, we expect, there, there have to be contributions given back. We owe something not just to our classmates, whatever color they are, but we also owe something to our communities."

ME: "So how much time do you think . . . do you put [into LLSA]?"

MARTA: "I think that the issue is . . . our numbers are so small that one of the things that we need to do to feel comfortable is to have these groups. We can't survive without these groups. . . . [Students of color] need these groups; it's a comfort zone. . . . [W]e need to have a family . . . [but], I mean, I was doing more [work on LLSA functions] during Latino Heritage Month than doing some of my class work. Like, I was . . . just going to the events, like six or seven hours a week. . . . And so, that's like going into work, like going to a job, like, once a week, and that's a lot of work. Um, and right now I'm kind of exhausted, but Diversity Week is starting, so I've gotta do it again."

The time that it takes to organize funding and speakers and to set up presentations is analogous to the work of a part-time job for many of the students of color. However, as Marta noted, these students also view it as essential for their law school education, as well as their survival in this white space.

Another issue that takes up both time and emotional energy for students of color is negotiating the demands of the law school community and the dominant racialized discourse. The LSAs get their funding from external sources (such as law firms or universitywide grant programs) and from law school funds administered by the law school governments. The funds inside the law school are limited ($500 to $800 per year), and fund-raising from law firms can be arduous, as Kimberly, a second-year Latina student, noted:

We're busting our humps, and it is not easy fund-raising law firms, because everybody's cutting back, and everyone wants to know what are you doing for me, or whatever. You know we're making up these proposals. . . . [T]hat's great, you know, we, we want to do it to a certain extent, but at the same time, we're in law school too, you know; it's not our primary job.

In order to any get funding, the LSAs have to put on a certain number of programs, but they also have to have successful program events. This means that both the number of programs put on and the number of people who attend these events are relevant to the amount of funding the LSAs will get for future programming. As David, a first-year American Indian student and an active member of the American Indian Law Students Association (AILSA), said, "We can't put on too many loser presentations without losing funding." The challenge, then, is to have presentations that address the issues that students of color want to discuss and see represented in the law school, while also maintaining the interest of the white students. In other words, in order for their organizations to continue to receive financial support, students of color involved in the LSAs must balance their own need to bring information into the law school that supports their issues and histories with the need to appeal to white students and the dominant racialized discourse in the law school.

Putting on academic programming in the law school is only one aspect of the work that the LSAs do. In my field notes from the BLSA meeting presented above, I noted that Melanie, the president of the BLSA, advised BLSA members about getting a job. In particular, she told them not to rely on the Career Services Office to find a job for them. Networking with the broader law community of color was a major activity for students of color. This was necessary for them not only to find resources to negotiate the legal profession, which is steeped in the same kinds of racialized practices and discourses as the law school, but also to find inroads into job possibilities.(see Pierce 2003). Again, white students also network with the legal community, but their networking is not racialized. As noted above, the job-search process is situated within a white normative discourse about affirmative action; thus, students of color look to the law community of color to help them negotiate the job market. Many of the LSAs conduct receptions during which they invite students in the organization, as well as alumni and attorneys of color in the community. Some of the complications of this process have already been addressed above, but one of the struggles student organizations face is negotiating the workload to make these receptions happen. When I attended a meeting of the AILSA, David told the group, "The more we facilitate networking, the better off we will be. That is how we get the jobs . . . BLSA and LLSA have a wine-and-cheese [reception] to network. . . . [O]ur numbers are not big enough, but we can get a speaker in per semester to be networking that way." David's comments are similar to Melanie's, as he notes that networking within the American Indian legal community is the key to getting a job. AILSA, however, does not have the resources in sheer numbers or finances to network on the same level as the BLSA or LLSA, so its members have to be more creative in their networking by bringing in speakers for academic programs, then raising the issue of jobs for American Indian law students.

Part of the job of networking for students of color is to meet people in the legal profession and search out job contacts. Another aspect of networking, however, is the role that students themselves play in networking with each other and with communities of color more broadly. The LSAs at both law schools were involved in both mentoring programs within the law school; that is, second- and third-year students' mentoring first-year students. But they also worked to create connections with communities of color around the law schools. As I mentioned above, the BLSA became involved in the Books for Africa program, but another BLSA activity was an outreach program to a local, predominantly minority high school. BLSA bussed in a group of students from this local high school, talked to them about law school and careers in the legal profession, fed them lunch, and then took them on a law school tour. They did this several times per year for different high schools. The entire event was funded by the BLSA. Activities like these kept students engaged in communities of color in a way that they felt was important as part of the process that many students identified as "giving back." However, all of these activities took an immense amount of planning, preparation, and facilitating time.

Students of color often felt compelled to take part in both presenting issues of race in the law school community and reaching out to communities of color outside the law school (as the sentiments of many students above have expressed). The workload of facilitating a climate in which they could be successful often left students of color tired and emotionally drained. But there was an expectation on the part of fellow law students and administration that students of color would do this labor. As Lisette, a third-year Latina student, explained,

> I found myself on so many committees and so many jobs because I was the person they'd call. . . . I was like "Okay, I will do it because it needs to be done" . . . and so adding that on, not only did I have to do my own law school activities, but there was all this other stuff, and it's a double-edged sword because I resent the fact. . . . I feel like I was being used in the sense that it was, like, okay we have a [minority] representative, so we don't need to look for anyone else . . . but what I really wish they would do is look for more people who could fill these positions. . . . I was often finding myself expending my energies in areas that I valued, but it wasn't gonna get me ahead.

Lisette's comments reveal how exhausting the work of being the "minority representative" can be, as well as the fact that this labor is not recognized or rewarded.

Conclusion

Students of color resist the white institutional space of elite law schools in a wide variety of ways. The time and energy they put into these spaces, as Nathan noted, to bring in some of the best programming in the schools illustrates their resilience and dedication to themselves and to the profession of law. However, it should not be the responsibility of students to educate the law school community; nor should these students be responsible for having to create the institutional circumstances in which they can succeed. White students are not burdened with having to work to create an institutional space in which they can feel like insiders; the white institutional space provides these students with social and cultural capital to succeed as soon as they enter the institution. Furthermore, despite the vast amount of energy, as well as emotional and other forms of invisible labor, that students of color put into their legal education, they are still consistently marginalized within the space. Their perspectives are dismissed via rhetoric that asserts that they are there because of "preferential treatment" or that labels them as "angry" or "overly emotional." As a result, students of color find ways to resist and succeed in elite law schools, but the dominant rhetoric and racialized practices in the law schools function to maintain and reproduce white space despite this resistance.

White institutional space is deeply entrenched as a result of a long history of racist exclusion, as well as the consistent white culture, discourse, and practice that maintains and reproduces it. However, when people engage in discussions about making the law profession more diverse, or making law school more accessible to people of color, or creating a better racial climate in the law schools, or even creating legal policies like affirmative action that can help remedy the consequences of systemic racism, these discussions get constrained within the same white frame that functions to reproduce white institutional space in the law schools. This is often true in academic race scholarship as well. Deconstructing white institutional space will require that we discard this constraining white frame and center the experiences and voices of students of color in the project of identifying and eliminating the structural remnants of our white racist past.

Notes

1. While emotional labor may be undervalued in the service industry or in gendered occupations, it has value in the sense that it is an expected aspect of these work roles, which are compensated through wages. Yet, as feminist studies of household work have noted, not all labor is compensated through wages (Arlie Hochschild, *The Managed Heart: The Commercialization of Human Feeling, Twentieth Anniversary Edition* [Berkeley: University of California Press, 2003]). Here I suggest that the emotional labor that law students must perform, though it is not work in the sense that it is connected to a wage, is a required aspect of their participation in the law school institution and, therefore, is required in order to successfully complete law school. Thus, it becomes a necessary component of their law school experience, compensated by their law school diplomas.

2. Thanks to Roderick Ferguson for helping me articulate the way in which people of color in white institutional space become responsible for creating the institutional conditions by which they can succeed in these institutions.

3. Several (though not all) of the students I quote in this chapter were also quoted in chapter 5 discussing their experiences with racism. In this chapter, I speak to the issues of resistance and invisible labor as part of the process of dealing with racism, so

the use of the quotes of these students connects to the ways in which they respond to the racism they have faced. I do want to reiterate that I received feedback from very many students of color who agreed with the sentiments expressed by the students I have quoted here.

4. See, for example, Linda Chavez, "Promoting Racial Harmony," in *The Affirmative Action Debate*, ed. George E. Curry (Reading, MA: Addison-Wesley Books, 1996); Stephan Thernstrom and Abigail Thernstrom, *America in Black and White: One Nation Indivisible* (New York: Simon & Schuster, 1997); Shelby Steele, "A Negative Vote on Affirmative Action," in *Debating Affirmative Action: Race, Gender, Ethnicity, and the Politics of Inclusion*, ed. Nicolaus Mills (New York: Delta, 1994).

5. *Hunt v. Washington State Apple Advertising Commission*, 432 U.S. 333 (1977).

6. See Kimberle Williams Crenshaw, "Race, Reform, and Retrenchment: Transformation and Legitimation in Antidiscrimination Law," *Harvard Law Review* 101 (1988): 1331–1383, for a discussion of patterns of resistance to white racism and the corresponding retrenchment of whites in U.S. society.

7. For more discussions of the rejection of these types of emotion in the law school, see Lani Guinier, Michelle Fine, and Jane Balin, *Becoming Gentlemen: Women, Law School, and Institutional Change* (Boston: Beacon Press, 1997); Debra Schleef, "Thinking Like a Lawyer: Gender Differences in the Production of Professional Knowledge," *Gender Issues* (Spring 2001): 69–86; Lawrence S. Krieger, "Institutional Denial about the Dark Side of Law School and Fresh Empirical Guidance for Constructively Breaking the Silence," *Journal of Legal Education* 32, nos. 1–2 (2002).

8. In fact, as bell hooks has suggested, the physical and psychological violence of racial oppression in the United States should provoke rage. The fact that it does not is evidence of the extent to which white people have been able to disconnect themselves from normal human emotion in order to protect white race privilege. See bell hooks, *killing rage: Ending Racism* (New York: Henry Holt & Company, 1995). See also Joe Feagin, *Systemic Racism* (New York: Routledge, 2006).

Conclusion

In the Elephant

NEAR THE END of the affirmative action debate at Georgetown Law Center, which I discuss in the introduction to this book, an African American man stood and said to the panel and the audience that in U.S. society, it is typical to ignore the relevance of racism. Referring to the common metaphor of the elephant in the room that everyone ignores, he said, "We're not just ignoring the elephant in the room; we're in the elephant." The extension of this metaphor brilliantly sums up the phenomenon of systemic racism and white institutional space. Racism and the structural organization of racial hierarchy are not merely present in the "room" of this society; rather, U.S. society *is* the elephant. Racism is a part of the very fabric of our nation, and we are embedded within a fundamentally racist state.[1] As a result, the elite institutions that organize and rationalize our society are both constituted by, and function to constitute, systemic racism. The conception of white institutional space, then, refers to the integrated functioning of the racialized structures, cultures, and practices, as well as dominant ideologies and discourses of social institutions, which interact to create a totally whitewashed space.

The political and structural location of elite law schools makes them especially relevant institutions within which to examine the functioning of white institutional space. The relationship between law schools and the law, as well as the creation and enforcement of race and racial hierarchy, implicates law schools in the reproduction of white privilege and power in U.S. society. Elite law schools developed as exclusively white institutions. Further, they were formed within a social context characterized by explicit white material and ideological racial supremacy. The norms and assumptions employed in the construction of the law school curriculum were based upon that white racist frame, which naturalized white intellectual and political superiority. As a result, law schools, particularly elite law schools, were deliberately constructed as white institutional spaces within which students were taught to internalize a form of "thinking" patterned after the reasoning of elite white men who sought to protect and extend their power.

From this deliberately racist foundation, elite law schools came to represent that figurative elephant, characterized by deep structures of white power within which law students, faculty, and administration acted. When students of color entered these schools as a result of the legal changes born out of the civil rights movement that prohibited their deliberate exclusion, these spaces and the actors within them relied upon the tacit, racialized deep structures, as well as contemporary cultural practices and discourses, to retrench and thereby maintain and reproduce white space. Largely as a result of their exclusionary past (though this was not the necessary result), most every facet of the structure of law schools signifies white privilege and power. The faces of white lawyers, judges, and other legal actors line these schools' walls, and these images are reconstituted in the present by the continuing racial disparities in law schools and, more importantly, the continued concentration of white people in positions of power in legal academia. Furthermore, racism, historical and contemporary, is consistently minimized and naturalized through a curricular assertion of objectivity. Through a so-called rational or neutral lens, legal cases concerning issues central to the state enforcement of violent racial oppression, for example, cases concerning the enslavement of African Americans, are presented as cases about "state's rights." Alternately, contemporary cases concerning race are framed within an ideology of individualism in the law, a rhetorical dishonesty that becomes a tacit assumption in the process of legal reasoning in law school classes.

Abstract individualism and other color-blind racist frames represent the dominant racial discourse in the post–civil rights era. The story lines of these frames are embedded in contemporary race jurisprudence and law school curricula and discourse. The abstract individualist frame becomes a mechanism through which legal analyses of, and discussions about, racism and racial inequality get removed from the long history of legally enforced racist oppression. Furthermore, abstract individualism works in concert with other color-blind racist frames, including the minimization of racism, the naturalization of racial inequality, and the assertion of pathological culture in communities of color. This allows whites to engage in racialized practices and discourses while simultaneously absolving themselves of responsibility for racial hierarchy. The power of this discourse in the law schools resides in the contemporary legal frame that lends legal authority to the color-blind racist discourse. As a result, the dominant white culture and patterns of white racist practices that characterize the everyday experience in law school get minimized and reduced to isolated incidents or mere expressions of humor by students and faculty, as well as the law school administration.

The racialized structure, culture, and discourse in law schools systematically impose hurdles that students of color must negotiate in their legal education. Students of color are made to feel as though they are outsiders—not legitimately in the law school space—almost the instant they arrive in law school as a result of the white-framed affirmative action narrative. Furthermore, students regularly face racist insults, subtle and overt, and have to negotiate the contradictory space of being both invisible and hypervisible in the law school. Because the law school administration views the experiences of students of color through the same color-blind racist lens that creates the very institutional space that facilitates the racism with which students of color must contend, these students find very little support from the only source of institutional power to which they can turn. Thus, students are left to find individual or student (and sometimes faculty) community support systems. Naturally, the racism with which students of color must contend produces anger, frustration, and sadness. Unfortunately, the institutional logic of the law school rejects the legitimacy of expressions of these emotions, yet another institutional constraint on students of color that facilitates the white discursive frame. As a result, students of color must manage their feelings about race and racism, sometimes having to objectify themselves through the process of disassociating themselves from their histories, the experiences of their communities, and their own personal experiences in order to maintain legitimacy in the constraining frame of so-called neutrality, objectivity, and rationality. As a result, students often disengage and sometimes create peer networks that exclude whites. Unfortunately, however, this often functions to reinforce their invisibility in the law school space.

Despite all of the hurdles students of color face, they succeed in elite law schools because they create supportive peer networks and a separate law school community where the white frame cannot dominate. Students take on the responsibility of doing the work themselves to create institutional settings in which they can succeed. As a consequence, however, in order to resist white institutional space, students of color expend a great deal of emotional and other forms of invisible labor that their white counterparts do not have to perform. This labor is silently and institutionally *expected* of students of color, yet it is valued neither in the law schools nor the profession at large.

Given the centrality of law schools in contemporary debates concerning affirmative action, it is telling that the additional costs paid by students of color in elite law schools remain unaccounted for in policy debates about affirmative action. There is a deep irony in the fact that as students of color engage in vast amounts of unrecognized labor to negotiate the space of the law schools, they must simultaneously contend with the rhetoric of affirmative action, which fails to account for this labor, yet continually challenges their talents and abilities. This fact presents one of the most exposing contradictions in the policy discussions and debates concerning affirmative action. When viewed through the lens of white institutional space, which accounts for the extraneous labor required of students of color, the current framing of discussions about affirmative action look hollow and merely reflective of white power.

White Institutional Space and Affirmative Action in Elite Law Schools

> White people don't have to deal with race the way that we have to—that's one less problem that you have to deal with.
>
> —Marta, a second-year Mexican American student

In the fall of 2004, the *Stanford Law Review* published an article by Richard Sander positing that affirmative action in law school admissions is harmful to African Americans (Sander 2004). Sander comes to this conclusion by comparing law school grades and first-time bar-passage rates for white students and African American students (he does not include other racial groups in this study, though he promises that a broader analysis will be forthcoming). His article created a fervor even before it was published. Northwestern University law professor James Lindgren commented to a reporter, "With Sander's new study . . . we are finally able to move to a less fevered and more nuanced discussion of the scope of affirmative action."[2] In fact, Sander's argument is not new, as others have presented similar arguments about undergraduate admissions (see, for example, Thurnstrom and Thurnstrom 1997). Furthermore, while Sander does examine the racial differences in performance on the indicators used in law school admissions (LSAT and undergraduate grades), combined with several outcome-based measures of law school performance, his argument is not particularly nuanced.

Just as arguments about the racial stigma that may arise from affirmative action appear to be magnanimous and empathic before critical examination, Sander presents an argument seemingly filled with concern for African Americans in legal education; on closer examination, however, it is both paternalistic and methodologically problematic. Sander begins his article with an emotional plea, noting that "much of [his] adult career has revolved around issues of racial justice" and that he has a biracial son, "part black and part white, and so the question of how nonwhites are treated and how they fare in higher education gives rise in [him] to all the doubts and worries of a parent" (Sander 2004, 370). Unfortunately, despite Sander's concern for "how nonwhites are treated," based in part on having a biracial son, Sander remains deeply embedded in a white frame, and, unfortunately, his inability to see beyond that frame belies this concern.

The thrust of Sander's argument is that race-based affirmative action in elite law schools places African American students into schools in which they cannot compete academically. If these African American students went to lower-tier schools, he argues, they would get better grades and, as a result, would be able to compete for jobs more effectively. Thus, Sander concludes that affirmative action is not beneficial to African Americans and is not worth the "sacrifice of the principle of color blindness" and the "enormous social and political capital spent to sustain affirmative action" (2004, 371). This argument contains two tacit assumptions that are problematic. First, the argument that it is undesirable to sacrifice "the principle of color blindness" only holds if one believes that color blindness, in the context of contemporary American society, is desirable. To get there, one must again remove the argument about the "principle" of color blindness, an abstract individualist assertion, from the substantive reality of structural racial inequality. By presuming that everyone will agree that the principle of color blindness is legally desirable, Sander tacitly enforces the boundaries of a white frame within which his analysis will take place. Second, the "enormous social and political capital spent to sustain affirmative action" mentioned by Sander is obviously spent *by* people of color, and this expenditure of capital is only required because of *white resistance* to affirmative action. Sander's implicit warning, which he states only indirectly, is that people of color do not have much social and political capital to spend with whites, so what capital they have must be spent cautiously. In other words, the argument centers on the reactions and feelings of white people. Moreover, his analysis revolves around the presumption that we passively accept the limits of social and political capital imposed upon people of color in discussions about progressive racial reform, rather than interrogating whether it is desirable in a democracy for whites to impose such limits.

Even though Sander begins by framing his arguments squarely within a white frame, he goes on to suggest that he would be willing to move beyond the "problems" he identifies if there were a sufficient benefit to African Americans as a result of affirmative action. In his analysis, however, he concludes there is no such benefit. Sander's empirical research reveals that African American law students do not perform as well as white students on outcome-based measurements like law school grades and first-time bar-passage rates. As mentioned, he attributes this racial gap to the admission of African Americans (with lower grade point averages and LSAT scores) into schools for which they are not academically prepared. Problematically, though Sander acknowledges that a wide range of empirical evidence has suggested that LSAT scores are culturally biased, he dismisses the relevance of this bias because, he says, the racial gap in grades and bar-passage rates reveals that LSAT scores do have predictive value. He goes on to say,

> One might respond that law school exams and bar exams simply perpetuate the unfairness of tests like the LSAT—they are all timed and undoubtedly generate acute performance anxiety. But almost all first-year students take legal writing classes, which are graded on the basis of lengthy memos prepared over many weeks, and which give students an opportunity to demonstrate skills entirely outside the range of typical law school exams. My analysis of first-semester grade data from several law schools shows a slightly larger black-white gap in legal writing classes than in overall first-semester grades. (Sander 2004, 424)

His conclusion that grades in legal writing are free from bias is baffling if for no other reason than that he fails to consider the possibility that the law, which is the subject of the legal writing assignments, may contain racialized assumptions that place students of color at odds with the writing assignment topics (not to mention the potential bias in grading by legal writing instructors as a result of different legal interpretations or cultural assumptions about writing styles). However, his more critical mistake is his passive acceptance of *all* of these outcomes as the complete measures of law student success or "merit."

In Sander's work, as well as in the broader societal affirmative action rhetoric, scholars often identify the need to discuss how we define "merit," then proceed to restrict their analyses to the standard measures, like LSAT scores and grades. Accepting measures constructed and instituted by whites in white institutional spaces seems intuitively problematic. Beyond that, if we think of merit as the totality of skill sets that facilitate productivity in a particular endeavor, students of color are repeatedly and severely shortchanged by the limited definitions of merit that get passively accepted in these policy discussions. Sander's analysis fails completely to recognize the development of tacit knowledge with regard to negotiating white spaces and the emotional and invisible labor that students of color must expend to succeed in these spaces, as does the broader societal rhetoric concerning the racial gap in educational outcomes and affirmative action. Sander's analysis actually reveals not that African American students cannot succeed in elite law schools to the same extent as white students, but rather that there is a glaring shortcoming in our ability to define and identify merit and success within the elephant of societal and institutional systemic racism. This revelation presents scholars like Sander with a serious methodological problem. Obviously, comparing outcomes for substantively different processes is not methodologically sound.

In the elite law schools in which I conducted my research, students of color were regularly required to perform additional labor to negotiate white institutional space. They faced daily challenges to their presence in the schools, and they had to contest subtle and overt racist practices and discourses, publicly as well as privately, to protect their own mental health. Students of color must perform work that should not be expected of students, who are in educational institutions to learn, not to teach. White students are not required to perform any of this labor; every facet of the institution is designed to recognize white intellectual competence and the history (if only a selective history that ignores the violence of whiteness) of white success, privilege, and power. Clearly, students of color and white students engage in a very distinct process of legal education as a result of white institutional space, and because it is systemic, we have no way to measure how well students of color might do in law school if they were not required to perform this additional labor. Thus, drawing conclusions about outcome-based assessments of success or merit is clearly methodologically suspect. Any truly nuanced discussion about affirmative action or any policy designed to remedy racial inequality would have to reject assumptions inherent in the white frame concerning "merit" and take into consideration the additional labor of students of color in order to adequately compare the academic performance of students of color with that of white students.

As I mentioned above, Sander's argument about affirmative action, though it may contain some subtle differences, does not really add anything to the affirmative action debate. His final policy suggestion is that African American students (and presumably other students of color) would be better off attending lower-tier law schools so that they could achieve better grades; this, he says, would make them more competitive in the job market. His conclusion is as disingenuous as it is paternalistic. As William Bowen and Derek Bok (1998) have pointed out with regard to undergraduate education, those students of color who attend elite institutions end up getting more prestigious and better-paying jobs than those who do not attend these schools. Similarly, statistics from all top-tier law schools (those in the top fifty) reveal that over 90 percent of students who graduate are employed within a year of graduating, and over 90 percent of students who graduate pass the bar examination. At very highly selective schools (top ten), the numbers are even higher, with above 97 percent employment and bar-passage rates. Clearly, all students who attend elite law schools benefit from the educational training of the schools with regard to these indicators.[3] Furthermore, it is widely recognized in the profession of law that law school prestige and status open many informal doors. For example, it is well known that many higher-level judges restrict their judicial clerkships for students who have graduated from top law schools.[4] Sander's assertion that students of color would be better off in lower-tier schools is less than persuasive when viewed in this context. More importantly, however, students of color are themselves savvy enough to make reasoned decisions about where they can be most successful in law school. They do not need researchers or policy makers to paternalistically remove options for them out of so-called concern for their well-being.

Researching Race: The Relevance of White Institutional Space

> I know that somewhere, sometime in urban America, when an ethnographer, social worker, or sexologist asked a wayward ghetto youth if he had any "illegitimate children," he came back with the classic retort: "Ask your mama."
>
> —Robin D. G. Kelley[5]

As much race-critical scholarship suggests, the manifestation of white racism morphs as communities of color challenge and resist white racial supremacy. When resistance to racial oppression results in progressive racial reforms, white people and institutions of white power retrench in order to stifle progressive change that threatens white privilege and power. The mechanisms by which white privilege and power are maintained then shift and change. As a result, the social science community must continually scrutinize the contemporary operation of racial reproduction, or else we run the risk of merely producing better frameworks for understanding our past, which will have little application in the present. This means that as scholars, we must examine both the structural attributes of white racial supremacy and the discursive mechanisms and frames that constrain the ways in which we analyze and respond to structural inequality. For mainstream social science research on race, this will require a shift in paradigm, away from looking down toward the social problems of poor communities of color toward an upward glance at power to problematize the reproduction of systemic and institutionalized white power.

The vast majority of mainstream social science research on race has focused on issues surrounding urban poverty and the connection between the reproduction of poverty in black communities and black culture.[6] This construction has frequently occurred as scholars have drawn upon Oscar Lewis's (1961) "culture of poverty" theory either explicitly or tacitly, as an explanation for racialized urban poverty.[7] The result has been the construction of a dominant discourse in the social sciences that pathologizes the black community, as well as other communities of color.[8] And as my research illustrates, within white institutional spaces like elite law schools, these assumptions of pathological culture in communities of color are deployed to discursively reinforce white intellectual superiority and to challenge the right of students of color (and faculty of color) to be in the schools. Thus, a rarely stated byproduct of the social science focus on poor communities of color is the way it legitimates white elite power structures. If poor urban black communities represent dysfunction, then white elite institutions represent the normative and functional.

Scholars like Ruth Frankenberg (1993) and David Roediger (1991) paved the way for a critique of normative notions that infer the functionality and cultural superiority of whiteness. These scholars, as well as others who have analyzed whiteness, suggest that the concept of whiteness exists only as an invisible and oppressive source of power and privilege.[9] In other words, whiteness operates as a "location of structural advantage," from which the racial "other" gets constructed (Frankenberg 1993, 1). Looking back at the concept of whiteness in the law discussed in chapter 3, we see that whiteness was, in fact, legally constructed through a process of identifying those who were outside the boundaries and were therefore not entitled to the privileges that attached to the status of this classification. Roediger has gone so far as to say that whiteness is *nothing more* than "the empty and therefore terrifying attempt to build an identity based upon what one is not and whom one can hold back" (1994, 13). The sociolegal process of constructing whiteness requires a reference to the degraded racial other, and, as a result, the attributes of whiteness become the tacit norm of functionality. Exposing this tacit norm, which gets perpetuated through the color-blind racist discourse, presents a challenge to the notion of pathological culture by suggesting that the taken-for-granted cultural markers used to measure the "black underclass" are in fact problematic.

If white middle- and upper-class culture operates solely as a privileged structural location and an identity that reifies itself by constructing a pathological "other," then the pathologies of the black underclass are merely a teleological lie, a construction built upon a construction that collapses upon itself. This is not to suggest that real material inequalities do not plague working-class and poor communities of color; rather, it suggests that the cause of the reproduction of these material relations is not the cultural pathology of communities of color but the pathological operation of whiteness upon those communities. It is the oppressive power of white racism that functions to reproduce racial inequality, particularly in powerful social institutions like elite law schools. This calls into question both the so-called pathologies assumed of urban poor black communities, as well as the assumption that white middle- and upper-class norms are desirable.

Turing a critical eye upon white institutional spaces reveals the mechanisms by which white power and privilege are enforced and reproduced in the post–civil rights era. Understanding these mechanisms helps us analyze white institutional space and exposes the centrality of institutions like elite law schools in the process of racial reproduction. While I have discussed the particular political relevance of elite law schools, I also suggest that the conception of white space offered herein likely applies to most powerful U.S. institutions. The vast majority of studies of whiteness have not gone far enough in their critical analysis of the coercive, not to mention undemocratic, mechanisms by which white supremacy gets reproduced in American society, particularly in powerful institutional settings.[10] My hope is that this research will pave the way for a more critical examination of the way in which white institutional space operates to maintain white racial supremacy in a wide range of social institutions.

Getting Out of the Elephant

The question that remains is, if we are in the metaphorical elephant, how can we get out? In other words, given how totalizing white institutional space is and how connected it is to other racialized institutions of power (like the law), can anything be done to deconstruct white space, short of rejecting our entire system of law and government and conducting a new constitutional convention with real democratic participation?[11] This question is particularly important given the resistance we have seen on the part of U.S. courts to create any racial reforms that significantly alter the dynamics of racial hierarchy. Further, the answer must consider the historically demonstrated ability of whites to transform racial progress into stagnation.[12] In looking for the answer to this question, the most obvious place to begin is with the foundations of the theoretical framework that developed out of the white institutional space of law schools—critical race theory.

A central problem for the project of deconstructing white institutional space is the fact that rejecting a white frame will put law schools in conflict with the very curriculum they are intended to teach. The tenets of color-blind racism are embedded within the law taught to students in law school. As I discussed in chapter 1, the interaction between these two societal institutions, law and education, makes deconstructing white space in law schools particularly challenging. However, steps can be taken short of a complete rejection of the American legal system.[13] Looking to the body of critical race theory and its conscious focus upon the subject and the standpoint of social actors, we can glean that an essential place to begin must be a rejection of the notion of impartiality and objectivity in the law and in legal education. It is worth repeating here the quote of scientist Stephen Jay Gould presented in chapter 2 as it provides a most thoughtful and developed conception of scientific objectivity:

Impartiality (even if desirable) is unattainable by human beings with inevitable backgrounds, needs, beliefs, and desires. It is dangerous for a scholar even to imagine that he might attain complete neutrality, for then one stops being vigilant about personal preferences and their influences—and then one truly falls victim to the dictates of prejudice. Objectivity must be operationally defined as fair treatment of data, not absence of preference. Moreover, one needs to understand and acknowledge inevitable preferences in order to know their influence— so that fair treatment of data and arguments can be attained. (1996, 36)

If we are to challenge white space, while teaching a legal framework that is within the white frame, we must begin to be vigilant about exposing the power relations that the law facilitates. Law school education does not have to indoctrinate students into a way of thinking patterned after the reasoning of elite white men, most of whom were writing during a historical moment characterized by brutal racism. Instead, legal education could shift its focus to teaching from a critical standpoint. Thinking like a lawyer should mean being able to assess whose interests particular legal doctrines serve and how the power dynamics in our legal system fit within our national ideals of freedom, individuality, and democracy.

To change the focus of legal education, not only would we have to reject traditional notions of objectivity in favor of a more nuanced conception of the term, but we would have to institute changes in curricular focus. To do this effectively, we would need to ensure that critical race theory became a required component of legal education—not to mention other forms of critical legal scholarship. During my research, many students and faculty members suggested that they would like to see a required course component, for example a law and inequality course, that examined the way in which the law operates with structures of inequality in the United States. However, many students, faculty, and administrators bristled at this suggestion. Most noted that requiring a course like this would exacerbate current racial tensions because white students would resent taking the class. Again, a tacit focus upon white reaction (particularly, in this context, the reaction of white elite men) echoes the sentiments of Richard Sander above, when he notes that people of color do not have much social and political capital with which to bargain for the right to a nonracist legal education. I note that we must reject this framing if we are to deconstruct white space. However, this reaction does highlight a major problem associated with merely adding a course while failing to change the entire curriculum. Thus, the addition of critical race, class, and gender perspectives would have to be integrated into the full law school curriculum.

Nothing short of this major refocusing of the law school curriculum could disembed legal education from a white frame, and even this could not eliminate the white frame that characterizes the U.S. legal framework. Yet, this would be only one necessary change; truly deconstructing white space would require many more small- and large-scale changes to the institution. As critical race theory developed, one of the central aspects of the theoretical framework became the prioritization of the voices of people of color. In order to resist the constraints placed upon the legal discourse surrounding racial inequality by the white frame, legal scholars of color suggested that a new frame must be developed and that it *must* be developed by people of color. The result has been a prolific and enlightening new frame with which to critically analyze the law and sociolegal constructions of race and racial inequality (material and ideological). Taking a lesson from the successes of this body of theory, another important step in dismantling white institutional space will be to give priority to the voices of people of color in these spaces. This must occur in several ways. First, rather than allowing whites to define what constitutes racism in the space of the law school and in broader American society, we must look to the experiences and narratives of students and faculty of color. This would mean allowing people of color to describe and interpret their own life experiences, as they have done in this research, without a rush to a white frame that dismisses or reinterprets their stories in a way that naturalizes and minimizes racism. By doing this, we will secure a more genuine understanding of how racism is manifested in white institutional space.

Once we have a better and more nuanced understanding of how racism impacts the space, we must again look to those who have experienced racism to construct potential changes to the space to reduce or eliminate the manifestation of racism. In other words, white people must reject the common paternalistic notion that they should be in charge of creating solutions to racism. *As white people are not the target of racism in white institutional spaces, they are the least likely group of people in law schools to understand how racism works.* Thus, they are not in the best position to construct effective solutions to racism. Just as critical race scholarship centered the experiences and perspectives of people of color in analysis of the racist operation of U.S. law, people of color must lead the project to identify and eliminate racism in white institutional spaces. This means that once we have centered the experiences of people of color, we must ensure that people of color are in the central positions of institutional power in the law schools.

Deconstructing white space will require a conscious rejection of the notion of the principle of color blindness. In a society characterized by systemic racism, color blindness is neither desirable, nor effective for creating racial change. The "principle" of color blindness effectively denies people of color the full recognition of their humanity in that it ignores the real relevance of race in their life experience (see Feagin, Vera and Imani 1997). Resisting white racism is impossible within a frame that tends to reproduce the racist relations that already exist as a result of hundreds of years of racist color consciousness. To deconstruct white space, we must deliberately consider race, and in doing so, we must center the perspectives of people of color in locations of authority and power within white institutions. This does not mean putting one or two people of color in symbolic positions in which they have relatively little institutional power; rather, people of color must be placed into a critical mass of powerful institutional positions so that they can take action without having to negotiate with white people. Whites will have to relinquish some of their coercively attained power so that people of color will no longer have to be concerned about the expenditure of social and political capital in the process of creating institutional responses to racism.

Creating institutional change in elite law schools or other white institutional spaces in the context of a society marked by systemic racism will require a constant interrogation of the racial demographics of power in these spaces, as well as of the frames and underlying normative assumptions that constrain this interrogation. It will require serious curricular change—the conscious and deliberate centering and empowering of the voices of students, faculty, and administrators of color. As Joe Feagin has suggested, "White Americans have not been the main carriers of robust ideals of freedom and justice. For centuries the strongest commitment to fully implementing the ideals of freedom, justice, and equality has been that of black Americans" (2000, 246).

At stake for elite law schools in the deconstruction of white institutional space is not merely the racial diversification of the legal profession but the future of our commitment to American ideals that have long been purely rhetoric—our national commitment to the values of democracy, individual liberties, freedom, and justice.

Notes

1. This is also captured in Joe Feagin's quotation, cited in chapter 1, in which he notes that "race relations—or more accurately, racist relations—are not *in*, but rather *of*, this society" (*Racist America: Roots, Current Realities and Future Reparations* [New York: Routledge, 2000], 17, emphasis added).

2. Katherine S. Mangan, "Affirmative Action Hurts Black Law Students, Study Finds," Associated Press, October 2004.

3. See the Law School Admission Council website (www.lsac.org) for statistics on law school employment placement.

4. It is well known that there are judges who will not even interview students who did not go to top-tier schools for clerkships on their courts. Also, see the discussion concerning law-faculty hiring in Derrick Bell, *Confronting Authority: Reflections of an Ardent Protestor* (New York: Basic Books, 1996).

5. Robin D. G. Kelley, *Yo' Mama's DisFunktional: Fighting the Culture Wars in Urban America* (Boston: Beacon Press, 1997), 3.

6. For a more in-depth discussion of this phenomenon, see Carole Marks, "The Urban Underclass," *Annual Review of Sociology* 17 (1991): 445–66; Robin D. G. Kelley, *Yo' Mama's DisFunktional: Fighting the Culture Wars in Urban America* (Boston: Beacon Press, 1997); Eduardo Bonilla-Silva, *Racism without Racists: Color-Blind Racism and the Persistence of Racial Inequality in the United States* (Lanham, MD: Rowman & Littlefield, 2003).

7. Bonilla-Silva, in *Racism without Racists: Color-Blind Racism and the Persistence of Racial Inequality in the United States* (Lanham, MD: Rowman & Littlefield, 2003), has pointed out that Lewis's culture-of-poverty argument was fundamentally racialized and, thus, easily extrapolated to the experience of minorities in the United States because Lewis constructed the concept by analyzing poverty in Mexico and Puerto Rico (51).

8. See, for example, the works of Dinesh D'Souza, *The End of Racism: Principles for a Multicultural Society* (New York: The Free Press, 1995); William Julius Wilson, *The Truly Disadvantaged: The Inner City, the Underclass, and Public Policy* (Chicago: University of Chicago Press, 1987); William Julius Wilson, *When Work Disappears: The World of the New Urban Poor* (New York: Knopf: Distributed by Random House, 1996); and Richard Hernstein and Charles Murray, *The Bell Curve: Intelligence and Class Structure in the United States* (New York: Free Press, 1994).

9. See also Toni Morrison, *Playing in the Dark: Whiteness in the Literary Imagination* (Cambridge, MA: Harvard University Press, 1992).

10. See Margaret L. Andersen, "Whitewashing Race: A Critical Perspective on Whiteness," in *White Out: The Continuing Significance of Racism*, ed. Ashley Doane and Eduardo Bonilla-Silva (New York: Routledge, 2003), for a critique of whiteness studies.

11. See Joe Feagin's conclusion in *Racist America: Roots, Current Realities and Future Reparations* (New York: Routledge, 2000) for a discussion of the possibility of creating a new, more democratic constitutional convention to form a representative legal structure.

12. See Derrick Bell, *Silent Covenants: Brown v. Board of Education and the Unfulfilled Hopes for Racial Reform* (New York: Oxford University Press, 2004); Derrick Bell, *Faces at the Bottom of the Well: The Permanence of Racism* (New York: Basic Books, 1992); Derrick Bell, *And We Are Not Saved: The Elusive Quest for Racial Justice* (New York: Basic Books, 1987); Joe R. Feagin, *Systemic Racism* (New York: Routledge, 2006); Joe R. Feagin, *Racist America: Roots, Current Realities and Future Reparations* (New York: Routledge, 2000).

13. I make these suggestions for pragmatic reasons; however, I believe that this nation will never live up to the ideals of democracy and freedom asserted in the Declaration of Independence unless we completely restructure the American legal system. But this is a topic of too much breadth to cover herein.

Appendix

Research Method

I CONDUCTED ETHNOGRAPHIC RESEARCH in two elite American law schools, which I call Presidential University School of Law and Midstate Law School. I defined "elite" law schools as those law schools that fall within the "top twenty" in the *U.S. News and World Report's* ranking system. I selected two top-twenty law schools with different racial demographics; both of these law schools were located in urban midwestern areas. The first, Midstate, is a public institution with a combined minority student population of just 16 percent, which is a low percentage of minority students relative to other top law schools. The breakdown of minority students at Midstate was approximately 2 percent African American, 2 percent American Indian, 10 percent Asian American, and 2 percent Chicano and Latino. The second school I selected, Presidential, was a private institution with a minority population of just over 30 percent, one of the highest percentages of students of color among top law schools. The racial breakdown at Presidential was approximately 8 percent African American, 1 percent American Indian, 14 percent Asian American, and 8 percent Chicano and Latino. In addition to having a relatively high percentage of minority students, Presidential was the only top law school in the country to have created an administrative position for a director of minority affairs. This position was added when the law school received a grant for diversity funding, and students requested that the grant be used to fund this permanent administrative position. The construction of this position indicated some level of institutional change based upon a perceived need to address issues of race in the law school, making this a unique and interesting second site.

I spent over fifteen weeks at each school over the course of two academic years, conducting observations of public spaces, law school events, meetings of student organizations, and classes. I observed first-year required classes at both law schools, including contracts, civil procedure, torts, and, for a more extended period, criminal law and constitutional law. I also observed jurisprudence (legal theory) classes at Midstate, as well as a critical race theory course. At Presidential, I observed a Fourteenth Amendment course, an elective that examined the jurisprudence of the Fourteenth Amendment in detail.

I was invited to attend various student organization meetings at both schools, including meetings of the Black Law Students Association, the Native American Law Students Association, the Women's Law Students Association, and the National Lawyers Guild. At Midstate, several student-of-color organizations got together to arrange a meeting with the dean concerning the recruitment of underrepresented minority students, and they invited me to sit in on the meeting. At Presidential, I was invited by administrators to sit in on several staff meetings in which issues of race were a topic of discussion. I also observed the new-student orientation at Presidential, including a session in which the school conducted diversity training and teambuilding workshops.

I formally interviewed thirty students at Midstate, including eighteen students of color. At Presidential, I interviewed twenty-three students, including fifteen students of color. Interviews with students lasted between one and three hours. The entire student bodies at both schools were notified of my research by two separate e-mails at the beginning and the middle of my years at each school. E-mail was an effective means of communication at the law schools because the administration regularly sent students information via e-mail, and the students knew that they were responsible for reading their e-mail for important announcements. I also sent e-mails to all of the law student organizations at both schools asking that someone from each organization volunteer to be interviewed. I did this to get at the full range of political and ideological viewpoints in the law schools. As a result, I interviewed members of a variety of very diverse student populations, including students from the student-of-color organizations like the Black Law Students Association and the American Indian Law Students Association, but also the National Lawyers Guild and the Federalist Society. I also sent e-mails to the law school journals and law reviews, so I interviewed several students who were on the law school journals. I spoke informally with many more students than the fifty-three that I formally interviewed over the course of my research at both schools. For example, on one of my last days at Presidential, I spent nearly six hours in the atrium talking with students who had experiences that they wanted to discuss with me before I left. These conversations are recorded in my field notes, which filled many notebooks and resulted in over one hundred pages of typed notes. In addition to the student interviews, I formally interviewed nine faculty members and two administrators at Midstate and ten faculty members and four administrators at Presidential.

In addition to the participant observation I did at both law schools, in the spring of 2002, when the Supreme Court was scheduled to hear the Michigan affirmative action cases, the Coalition to Defend Affirmative Action By Any Means Necessary (BAMN) organized a March on Washington on the day of the oral arguments, which I attended. Several students from Midstate organized a group of students to participate in the march, and I went along and conducted participant observation at several events leading up to the march and at the march. I attended several debates organized by law students at Georgetown School of Law and Howard Law School.[1] I also went to the Supreme Court the night before the march and talked with people who were already there. There was a group of people waiting in line to get in to hear the oral arguments who had been there for several nights, as well as a group of students from Howard University who had organized a vigil and who marched around the Supreme Court building for the entire night. Finally, I participated in the march and talked with several of the key organizers from BAMN.

The overall research design was based upon the concept of triangulation (see Denzin and Lincoln 2003, Lewis 2003). Thus, I utilized a variety of forms of empirical investigation, including observation, formal interviews, and informal discussions with a diverse range of social actors in the institutions in order to bolster validity. The sample of students of color who were interviewed, formally and informally, was disproportionate to their demographics in the schools. This was done intentionally to ensure that the voices of students of color were adequately represented in the data. I also paid specific attention to having a wide variety of political and ideological perspectives represented in my interviews with white students and students of color.

I use pseudonyms for the law schools, as well as for individuals I came into contact with in the law schools. I did inform both law schools that there would be enough identifying information that people familiar with elite law schools would be able to identify the schools. As a result of this potential for identification, and because the patterns I discuss herein were found at both law schools, I refrain from identifying which law school individual interview participants attended. I do this specifically to protect my research participants, particularly students of color who are easily identifiable because of their small numbers in the schools.

Note

1. The debate at Georgetown School of Law is referred to in the opening of the introduction.

Bibliography

Acker, Joan. 1990. "Hierarchies, Jobs, Bodies: A Theory of Gendered Organizations." *Gender & Society* 4, no. 2 (June): 139–58.

"Administration Responds to BLSA Demands as Students Stage Protest," *Harvard Law Record*, April 18, 2002.

Allen, Theodore W. 1997a. *Racial Oppression and Social Control*, vol. 1 of *The Invention of the White Race*. London: Verso.

———. 1997b. *The Origin of Racial Oppression in Anglo-America*, vol. 2 of *The Invention of the White Race*. London: Verso.

Allen, Walter R. and Daniel Solorzano. 2001. "Affirmative Action, Educational Equity, and Campus Racial Climate. A Case Study of the University of Michigan Law School," *Berkeley La Raza Law Journal* 12:237–363.

Andersen, Margaret L. 2003. "Whitewashing Race: A Critical Perspective on Whiteness." In *White Out: The Continuing Significance of Racism*, ed. Ashley Doane and Eduardo Bonilla-Silva: 21–34. New York: Routledge.

Apple, Michael. 1982. *Cultural and Economic Reproduction in Education*. London: Routledge & Kegan Paul.

———. 1986. *Teachers and Texts: A Political Economy of Class and Gender Relations in Education*. New York: Routledge.

———. 1990. *Ideology and Curriculum*. 2nd ed. New York: Routledge.

Banks, Taunya Lovell. 1988. "Gender Bias in the Classroom." *Journal of Legal Education* 38:137–46.

———. 1990. "Gender Bias in the Classroom." *Southern Illinois Law Journal* 14:527–537.

Becker, Howard S., Blanche Geer, Everett C. Hughes, and Anselm L. Strauss. 1961. *Boys in White: Student Culture in Medical School*. New Brunswick, NJ: Transaction Publishers.

Bell, Derrick. 1987. *And We Are Not Saved: The Elusive Quest for Racial Justice*. New York: Basic Books.

———. 1992. *Faces at the Bottom of the Well: The Permanence of Racism*. New York: Basic Books.

———. 1996. *Confronting Authority: Reflections of an Ardent Protestor*. New York: Basic Books.

———. 2000. *Race, Racism and American Law*. 4th ed. New York: Aspen Press.

———. 2004. *Silent Covenants: Brown v. Board of Education and the Unfulfilled Hopes for Racial Reform*. New York: Oxford University Press.

Bellah, Robert, Richard Madsen, William Sullivan, Ann Swidler, and Steven Tipton. 1985. *Habits of the Heart: Individualism and Commitment in American Life*. New York: Harper & Row.

Blauner, Robert. 1972. *Racial Oppression in America*. New York: Harper & Row.

Bobo, Lawrence, and James R. Kluegel. 1993. "Dimensions of Whites' Beliefs about the Black-White Socioeconomic Gap." In *Prejudice, Politics, and the American Dilemma*, ed. Paul M. Sniderman, Philip E. Tetlock, and Edward G. Carmines, 127–47. Stanford, CA: Stanford University Press.

Bobo, Lawrence, James R. Kluegel, and Ryan Smith. 1997. "Laissez-Faire Racism: The Crystallization of a Kinder, Gentler Antiblack Ideology." In *Racial Attitudes in the 1990s: Continuity and Change*, ed. Steven A. Tuch and Jack K. Martin, 15–41. Westport, CT: Praeger.

Bonilla-Silva, Eduardo. 1997. "Rethinking Racism: Toward a Structural Interpretation." *American Sociological Review* 62:465–80.

———. 2001. *White Supremacy and Racism in the Post–Civil Rights Era*. Boulder, CO: Lynne Rienner.

———. 2003. *Racism without Racists: Color-Blind Racism and the Persistence of Racial Inequality in the United States*. Lanham, MD: Rowman & Littlefield.

Bonilla-Silva, Eduardo and Tyrone Forman. 2000. "'I'm Not a Racist But. . .' Mapping White College Students' Racial Ideology in the USA," *Discourse & Society* 11:50–85.

Bourdieu, Pierre. 1990. *The Logic of Practice*. Stanford, CA: Stanford University Press.

Bourdieu, Pierre, and Jean-Claude Passeron. 1990. *Reproduction in Education, Society and Culture*. London: Sage.

Bowen, William G., and Derek Bok. 1998. *The Shape of the River: Long-Term Consequences of Considering Race in College and University Admissions*. Princeton, NJ: Princeton University Press.

Branch, Taylor. 1988. *Parting the Waters: America in the King Years, 1954–1963*. New York: Simon and Schuster.

Brodkin, Karen. 1998. *How Jews Became White Folks and What That Says about Race in America*. Piscatanay, N.J.: Rutgers University Press.

Brooks, Roy L. 2002. *Structures of Judicial Decision Making from Legal Formalism to Critical Theory*. Durham, NC: California Academic Press.

Brown, Michael K., Martin Carnoy, Elliott Currie, Troy Duster, David B. Oppenheimer, Marjorie M. Shultz, and David Wellman. 2003. *Whitewashing Race: The Myth of a Color-Blind Society*. Berkeley: University of California Press.

Buckner, Carole J. 2004. "Realizing Grutter v. Bollinger's 'Compelling Educational Benefits of Diversity'—Transforming Aspirationall Rhetoric into Experience," *U.C. Davis Law Review* 38:1209–58.

Carmichael, Stokely (Kwame Ture), and Charles V. Hamilton. 1977. *Black Power: The Politics of Liberation in America*. New York: Random House.

Carmines, Edward G., and W. Richard Merriman Jr. 1993. "The Changing American Dilemma: Liberal Values and Racial Policies." In *Prejudice, Politics, and the American Dilemma*, ed. Paul M. Sniderman, Philip E. Tetlock, and Edward G. Carmines, 237–55. Stanford, CA: Stanford University Press.

Chase, Susan. 1995. *Ambiguous Empowerment*. Amherst: University of Massachusetts Press.

Chavez, Linda. 1996. "Promoting Racial Harmony." In *The Affirmative Action Debate*, ed. George E. Curry. Reading, MA: Addison-Wesley Books.

Clinton, Robert N., Nell Jessup Newton, and Monroe E. Price. 1991. *American Indian Law: Cases and Materials*. 3rd ed. Charlottesville, VA: The Michie Company Law Publishers.

Coleman, James S. 1986. "Social Theory, Social Research, and a Theory of Action." *American Journal of Sociology* 91, no. 6:1301–1335.

Collins, Patricia Hill. 2000. *Black Feminist Thought: Knowledge, Consciousness, and the Politics of Empowerment, Second Edition*. New York: Routledge.

"Comments Concerning Race Divide Harvard Law School," *New York Times*, April 20, 2002.

Costello, Carrie Yang. 2001. "The (Re)production of Social Stratification in Professional School Settings." In *The Hidden Curriculum in Higher Education*, ed. Eric Margolis, 43–60. New York: Routledge.

———. 2005. *Professional Identity Crisis: Race, Class, Gender, and Success at Professional Schools*. Nashville, TN: Vanderbilt University Press.

Cox, Oliver. 1948. *Caste, Class, and Race*. New York: Modern Reader Paperbacks.

Crenshaw, Kimberle Williams. 1988. "Race, Reform, and Retrenchment: Transformation and Legitimation in Antidiscrimination Law." *Harvard Law Review* 101: 1331–1383.

———. 1994. "Forward: Toward a Race-Conscious Pedagogy in Legal Education." *National Black Law Journal* 1:1–14.

Crenshaw, Kimberle, Neil Gotanda, Gary Peller, and Kendall Thomas, eds. 1995. *Critical Race Theory: The Key Writings That Formed the Movement*. New York: The New Press.

Davis, Adrienne D. 1996. "Identity Notes Part One: Playing in the Light." *American University Law Review* 45:695–720.

Delgado, Richard. 1995. *Critical Race Theory: The Cutting Edge*. Philadelphia: Temple University Press.

———. 2001. *Critical Race Theory: An Introduction*. New York: New York University Press.

Denzin, Norman and Yvonna Lincoln, ed. 2003. *Collecting and Interpreting Qualitative Materials*. Thousand Oaks, CA: Sage.

De Tocqueville, Alexis. 1988 (1876). *Democracy in America.* Herdfortshire, England: Wadsworth Edition Limited.

D'Souza, Dinesh. 1995. *The End of Racism: Principles for a Multicultural Society.* New York: The Free Press.

Dowd, Nancy E. 2003. "Diversity Matters: Race, Gender, and Ethnicity in Legal Education," *Florida Journal of Law and Public Policy* 15:877–908.

DuBois, W. E. B. 1903. *The Souls of Black Folk.* New York: A.C. McClug & Company.

Durkheim, Emile. 1956 (1922). *Education and Sociology.* Glencoe, IL: The Free Press.

Epstein, Cynthia Fuchs. 1999. "Knowledge for What?" *Journal of Legal Education* 49, no.1:41–49.

Erlanger, Howard S., and Douglas A. Klegon. 1978. "Socialization Effects of Professional School: The Law School Experience and Student Orientations to Public Interest Concerns." *Law and Society Review* 13:11–35.

Feagin, Joe R. 2000. *Racist America: Roots, Current Realities and Future Reparations.* New York: Routledge.

———. 2006. *Systemic Racism.* New York: Routledge.

Feagin, Joe R., and Karyn D. McKinny. 2003. *The Many Costs of Racism.* New York: Routledge.

Feagin, Joe R., and Melvin Sikes. 1994. *Living with Racism: The Black Middle Class Experience.* Boston: Beacon Press.

Feagin, Joe R., and Hernan Vera. 1995. *White Racism: The Basics.* New York: Routledge.

Feagin, Joe, Hernan Vera, and Nikitah Imani. 1997. *The Agony of Education.* New York: Routledge.

Flagg, Barbara J. 1993. "'Was Blind but Now I See': White Race Consciousness and the Requirement of Discriminatory Intent." *Michigan Law Review* 91:953–1017.

Foucault, Michel. 1977. *Discipline and Punish: The Birth of the Prison,* trans. Alan Sheridan. New York: Vintage Books.

Frankenberg, Ruth. 1993. *White Women, Race Matters: The Social Construction of Whiteness.* Minneapolis: University of Minnesota Press.

Franklin, John Hope. 1967. *From Slavery to Freedom.* 3rd ed. New York: Alfred A. Knopf, Inc.

Glenn, Evalyn Nakano. 2002. *Unequal Freedom: How Race and Gender Shaped American Citizenship and Labor.* Cambridge, MA: Harvard University Press.

Goodrich, Peter, and Linda G. Mills. 2001. "The Law of White Spaces: Race, Culture, and Legal Education." *Journal of Legal Education* 51, no.1:15–38.

Gould, Stephen Jay. 1996. *The Mismeasure of Man, Revised and Expanded.* New York: W. W. Norton & Company.

Granfield, Robert. 1986. "Legal Education as Corporate Ideology: Student Adjustment to the Law School Experience." *Sociological Forum* 1:514–523.

———. 1991. "Making It by Faking It: Working-Class Students in an Elite Academic Environment." *Journal of Contemporary Ethnography* 20, no. 3:331–51.

———. 1992. *Making Elite Lawyers: Visions of Law at Harvard and Beyond.* New York: Routledge.

Granfield, Robert, and Thomas Koenig. 1992. "Learning Collective Eminence: Harvard Law School and the Social Production of Elite Lawyers." *The Sociological Quarterly* 33, no. 4:503.

Greene, Linda S. 1997. "Tokens, Role Models, and Pedagogical Politics: Lamentations of an African American Female Law Professor." In *Critical Race Feminism*, ed. Adrien Katherine Wing, 88–95. New York: New York University Press.

Gross, Ariela. 1998. "Litigating Whiteness: Trials of Racial Determination in the Nineteenth-Century South." *Yale Law Journal* 108:109–185.

Guinier, Lani, Michelle Fine, and Jane Balin. 1997. *Becoming Gentlemen: Women, Law School, and Institutional Change*. Boston: Beacon Press.

Harding, Sandra. 1991. *Whose Science? Whose Knowledge? Thinking from Women's Lives*. Ithaca, NY: Cornell University Press.

———, ed. 1993. *The Racial Economy of Science: Toward a Democratic Future*. Bloomington: Indiana University Press.

Harris, Cheryl. 1993. "Whiteness as Property." *Harvard Law Review* 106:1709–89.

Hernstein, Richard and Charles Murray. 1994. *The Bell Curve: Intelligence and Class Structure in the United States*. New York: Free Press.

Herring, Cedric. 2002. "Bleaching Out the Colorline?: The Skin Color Continuum and The Tripartite Model of Race." *Race & Society* 5:17–31.

Higginbotham, A. Leon, Jr., and Barbara Kopytoff. 1989. "Racial Purity and Interracial Sex in the Law of Colonial and Antebellum Virginia." *Georgetown Law Journal* 77:1967–2028.

Higginbotham, Elizabeth. 2001. *Too Much to Ask: Black Women in the Era of Integration*. Chapel Hill: University of North Carolina Press.

Hochschild, Arlie. 2003. *The Managed Heart: The Commercialization of Human Feeling, Twentieth Anniversary Edition*. Berkeley: University of California Press (first published in 1983).

hooks, bell. 1987. *Ain't I a Woman: Black Women and Feminism*. Boston: South End Press.

———. 1992. *Black Looks: Race and Representation*. Boston: South End Press.

———. 1995. *killing rage: Ending Racism*. New York: Henry Holt and Company.

Ignatiev, Noel. 1995. *How the Irish Became White*. New York: Routledge.

Jackman, Mary. 1996. "Individualism, Self Interest, and White Racism." *Social Science Quarterly* 77:760–767.

Jacobson, Matthew Frye. 1998. *Whiteness of a Different Color: European Immigrants and the Alchemy of Race*. Cambridge, MA: Harvard University Press.

Jargowsky, Paul A. 1997. *Poverty and Place: Ghettos, Barrios, and the American City*. New York: Russell Sage Foundation.

Jhally, Sut, and Justin Lewis. 1992. *Enlightened Racism: The Cosby Show, Audiences, and the Myth of the American Dream*. Boulder, CO: Westview.

Katznelson, Ira. 2005. *When Affirmative Action was White: An Untold History of Racial Inequality in Twentieth-Century America*. New York: W. W. Norton & Company.

Kelley, Robin D. G. 1997. *Yo' Mama's DisFunktional: Fighting the Culture Wars in Urban America*. Boston: Beacon Press.

Kennedy, Duncan. 1983. *Legal Education and the Reproduction of Hierarchy: A Polemic against the System*. Cambridge, MA: AFAR Press.

Kluger, Richard. 2004. *Simple Justice: The History of Brown v. Board of Education and Black America's Struggle for Equality*. New York: Vintage Books.

Knowles, Louis L., and Kenneth Prewitt. 1969. *Institutional Racism in America*. Englewood Cliffs, NJ: Prentice Hall.

Krauskopf, Joan M. 1994. "Touching the Elephant: Perceptions of Gender Issues in Nine Law Schools." *Journal of Legal Education* 44:311–340.

Krieger, Lawrence S. 2002. "Institutional Denial about the Dark Side of Law School and Fresh Empirical Guidance for Constructively Breaking the Silence." *Journal of Legal Education* 52, nos. 1–2:112–129.

"Law Schools Boycotted Over Lack of Minority Teachers," *New York Times*, April 6, 1990.

"Law Students, Faculty Protest Racial Incidents," *Harvard Crimson*, April 16, 2002.

Lawrence, Charles R., III. 1995. "The Word and the River: Pedagogy as Scholarship as Struggle." In *Critical Race Theory: The Key Writings That Formed the Movement*, ed. Kimberle Crenshaw, Neil Gotanda, Gary Peller, and Kendall Thomas: 235–56. New York: The New York Press.

Lewis, Amanda E. 2003. *Race in the Schoolyard: Negotiating the Color Line in Classrooms and Communities.* New Brunswick, NJ: Rutgers University Press.

Lipsitz, George. 1998. *The Possessive Investment in Whiteness.* Philadelphia: Temple University Press.

Lopez, Ian Haney. 1994. "The Social Construction of Race: Some Observations on Illusion, Fabrication, and Choice." *Harvard Civil Rights–Civil Liberties Law Review* 29: 1–62.

———. 1996. *White by Law: The Legal Construction of Race.* New York: New York University Press.

Lorde, Audre. 1984. *Sister Outsider.* Berkeley: The Crossing Press.

Mangan, Katherine S. 2004. "Affirmative Action Hurts Black Law Students, Study Finds." Associated Press, November 11, 2004.

Margolis, Eric, ed. 2001. *The Hidden Curriculum in Higher Education.* New York: Routledge.

Margolis, Eric, Michael Soldatenko, Sandra Acker, and Marina Gair. 2001. "Peekaboo: Hiding and Outing the Curriculum." In *The Hidden Curriculum in Higher Education*, ed. Eric Margolis, 1–19. New York: Routledge.

Marks, Carole. 1991. "The Urban Underclass." *Annual Review of Sociology* 17:445–66.

Massey, Douglas S., and Nancy A. Denton. 1993. *American Apartheid: Segregation and the Making of the Underclass.* Cambridge, MA: Harvard University Press.

McClintock, Jessica. 1995. Imperial Leather: Race, Gender and Sexuality in the Colonial Context. New York: Routledge.

Mertz, Elizabeth, Wamucii Njogu, and Susan Gooding. 1998. "What Difference Does Difference Make? The Challenge for Legal Education." *Journal of Legal Education* 48, no.1:1–87.

Miles, Robert. 1989. *Racism.* London: Routledge.

———. 1993. *Racism after Race Relations.* London: Routledge.

Miller, Mark C. 1995. *The High Priests of American Politics.* Knoxville: University of Tennessee Press.

Mills, Charles. 1997. *The Racial Contract.* Ithaca, NY: Cornell University Press.

Morris, Aldon. 1999. "A Retrospective on the Civil Rights Movement: Political and Intellectual Landmarks." *Annual Review of Sociology* 25:517–39.

Morrison, Toni. 1992. *Playing in the Dark: Whiteness in the Literary Imagination.* Cambridge, MA: Harvard University Press.

Mutua, Athena D. 1999. "Shifting Bottoms and Rotating Centers: Reflections on LatCrit III and the Black/White Paradigm." *University of Miami Law Review* 53: 1177–1217.

"*New York Times*' Comments Concerning Race Divide Harvard Law School," April 20, 2002.

"Old Rights Campaigner Leads a Harvard Battle," *New York Times*, May 21, 1990.

Omi, Michael, and Howard Winant. 1994. *Racial Formation in the United States from the 1960s to the 1990s*. New York: Routledge.

Orfield, Gary, and Susan Eaton. 1996. *Dismantling Desegregation: The Quiet Reversal of Brown v. Board of Education*. New York: The New Press.

Perea, Juan F. 1997. "The Black/White Binary Paradigm of Race: The 'Normal Science' of American Racial Thought." *California Law Review* 85:1213–58.

Pierce, Jennifer. 1995. *Gender Trials: Emotional Lives in Contemporary Law Firms*. Berkeley: University of California Press.

Pierce, Jennifer. 2003. "Racing for Innocence: Whiteness, Corporate Culture, and the Backlash against Affirmative Action." *Qualitative Sociology* 26, no. 1:53–70.

Picca, Leslie Houts and Joe R. Feagin. 2007. *Two-Faced Racism: Whites in the Backstage and Frontstage*. New York: Routledge.

powell, john. 1999. "Race and Space." *Poverty and Race* 8:3–4.

———. 2000. "Whites Will Be Whites: The Failure to Interrogate Racial Privilege," *University of San Fransisco Law* Review 34:419–464.

———. 1994. *Towards the Abolition of Whiteness*. London: Verso.

———. 1998. *Black on White: Black Writers on What It Means to Be White*. New York: Schocken Books.

———. 2002. *Colored White: Transcending the Racial Past*. Berkeley: University of California Press.

Sander, Richard H. 2004. "A Systematic Analysis of Affirmative Action in American Law Schools." *Stanford Law Review* 57:367–483.

Sarat, Austin, and William L. F. Felstiner. 1989. "Lawyers and Legal Consciousness: Law Talk in the Divorce Lawyer's Office." *Yale Law Review* 98:1663–1688.

Schleef, Debra. 2001. "Thinking like a Lawyer: Gender Differences in the Production of Professional Knowledge." *Gender Issues* (Spring): 69–86.

Seligman, J. 1978. *The High Citadel: The Influence of Harvard Law School*. Boston: Houghton Mifflin Co.

Steele, Shelby. 1994. "A Negative Vote on Affirmative Action." In *Debating Affirmative Action, Race, Gender, Ethnicity, and the Politics of Inclusion*, ed. Nicolaus Mills: 132–41. New York: Delta.

Stevens, Robert. 1983. *Law School: Legal Education in America from the 1850s to the 1980s*. Chapel Hill: University of North Carolina Press.

Stone, Geoffrey R., Louis M. Seidman, Cass R. Sunstein, and Mark Tushnet. 1996. *Constitutional Law*. 3rd ed. Boston: Little, Brown and Company.

Takaki, Ronald. 1993. *A Different Mirror*. Boston: Little, Brown, and Company.

Tatum, Beverly. 1997. *"Why Are All the Black Kids Sitting Together in the Cafeteria?" And Other Conversations about Race*. New York: Basic Books.

Terdimann. 1987. "Editor's Translation: Pierre Bourdieu and the Force of Law." *Hastings Law Review* 38:805–853.

Thernstrom, Stephan, and Abigail Thernstrom. 1997. *America in Black and White: One Nation Indivisible.* New York: Simon & Schuster.

Thompson-Miller, Ruth and Joe Feagin. 2007. "The Oppression of Legal Segregation:Making a Case for Reparations for the Living?" Paper presentation, American Sociological Association Annual Conference.

Turow, Scott. 1977. *One L.* New York: Warner Books.

Urofsky, Melvin I. 1988. *A March of Liberty: A Constitutional History of the United States.* Vol. 1: To 1877. New York: McGraw Hill.

Valdes, Francisco, Jerome McCristal Culp, and Angela P. Harris, eds. 2002. *Crossroads, Directions, and a New Critical Race Theory.* Philadelphia: Temple University Press.

Wangerin, Paul T. 1986. "Skills Training in 'Legal Analysis': A Systematic Approach." *University of Miami Law Review* 40:409–85.

Weber, Max. 1925. *Max Weber on Law in Economy and Society,* trans. Edward Shils and Max Rheinstein. Cambridge, MA: Harvard University Press.

Wellman, David T. 1993. *Portraits of White Racism.* 2nd ed. Cambridge: Cambridge University Press.

White, James Boyd. 1987. "Lecture: Constructing a Constitution: 'Original Intention' in the Slave Cases." *Maryland Law Review* 47:239–270.

Wilkins, David E. 2007. *American Indian Politics and the American Political System.* Lanham, MD: Rowman & Littlefield.

Williams, Patricia. 1987. "Alchemical Notes: Reconstructing Ideals from Deconstructed Rights." *Harvard Civil Rights–Civil Liberties Law Review* 22:401–33.

———. 1991. *The Alchemy of Race and Rights.* Cambridge, MA: Harvard University Press.

Wilson, William Julius. 1987. *The Truly Disadvantaged: The Inner City, the Underclass, and Public Policy.* Chicago: University of Chicago Press.

———. 1996. *When Work Disappears: The World of the New Urban Poor.* New York: Knopf: Distributed by Random House.

Winant, Howard. 1997. *Racial Conditions: Politics, Theory, Comparisons.* Minneapolis: University of Minnesota Press.

———. 2001. *The World is a Ghetto: Race and Democracy Since World War II.* New York: Basic Books.

Wing, Adrien Katherine, ed. 1997. *Critical Race Feminism: A Reader.* New York: New York University Press.

Young, Iris. 2000. *Inclusion and Democracy.* New York: Oxford University Press.

Index

ABA. *See* American Bar Association
abstract individualism, 29, 30, 62, 65, 90, 92, 102, 104, 108, 112, 139, 166, 169; "equal access," 4
academic freedom: racist speech, 10
Acker, Joan, 26–28
adversarial approach, 20, 49, 56
affirmative action, 1, 4, 31, 104–12, 165, 167–70; white narrative, 147–49, 151, 158
African Americans, as outsiders, 43–44
alienation, in law school, 3
American Bar Association, 13, 39, 40
"Americanness" as whiteness, 124
Ames, James Barr, 40, 55
antimiscegenation laws, 15, 76
argumentation, 20, 127
Association of American Law Schools, 40

Bell, Derrick, 13
bifurcated bar, 39
biological racism, 14
"blackness," 68–69
blatant racism. *See* overt racism
Bonilla-Silva, Eduardo, 16, 29, 66, 84, 90–92

Bourdieu, Pierre, 17
boycott as protest, 13
Bradley, Justice Joseph, 41–42
Brown v. Board of Education of Topeka, 16, 78–80, 96

centering: people of color, 30, 117, 120, 163, 176–77; whiteness, 90, 113, 118, 120, 122, 139, 169, 175
citizenship, 15, 69–71, 72, 75, 123–25
Civil Rights Act, 1964, 57, 79, 133
civil rights movement, 43, 78, 166
classed institution, 20
classism, 20–21
collective consciousness, 130
color blindness, principle of, 38, 62, 84, 169; rejection of, 176
color consciousness, 177
colorblind racism, 30, 84, 174; abstract liberalism, 29, 30, 65, 108, 112, 139, 166, 169; discourse, 90, 91–92, 103–5, 108, 111–12, 120, 122, 149, 161, 173; justification of, 31, 126–27; lens, 167; minimization of racism, 12, 13, 30, 57–58, 84, 91, 103, 112, 122–23, 132, 139, 165, 166, 176; naturalization of,

About the Author

Wendy Leo Moore is an assistant professor at Texas A&M University. She received her Ph.D. in sociology from the University of Minnesota and her J.D. from the University of Minnesota Law School. Her work focuses on the intersections of race, racism, and U.S. law.